A Continual Feast

A Continual Feast

A cookbook to celebrate the joys
of family and faith throughout the Christian year

EVELYN BIRGE VITZ

Drawings by Parker Leighton

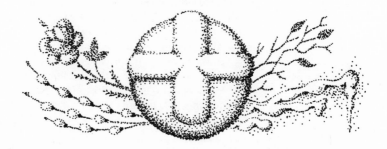

1817

HARPER & ROW, PUBLISHERS, New York
Cambridge, Philadelphia, San Francisco, London
Mexico City, São Paulo, Singapore, Sydney

For my children—Rebecca, Jessica, Daniel, Peter, and Michael—
with my love. You made it all a joy.

Copyright acknowledgments begin on page 295

A CONTINUAL FEAST. Copyright © 1985 by Evelyn Birge Vitz.
Illustrations copyright © 1985 by Parker Leighton. All rights reserved.
Printed in the United States of America. No part of this book may be
used or reproduced in any manner whatsoever without written
permission except in the case of brief quotations embodied in critical
articles and reviews. For information address Harper & Row,
Publishers, Inc., 10 East 53rd Street, New York, N.Y. 10022. Published
simultaneously in Canada by Fitzhenry & Whiteside Limited, Toronto.

FIRST EDITION

Designer: Gayle Jaeger

Library of Congress Cataloging in Publication Data
    Vitz, Evelyn Birge.
        A continual feast.

        Includes index.
        1. Cookery.   2. Fasts and Feasts.   3. Holidays.
I. Title.
TX739.V57   1985   641.5′66   84-48629
ISBN 0-06-181897-6

85 86 87 88 89 FG 10 9 8 7 6 5 4 3 2 1

Contents

Preface

This is a cookbook full of wonderful dishes drawn from throughout the Christian tradition, with suggestions about when, and why, these dishes might be served. But it is also a book about how the food we cook, the meals we serve, can enrich and deepen our lives, not merely as individuals, but as families and communities as well. It is a reminder that all we eat, all the fruits of the earth, come to us from the hand of God. It is a reminder as well of how important a meal is, as a shared experience. I hope it will spur you to make sure your family sits down to eat together as often as possible. "Breaking bread together," as the beautiful old expression goes, encourages the growth of bonds of love and commitment. And how many of the memorable moments of our lives occur at meals!

We all want our families to be as united, as happy, as loving as possible. And we want to deepen our understanding that we are part of a greater family scattered around the world and across the centuries.

It is with such thoughts in mind that this cookbook was written.

———————————————

More friends and relatives than I can enumerate here have contributed to this book by generously sharing their recipes, expertise, and general lore and by lending me books. But I particularly want to thank my husband, Paul, for all his loving and wise support—and for being willing on occasion to eat five versions of the same dish five days in a row; my mother, Evelyn C. Denny, and my mother-in-law, Alda C. Vitz, for their encouragement and invaluable aid along the way; and my friends Kathryn Talarico, Roger Sorrentino, Steven Gordon, Jimmie Ritchie, Laurie Postlewate, Martha Moon, Barbara Kirschenblatt-Gimblett, Colleen Crowell Rooney, Justin Gennaro, Wendy Zuckerman and Mary Elizabeth Podhaizer. I am grateful to my editor Ann Bramson for her patience and counsel throughout the extended labor and various revisions of this book. Finally, without the guidance of my extraordinary friend Nona Aguilar, this book would, quite simply, never have gotten done.

". . . the cheerful heart has a continual feast."

Proverbs 15:15 (NIV)

"Tell me what you eat, and I will tell you what you are."

Brillat-Savarin, *The Physiology of Taste*

Why is any day better than another, when all the daylight in the year
is from the sun?
By the Lord's decision they were distinguished, and he appointed the
different seasons and feasts;
some of them he exalted and hallowed, and some of them he made
ordinary days.

Ecclesiasticus (also called Sirach) 33:7–9 Apocrypha, RSV

PART ONE *All the days of our lives*

We start with all the many days of our lives and the meals that are part of them with recipes for delicious dishes for Sunday dinners, church picnics, baptismal parties, and other such happy occasions. We will look as well at the importance of everyday living as we all want our family meals to be delicious and memorable, festive in their own special way, through the joys of companionship and collaboration.

Here I am! I stand at the door and knock. If anyone hears my voice and opens the door, I will come in and eat with him, and he with me.

Revelation 3:20 (NIV)

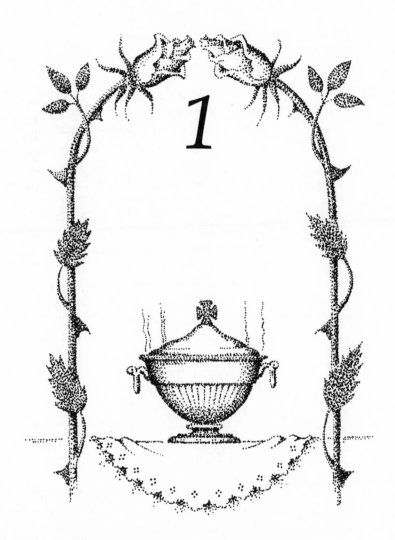

1

Days of rejoicing
and celebration

I once asked a friend of mine who comes from a very close-knit family why they were so united. She answered that her mother had been wonderfully able to find occasions for the family to rejoice together. There was always a sense of festivity in the family, and she and her brothers and sisters have never been willing to let go of that sense of unity and joy.

There are so many occasions in our lives as families and in our relationships with friends that invite celebration. Let's learn to make the most of them.

The Bible is full of references to feasting and celebration. In the Old Testament there are feasts of welcome and many others celebrating happy occasions in the lives of individuals. And all the great events in the history of the Jews, those commemorating the actions of the Lord in their behalf, are kept with feasts, shared meals, at the command of the Lord himself.

As to the New Testament, Jesus performed his very first miracle at a wedding feast, at Cana, where he turned water into wine for the thirsty guests. And, in many of his stories and parables, feasting plays a major role, taking on a new, spiritual meaning. Often in Jesus' words earthly rejoicing is symbolic of, and looks forward to, the heavenly banquet. In fact, this idea that heaven will be a great shared feast permeates and enriches the Christian ideal of the banquet.

There is another dimension to the Christian feast: all communal eating is seen as intimately connected to the Lord's Supper, in which Christians become one with Christ and also with each other.

SUNDAY

Sunday, the Christian Sabbath, is the high point of the Christian week. From a secular perspective, Friday is no doubt the high point. Just think of the Thank-God-it's-Friday party; the work week is finishing, the weekend lies ahead: all hope, no fatigue or disappointments (yet). But, from the Christian perspective, Sunday has

4

always held pride of place among the days. It is the great day, the "first" day in every sense. And since the early centuries, Christians have gathered together on Sunday to eat their most special meal of the week, in honor of Christ. Many people today who had lost touch with this tradition are rediscovering it. If anything, the Sunday dinner has gained in importance and meaning today, when families are having a hard time arranging to eat other meals together. It can be, as many are finding, a time at which the whole family gathers, perhaps with invited friends or relatives, for a special hour or two. It is a shared meal, but more: a time when the family recollects itself, in the various meanings of this word, and reconsecrates itself and the coming week to God.

This day is a reminder of all the richness of our heritage. Foremost among the days that the Jews celebrated as holy was the Sabbath, the seventh and last day of the week—Saturday—on which the Lord rested after completing the work of creation. Christ himself kept this day as holy though he did scandalize some by working miracles and plucking grain to eat, declaring, "The Sabbath was made for man, not man for the Sabbath."

But, after the death and resurrection of Christ, the earliest Christians began to celebrate a new day as holy: the first day of the week, the day on which Christ rose from the dead. This day, the new Lord's Day, came to be celebrated as a little, a weekly, Easter.

The Lord's Day was understood to be a day of rest, but not in so complete a way as the Jewish Sabbath. It was, rather, a "rest for the heart," a day to restore the spirit as well as the body. And it was a day of rejoicing, a triumphant, happy day. Sunday was also the day on which new projects, new plans, should be inaugurated, since it imparted a blessing on all that was undertaken.

Sunday was, then, a day for thanksgiving and communion, and the very earliest Christians shared an "agape meal," or "love feast." The Eucharist, or Lord's Supper, was originally celebrated at the end of the love feast. Eventually the Lord's Supper was set off as a separate liturgy, to stress the reverence and spirit of prayer that must surround this sacred meal.

At the time of the Protestant Reformation, Sunday came often to be referred to as the Sabbath. The point was to renew an Old Testament sense of the holiness of the Lord's Day.

This day has retained its character as one of rest, and as that on which the best meal of the week has been eaten, shared, in honor of the Risen Christ.

Wash on Monday
Iron on Tuesday
Mend on Wednesday
Churn on Thursday
Clean on Friday
Bake on Saturday
Rest on Sunday.

Early American saying

Edelweiss coffeecake

Part of setting Sunday apart from other days is the shared enjoyment of foods that we don't have during the week. Sitting down together after church for a homemade coffeecake, perhaps along with bacon and eggs—this is part of many a family's Sunday ritual. It is also traditional to serve such a coffeecake to Sunday-afternoon guests, with coffee.

Here is an Edelweiss, by my book one of the most delectable of all yeast coffeecakes.

2 packages dry yeast
½ cup warm water
 (100–110° F.)
½ cup sugar
1½ cups milk
1 stick (¼ pound) sweet
 butter
1 teaspoon salt
Grated rind of 1 lemon
½ teaspoon cinnamon
2 eggs
About 6 cups flour
1 cup confectioners' sugar
⅔–1 cup butter at room
 temperature
1 teaspoon vanilla
1 cup finely chopped or
 ground blanched almonds

Dissolve the yeast in the warm water in a large bowl. Stir in 1 tablespoon of the sugar. Let sit until frothy.

In a saucepan, scald the milk. Add the 1 stick butter, the remaining sugar, and the salt. Stir until the butter is melted. Cool to lukewarm. Add the lemon rind and cinnamon and beat in the eggs. Add to the yeast mixture.

Stir in 2 cups of the flour, and beat with a wooden spoon until the mixture is smooth. Gradually add just enough of the remaining flour to make a soft, nonsticky dough. Turn the dough out onto a lightly floured surface and knead for about 10 minutes, until the dough is smooth and elastic and blisters form on the surface.

Place the dough in a greased bowl, turning to grease the top. Cover with a towel or plastic wrap and let rise in a draft-free spot until doubled in bulk, about 1½ hours.

Preheat oven to 350° F.

Punch the dough down. Divide in 2 or 3 parts, depending on whether you wish to make 2 large or 3 smaller coffeecakes. Grease 2 baking sheets or 3 pie pans. Form the dough into 2 large, round flat coffeecakes on the baking sheets. Or pat it into pie pans.

Prepare the topping: Cream the confectioners' sugar with the butter. Stir in the vanilla and almonds. Sprinkle onto the dough.

Let rise again until doubled in bulk, about 45 minutes.

Bake at 350° F. for about 45 minutes, or until golden brown.

Yield: 2 large or 3 smaller coffeecakes

Note: These coffeecakes freeze well.

Variations:

Add raisins, dried currants, or chopped candied fruit peel to the dough or topping; for the almonds, substitute chopped hazelnuts, walnuts, or pecans.

STICKY BUNS

Make a slightly stiffer dough than that for the coffeecakes by adding a little more flour. Instead of forming the dough into coffeecakes, roll it out into two rectangles about ¼ inch thick, 12 inches wide, and 18 inches long. Cream ¾ cup brown sugar with 6 tablespoons butter. Add ½ cup chopped raisins and 1 teaspoon cinnamon; if you like, add ¼ cup or more chopped nuts. Sprinkle this filling onto the dough. Roll the dough up along the 12-inch side. Cut it into slices about 1 inch thick. Place the slices slightly apart on lightly greased pans and let rise for the second time. Bake at 375° F. for about 20 minutes. While still hot brush with confectioners' sugar mixed with lemon juice and a little vanilla.

Yield: about 3 dozen

Liver dumpling soup

In a number of countries—Germany and Belgium among them—there is a tradition of "Sunday soups." These are favorite soups of the house, which the cook produces on Sundays—and only on Sundays—to the anticipation and delight of the family. These soups often contain dumplings or meatballs.

I have heard the monks at St. Vincent's Archabbey (in Latrobe, Pennsylvania) reminisce fondly about this wonderful liver dumpling soup. One of the elderly sisters from the nearby German Benedictine convent of St. Emma's used to cook it up on Sunday from time to time—the intervals always seemed too long. This recipe has been adapted from St. Emma's Cookbook.

¼ pound any liver
1 tablespoon butter
1 egg
¼ teaspoon salt
A few grindings of black pepper
2 tablespoons finely minced onion
1½ tablespoons finely minced parsley
¼ teaspoon grated lemon rind
Pinch of marjoram
Pinch of nutmeg
About ½ cup fresh breadcrumbs
Approximately 12 cups good beef broth

Skin the liver and remove any fibers. Grind or chop very fine. (Liver is easier to chop if it is slightly frozen.)

Cream the butter, add the egg and the finely chopped or ground liver. Mix in the remaining ingredients except broth, using enough breadcrumbs to make the mixture light and fluffy—about ½ cup.

Bring a large pot of lightly salted water to a simmer. Drop in 1 teaspoon after another of the mixture. Simmer the dumplings gently for about 10 minutes, or until they have become slightly fluffy, and a toothpick inserted in one comes out clean. The cooking time will vary according to the size of the dumplings.

Add dumplings to heated broth and simmer soup until ready to serve.

Yield: about 8 servings

Braised capon, Italian style

Sunday is a particularly nice day to prepare a roast, or at any rate something cooked and served "whole." Such a dish is handsome to present at the table—it always looks special. And when all partake of one common dish, it is a symbolic reminder that we are not isolated individuals, but are unified by bonds of love and faith.

In both Italy and France, capon is a favorite Sunday dish. This one is braised with a little Marsala wine, and flavored with onion, garlic, prosciutto, and tomatoes. Serve with Rice with Parmesan Cheese and Lemon Juice or Pasta with Walnut Sauce (both follow this recipe).

Salt
Freshly ground pepper
1 capon, about 5 pounds, or 1 large roasting chicken
3 tablespoons butter
3 tablespoons olive oil
3 onions, sliced
2 cloves garlic, mashed
⅔ cup Marsala wine
1½ cups seeded, coarsely chopped ripe tomatoes or canned Italian plum tomatoes, drained
¾ cup coarsely chopped prosciutto
1 bay leaf
½ cup chicken broth
3 tablespoons chopped fresh basil, or 1 tablespoon dried
¼ cup fresh parsley, chopped

Salt and pepper the cavity of the bird, and place it in a large flameproof casserole or high-sided frying pan with a lid. Over moderate heat cook and turn the capon in the butter and olive oil until it is nicely browned on all sides.

Remove the capon to a dish. Sauté the onions and garlic in the pan until the onions begin to brown. Stir in ⅓ cup of the wine, reserving the rest for the sauce. Add the tomatoes, prosciutto, and bay leaf. Return the capon to the pan.

Bring the liquid to a simmer. Cover the pan tightly and place it in the oven. Cook at 350° F. for about 2 hours or until the legs move freely at the joints and the juices run clear when the bird is pricked with a fork.

When the capon is done, remove it to a warmed serving dish. Surround it with the onion, tomato, and ham mixture. Keep warm.

Remove all but a few tablespoons of the cooking juices from the pan in which the capon was cooked and degrease those remaining in the pan. Add the chicken broth and the remaining ⅓ cup of Marsala, and boil the mixture down until it is thick and syrupy. In the last minute or two, stir in the basil and parsley. Serve with the capon.

Yield: 4 to 6 servings

I want every laborer in my realm to be able to put a fowl in the pot on Sunday.

Henri IV

Rice with Parmesan cheese and lemon juice

1½ cups Italian Arborio rice
  or long-grain rice
Chicken stock or water, or a
  mixture
Salt
6 tablespoons butter
1¼ cups freshly grated
  Parmesan cheese
6 tablespoons lemon juice

Cook the rice in the stock or water with salt, as directed on the package. Remove from the heat.

Stir in the butter, Parmesan cheese, and lemon juice. Blend well with a fork until the butter is melted and the mixture is smooth and creamy.

Serve immediately.

Yield: 6 servings

Variation:

Instead of the lemon juice, stir in a little dry white wine.

Pasta with walnut sauce

PASTA CON SALSA DI NOCI

Try this simple, classic sauce with any pasta, such as fettuccine, cappelletti or tagliatelle.

¾ cup shelled walnuts or
  ½ cup walnuts and ¼ cup
  pine nuts, coarsely
  chopped
½ teaspoon marjoram
¼ cup olive oil
¼ cup heavy cream
¼ cup ricotta cheese
2 tablespoons chopped
  parsley
Milk
Salt and freshly ground
  black pepper
Pinch of nutmeg
1 pound pasta
½ cup freshly grated
  Parmesan cheese

In a food processor or blender combine nuts, marjoram, olive oil, cream, ricotta, and parsley. If the sauce seems too thick, add a tablespoon or two of milk. Season with salt, pepper, and nutmeg to taste.

Cook the pasta in a large pot of boiling salted water until just tender.

Toss with walnut sauce. Sprinkle with Parmesan cheese.

Yield: 4 servings

No man is lonely while eating spaghetti; it requires so much attention.

Christopher Morley

Pot roast

Always delicious, always well received.

Salt
Freshly ground pepper
Nutmeg
5-pound beef roast (rump, chuck, or round)
Flour
2–3 tablespoons oil, butter, or bacon grease
¼ cup brandy, warmed (optional)
1½ cups red wine, beef stock or tomato juice
1 clove garlic, peeled
1 stick celery
1 onion, studded with a few cloves
10–15 small carrots, peeled, or 6–8 large carrots, peeled and cut into uniform pieces
10–12 small white onions, peeled
4 turnips, peeled, diced
2 tablespoons butter

BEURRE MANIÉ:
About 2 tablespoons flour
About 2 tablespoons softened butter

Rub the salt, pepper, and nutmeg into the meat; roll it in flour. In a large pan with a tight-fitting lid, brown the meat on all sides in the oil or fat. Pour out most of the grease. (Optional: Pour in the brandy and carefully ignite it.) Add the liquid and the garlic, celery, and clove-studded onion.

Cover the pot and simmer for about 1¾ hours. While the meat is simmering, sauté the carrots, onions, and turnips in 2 tablespoons butter until lightly browned.

After the meat has cooked for 1¾ hours, add the vegetables to the pan. Cover again and continue simmering until the meat is done and the vegetables are tender, about 15 minutes.

Transfer the meat to a serving platter; surround with the vegetables (except for the celery and clove-studded onion). Keep warm.

Degrease the pan. Make little balls of *beurre manié* with the flour and softened butter: knead the two together until well blended, and form little pea-sized balls. Stir these little balls into the degreased liquid until the sauce is of the desired consistency. Pour some over the meat and serve the rest in a gravy boat.

Carve the meat across the grain—that way you will get no stringy slices.

Yield: 6 to 8 servings

> Better a good dinner than a fine coat.
>
> French saying

Giant dumpling

MIQUE

With your Pot Roast try serving Mique *(pronounced "Meek"). This great beautiful dumpling from Normandy is, when sliced, very like bread.*

⅔ cup milk
2 tablespoons yeast
3¼ cups flour

Warm ⅓ cup of the milk to 100–110° F. Sprinkle in the yeast.

Place a generous ¾ cup flour in a large bowl, or on a floured surface. Add the butter and the yeast, a little at a time. Knead until the flour is completely incorporated. Form the dough into a

6½ tablespoons butter,
softened
1 pinch salt
2 eggs

ball, and cover it with the rest of the flour. Let it rise for 20 minutes at room temperature.

Make a well in the dough. Put in it the salt, eggs, and remaining milk. Knead and mix. Work in the flour until the dough is firm and elastic.

Form the dough into a ball. Wrap it loosely in cheesecloth and place it in a bowl. Let it rise for 2½ to 3 hours.

Bring a large pot of salted water to a boil. Set the dough—still wrapped in cheesecloth—in the water, and let it simmer for 35 to 40 minutes.

Serve hot with the Pot Roast.

Yield: 8 to 10 servings

Sabbath bread

CHALLAH

The members of the Word of God ecumenical Christian community in Ann Arbor, Michigan, commence the Sabbath with a family ceremony on Saturday night before dinner. (As in the Jewish tradition the Sabbath is observed from sundown to sundown.) The father or head of the household leads the ceremony; the wife or other designated person lights the candle and reads a meditation prayer. In the course of the ceremony a cup of wine (or grape juice) is blessed and shared by all present. The traditional Jewish Sabbath bread, Challah, is shared by all. This recipe for Challah was given to me by my friend Mary Perrotta of the community.

Challah also makes a wonderful addition to any Sunday dinner.

½ cup warm water
(100–110° F.)
2¼ teaspoons plus 2
heaping tablespoons sugar
1 rounded tablespoon yeast
½ cup oil
1 heaping tablespoon salt
½ cup cold water
7½–8 cups unbleached flour
1 cup boiling water
3 eggs, plus 1 lightly
whipped egg

Sprinkle the yeast and 2¼ teaspoons sugar into the warm water. Set aside till the yeast is bubbling.

Mix the oil, 2 heaping tablespoons sugar, and the salt in a large bowl. Add the cold water. Mix in ½ cup flour. *Whip* with a wire whisk, until the mixture is *very smooth.* (This is essential.) Add the boiling water and another ½ cup of flour. Again whip until *very smooth.* Add the 3 eggs; stir in the yeast. Mix well. Add the remaining flour gradually, beating constantly with a spoon. The dough will be sticky. With oiled fingers, knead the dough lightly in the bowl for 2 to 3 minutes.

Place the dough in an oiled bowl, turning it to grease the top. Let rise, covered, until doubled in bulk—from 1 to 2 hours.

Punch the dough down and knead for 2 or 3 minutes. Divide the dough into two pieces: a generous two-thirds, and a scant one-third.

Divide the larger piece into 3 parts. On a lightly floured

continued

Sabbath bread, continued

surface, roll each into an 18-inch-long rope. Braid the three ropes together. Form the braid into a long loaf, or into a circle, on a lightly greased pan.

Repeat this procedure with the smaller piece; that is, make three 18-inch ropes, and braid them. Place the smaller braid on top of the larger. Cover lightly, and let the dough rise again, until a little less than doubled, about 45 minutes.

Preheat the oven to 325° F.

Bake the bread for about 20 minutes at 325°. Then brush it with lightly beaten egg white (this will make it shiny). If the crust is not turning golden, raise the oven temperature to 350°. Bake for another 10 to 20 minutes, or until the crust is golden brown and when you lift the bread in a towel and rap it on the bottom, it sounds hollow. Careful: this bread dries out if overbaked.

Yield: 1 large loaf, serving 15 to 20

Scripture cake

1½ cups (3 sticks) Psalms 55:21 (butter)
2 cups Jeremiah 6:20 (sugar)
6 Jeremiah 17:11 (eggs)
½ cup Judges 4:19 (milk)
2 tablespoons I Samuel 14:25 (honey)
4½ cups Leviticus 6:15 (flour)
A pinch of Leviticus 2:13 (salt)
2 tablespoons Amos 4:5 (baking powder)
II Chronicles 9:9 (spices: 1 teaspoon cinnamon and ½ teaspoon freshly ground nutmeg)
2 cups I Samuel 30:12 (raisins)
2 cups Numbers 13:23 (figs), chopped
1 cup Numbers 17:8 (almonds), chopped or grated

How could we possibly omit this famous old New England favorite? It is a cake made from the words of the Bible—that is, only from ingredients that are mentioned in Scripture. The recipe for Scripture Cake was often set up as a puzzle or exercise and its underlying goal was to make you look up the reference, read the Bible. How many of us would recognize that "2 cups Jeremiah 6:20" means "2 cups sugar"? I have set it up here so that the answers are given.

Many recipes for Scripture Cake add to this list of ingredients only the words: "Follow Solomon's recipe for making a good boy and you will have a good cake, Proverbs 23:14"—"Beat well." I think I'll be a little more specific!

Preheat the oven to 350° F. Butter and flour loaf pans, small or larger disposable aluminum pans; or a bundt or tube pan.

In a large bowl, cream the butter until light and creamy. Beat in the sugar until fluffy. Add the eggs one at a time, beating well after each addition. Stir in the milk and the honey.

Sift the flour with the salt, baking powder, and dry spices.

Add the dry ingredients gradually to the wet. Mix only until thoroughly blended. Stir in the raisins, figs, and almonds.

Turn the mixture into the pans.

Bake for about 50 minutes, or until a straw inserted in the center comes out clean.

Yield: 1 large or several small cakes

Variation:

You can halve this recipe if you like.

"Good Christian" pear tart

TARTE RENVERSÉE AUX POIRES BON CHRÉTIEN

The pears that we call Bartlett today were originally called "Bon Chrétien," because it was claimed that the extraordinary Francis of Paola had brought them to King Louis XI of France in the fifteenth century. Here is, then, a lovely French "upside-down" tart, made of "Good Christian" pears. The pears are poached in a spiced wine, then baked with a pie crust on top. Just before serving the dish, you turn the tart out onto a serving platter. It is thus an "upside-down tart."

Whipped cream may be piped around the edges if desired.

4–7 Bartlett pears, firm and slightly under-ripe, peeled, halved, cored
½ cup sugar
½ teaspoon cinnamon
¼ teaspoon nutmeg, preferably freshly grated
1 piece lemon peel
2–3 cups red wine

SHORT CRUST:
2 cups flour
½ teaspoon salt
1½ sticks (¾ cup) cold sweet butter, cut into small pieces
6–8 tablespoons ice water
Optional:
   Whipped cream

Prepare the pears: The number used will be determined by the size of the pie pan. You may leave most of them in halves, or quarter some or all of them. This will depend on the pattern in which you wish to arrange them in the pie pan or baking dish. Pack the pears in in a tight, single layer, in an attractive design. Make a mental (or written) note of how you have arranged them.

Once you have decided on the design, place the pears in a large saucepan or frying pan. Sprinkle with the sugar and the spices; add the lemon peel and pour over them wine to cover. Bring the wine to a boil, cover, and poach the pears gently for about 10 minutes.

In the meantime, prepare the pie crust, following the pastry procedure on page 160. Roll it out to a shape a little larger than the pie pan. Preheat the oven to 400° F.

Remove the pears gently with a slotted spoon, and place them carefully in the pie pan in the design you chose. Try to keep them intact, but if a few get slightly broken, don't worry. Put the broken ones at the edges.

Boil the spiced wine down rapidly in the saucepan until only ½ to ⅔ cup remains. Pour this liquid over the pears.

Lay the pastry over the pears. Crimp or press down the edges, and prick the surface in several places.

Bake for about 40 minutes, or until the crust is golden. The tart can be served hot, at room temperature or cold. At any rate, it should not be reversed onto the serving platter until just before it is to be eaten.

Optional:
Pipe whipped cream around the edges

Yield: about 6 to 10 servings

Sundaes

One or more kinds of ice
   cream and/or sherbet
Chocolate, hot fudge,
   butterscotch, or
   marshmallow sauce
Fresh or frozen (thawed)
   strawberries or
   raspberries
Whipped cream
Chopped walnuts, pecans,
   or peanuts
Maraschino cherries
Bananas (For a Banana
   Split, slice a banana in
   two lengthwise, put
   scoops of ice cream on
   top, and pour hot fudge
   sauce over)

Another dessert possibility is Sundaes. What could be more appropriate? The word "sundae" comes apparently from "Sunday." Presumably this scrumptious dessert was sold or served only on this, the most special day of the week—just as "Sunday best" or "Sunday-go-to-meeting clothes" were worn only on that day.

Variation:
   For a more sophisticated sundae try:
   vanilla ice cream or raspberry sherbet with a little crème de cassis on top, or
   vanilla or coffee ice cream with Tía María or another coffee liqueur, or
   vanilla ice cream or lemon or lime sherbet with crème de menthe.

Green grapes with sour cream and brown sugar

An unusual and delicious dessert that is a cinch to prepare.

Green grapes (seedless or
   seeded), washed
Sour cream, lightly stirred
Dark brown sugar, stirred
   with a fork

Place the grapes, sour cream, and brown sugar in separate serving dishes. Pass, and allow the guests to combine them in their bowls in the proportions they wish.

CHURCH PICNICS

Sunday dinner is *the* fundamental festive meal. Another absolutely basic, and absolutely wonderful, Christian gathering is the church picnic. This is one variation on the church supper, which is about as old as the Church itself. St. Paul refers several times to communal, shared meals among Christians. The church supper is generally given in the church buildings—in a dining or meeting room. It is often scheduled to precede some sort of church meeting, whether for business, discussion, or prayer; and today, at least in large churches, it is commonly prepared by a special kitchen staff.

   Church picnics are quite different in that they are essentially festive, though the basic purpose of all shared meals is the same:

Christian fellowship. They are generally large outdoor gatherings, to which everyone contributes food to be shared. Down through the centuries there have been all manner of such gatherings. Originally, they were most often held in honor of a particular church's patron saint, at a yearly festival or fair; this is still common in many places. But it is thanks to the Protestants in America that we have the church picnic as we know it today—and this contribution has greatly enriched Christian communal life. Many churches today hold picnics in the summertime, as part of annual celebrations—or occasionally to rejoice at some special event. (Any pretext, I say, is good enough to schedule a church picnic!)

Such occasions can be marvelously enjoyable. Volleyball, badminton, and softball can be played. Young children can play tag and other popular group games. (If—as is often the case—there is no space on the church grounds for such activities, the picnic can be held at a park or picnic area.) There can be singing—with or without accompaniment—of songs from the whole breadth of the Christian tradition, including hymns, spirituals, and folksongs. (Try handing out copies of the words to less well-known songs.) And plenty of room should be left for conversation.

As to the food, it should be *good*—not everyday fare. (Leave your tuna casserole at home!) Below are some delectable church picnic recipes, many of them traditional. All recipes serve large numbers, and can be multiplied, if need be. There are selections from each of the categories of dishes that one is generally asked to provide on such occasions. And it is essential that each individual or family bring a dish to *share*; if people just bring their own food, the spirit of the event is very different: it does not function as a shared meal. It is essential too that a blessing be said—over the food, the group, the gathering: it is in the name of Christ that we come together.

Shout for joy to the Lord, all the earth. Serve the Lord with gladness;
  come before him with joyful songs.
Know that the Lord is God. It is he who made us, and we are his; we
  are his people, the sheep of his pasture.

Enter his gates with thanksgiving and his courts with praise; give
  thanks to him and praise his name.
For the Lord is good and his love endures forever.
                                                    Psalm 100:1–4 (NIV)

Fried chicken

It is hard to imagine an American church picnic without fried chicken. Here is an excellent traditional recipe. It has, however, an interesting little variation, which my friend Peggy Lopez of the People of Hope Community in New Jersey taught me: a bit of curry seasoning. Try it!

6 two-pound fryers (or the equivalent in weight), cut into serving pieces
1 cup milk
About 1 cup flour
2 teaspoons salt
A few grindings black pepper
2–3 teaspoons curry powder (optional)
Vegetable oil, or a mixture of lard and oil

Place the chicken in a large bowl and moisten it with the milk.

Combine the flour with 1 teaspoon salt, a little black pepper, and if you wish, 1 teaspoon curry powder. Roll the chicken in the flour mixture. Press the flour into the chicken so that it adheres well. Shake off excess.

Heat about 1 inch of oil in each of two large heavy skillets. Distribute the chicken pieces evenly between the two pans. Do not crowd the pieces. Cook until nicely browned on all sides.

Sprinkle the chicken with the rest of the salt, more pepper, and the rest of the curry powder, if you use it. Cover the pans, lower the heat, and cook the chicken gently until all the pieces are tender. This will take about 20 minutes. Turn the pieces several times during the cooking, and remove the white-meat pieces—which cook faster than dark meat—when they are done.

Drain all pieces thoroughly on paper towels.

Yield: 12 to 15 servings

Variation:

For the curry powder, substitute 1 to 2 teaspoons dried herbs such as thyme or oregano, mixed in with the flour. Another teaspoon or more of the herb can be sprinkled on during the cooking process.

> I feel a recipe is only a theme, which an intelligent cook can play each time with a variation.
>
> Madame Benoît

Broiled chicken

This recipe and the next are probably my two favorite meat dishes for church picnics.

10 half chicken breasts
Salt

Preheat the broiler. Salt the breasts lightly. Place on a broiler rack, skin side down, about 5 inches from the flame. Baste with a

¼ cup (½ stick) sweet
   butter, melted
¼ cup olive oil
3 tablespoons lemon juice
½ cup dry breadcrumbs
3–4 cloves garlic, pressed
¼ cup finely minced onion
¼ cup finely chopped
   parsley
1 teaspoon oregano or basil
   (optional)
A few teaspoons olive oil
3 or 4 lemons, cut
   lengthwise into quarters

mixture of butter, oil, and lemon juice. Broil for about 8 minutes, or until the chicken is beginning to brown.

Turn the breasts skin side up. Baste again with the butter mixture. Broil, basting frequently, until the tops are golden brown and the juices run clear when pierced with a knife: about 15 minutes.

Mix the breadcrumbs with the garlic, onion, parsley, and the oregano or basil. Moisten lightly with oil. Pat a little of this mixture on top of each piece of chicken, using a small metal spatula or the back of a spoon. Run the chicken back under the broiler until the tops are nicely browned.

Serve hot or at room temperature, with lemon quarters.

Yield: 10 servings

Variations:

To make the dish spicier, add a little cayenne or crushed red pepper to the butter-oil mixture.

Add a little dry mustard to the breadcrumbs.

Vary the herbs you add to the breadcrumbs: try tarragon, thyme, or dill.

Eliminate the bread crumbs, and just use a mixture of garlic, onion, and parsley, moistened with butter or oil, on the tops of the chicken pieces.

To make the dish less spicy, reduce or eliminate the garlic and onion.

Chinese barbecued spareribs

This is, to my mind, the ultimate sparerib recipe. It is good hot or at room temperature.

10 pounds spareribs
1⅓ cups hoisin sauce
4–6 teaspoons minced fresh
   ginger
4 tablespoons soy sauce
4 tablespoons sherry
2 teaspoons sugar
2–4 cloves garlic, pressed
   (optional)
4 scallions, chopped

Preheat the oven to 350° F.

Cut the spareribs into single- or double-rib sections. Place them on a rack over a roasting pan. Cook them in the oven for 1 hour, so that they render some of their fat. Turn them once or twice.

For the basting sauce, combine the hoisin sauce, ginger, soy sauce, sherry, sugar, and the garlic.

Brush the spareribs with the sauce and continue cooking for about another 60 minutes. Baste frequently and turn once or twice. After about 30 minutes, raise the temperature of the oven to 375° to brown the spareribs. Sprinkle them with the scallions about 10 minutes before they are done, which is when they look crisp and are beginning to blacken around the edges.

Yield: 10 to 12 servings

Pennsylvania Dutch baked beans

These spicy baked beans from the Pennsylvania Dutch tradition are appreciated any time, but they are especially popular at a picnic. They are good with pork prepared in almost any fashion, with fried or broiled chicken, and with barbecued meats or cold cuts. The combination of onion, molasses, mustard, and ketchup, and ginger— added to taste—can also liven up bland store-bought baked beans.

4 cups navy (pea) beans
½ pound salt pork, cut into slices about ¼ inch by 1 inch by 2 inches
3 onions, coarsely chopped
1 cup molasses
2 teaspoons salt
2 tablespoons dry mustard
1 cup tomato ketchup
Optional:
  1 teaspoon ground ginger
  Beer

Wash and pick over the beans, and soak them overnight in cold water to cover.

Drain the beans and cover them with fresh water. Bring to a boil. Cover and reduce heat. Simmer until the beans are tender. (Time of cooking can vary considerably.) Drain, reserving the liquid.

Lay half of the salt pork in a casserole or bean pot. Mix the onions with the beans, and add to the casserole.

Mix the molasses, salt, mustard, ketchup, ginger, and 1 cup of the reserved bean liquid. Pour over the beans. Add more bean liquid—or water, or beer—to cover. Strew the remaining pieces of salt pork over the top. Cover the pot tightly.

Bake at 300° F. for about 5 hours. Add liquid as necessary to keep the beans covered. Remove the cover for the last ½ hour of cooking to brown the top.

Yield: 10 to 12 servings

20 small red potatoes
3 purple onions, sliced thin
3 bell peppers (red, green, yellow) cut into thin strips
1 cup olive oil
⅓ cup lemon juice or wine vinegar
1–2 teaspoons Dijon mustard or Herbed Mustard (page 121)
3 cloves garlic, pressed
About 1½ teaspoons salt
Freshly ground black pepper
2 teaspoons dried or 4 teaspoons fresh chopped basil or dill
2 cups fresh chopped parsley, preferably Italian
Optional:
  Fresh basil leaves or sprigs of fresh dill weed

Potato salad

Another classic is potato salad. While the familiar German potato salad and its various relatives are always welcome on such occasions, why not try adding a new twist? Here is a marvelous and colorful variation.

Wash the potatoes. Boil them in a large pot of salted water to cover until just tender when pierced with a fork: about 15 to 20 minutes. Drain thoroughly.

Combine the potatoes with the onions and peppers on a serving platter.

Prepare the vinaigrette: mix the olive oil thoroughly with the lemon juice. Add the mustard, garlic, and salt and pepper to taste, and the basil or dill. Pour over the potatoes and vegetables. Let marinate for several hours, stirring occasionally.

A few minutes before serving, stir in the parsley. Adjust seasoning. Garnish with basil leaves or dill sprigs, if you wish.

Yield: about 10 to 12 servings

Cold pasta salad

Various forms of macaroni salad are among the most traditional and typical of American church picnic fare. Why not refresh and update this popular dish by widening the range of pasta shapes used as its base, and the dressings and seasonings as well? There are many possible variations, but here is an excellent and flavorful recipe.

¼ *pound green beans*
½ *pound* fusilli, *broken into short pieces*
½ *pound* mostaccioli rigati
A little under 1 cup olive oil
3 *red or green bell peppers, cut into thin strips*
1 *bunch scallions, chopped*
1 *pint cherry tomatoes*
2 *cucumbers, peeled, sliced*
2 *cans anchovies*
⅓ *cup wine vinegar*
1–3 *cloves garlic, pressed (optional)*
Salt
Freshly ground black pepper
1 *teaspoon oregano or marjoram*

Trim the ends off the green beans. Cut long beans in two. Cook in boiling salted water to cover until just tender. Plunge into cold water. Drain.

Cook the two kinds of pasta separately in large pots of boiling salted water until just tender: the pasta should be al dente—still a little chewy. Drain the pasta thoroughly.

Combine the two kinds of pasta in a large salad bowl and mix with a few tablespoons of the oil. When the pasta has cooled, add the green beans, peppers, scallions, cherry tomatoes, and cucumbers.

Mash half of the anchovies from one of the cans in a mixing bowl. Add the oil from both cans and enough olive oil to make ¾ cup. Stir in the vinegar and the garlic.

Add salt to taste (you may not need any as the anchovies are salty) and pepper. Add oregano or marjoram. Blend thoroughly.

Pour the dressing over the pasta and vegetables. Add the remaining anchovy fillets and mix thoroughly. Marinate for several hours before serving, stirring occasionally. Adjust seasoning.

Yield: about 10 to 12 servings

Variations:

The pasta: You can use different shapes, only one or several. Always cook different kinds of pasta separately, as they generally require different cooking times.

Vegetables: You can use Spanish or Bermuda onions instead of the scallions; fresh peas or other vegetables, cooked just until tender; or jarred foods like artichoke hearts.

Fish or meat: Add canned tuna or diced ham or thin strips of prosciutto.

The dressing: Eliminate the anchovies and flavor the dressing more intensely with any herb you like. Replace the vinaigrette with mayonnaise thinned to taste with oil and vinegar.

Seasoning is in Cookery what chords are in music.

Louis Eustache Ude, *The French Cook Book,* 1828

Sister Lettie's beet salad

The Shakers had wonderful and inventive vegetable dishes. Sister Lettie was a great cook in the 19th North Union (Ohio) Shaker Community.

This recipe is adapted from the Shaker Cookbook *by Caroline B. Piercy.*

4 tablespoons sugar
2 teaspoons salt
2 teaspoons prepared mustard
1 cup vinegar
12 cooked beets, sliced
8 hard-cooked eggs
Lettuce
8 small onions, sliced
4 green peppers, sliced

Make a dressing by combining sugar, salt, mustard, and vinegar. Heat to boiling and pour over the sliced beets. When they are cool add the whole shelled hard-cooked eggs, and let stand overnight.

On a serving dish arrange a bed of lettuce, and place the sliced beets in the center. Surround with rings of sliced onions, and garnish with slices of pickled eggs and green peppers. Pour some of the dressing over the salad.

Yield: 12 servings

Greek bread

Any homemade bread is certain to be welcomed at a church picnic. But one particularly large beautiful bread, from the Greek tradition, is Vasilopita (see page 161).

For a church picnic, make a large Greek cross on top of the bread: Before forming the loaf, take from it a piece about the size of an orange. Form it into two ropes about 14 inches long. With a sharp knife split the end of each rope for 2½ inches. Lay the two ropes over the top of the loaf, curling the ends around to form circular shapes. Place a half walnut or pecan in the middle of each of the eight circles.

The pleasures of the table are for every man, of every land, and no matter of what place in history or society; they can be a part of all his other pleasures, and they last the longest, to console him when he has outlived the rest.

Brillat-Savarin, *The Physiology of Taste*

Brownies

In my experience, hardly anything goes faster on a picnic buffet table (or elsewhere) than brownies. Here is a recipe that an old and dear friend of my mother was kind enough to share with me. She was given the recipe by an elderly friend of hers who was famous for her brownies.

¾ cup (1½ sticks) sweet butter, softened
2 cups sugar
4 eggs, well beaten
Pinch salt
4 squares Baker's unsweetened chocolate, melted, cooled
1 teaspoon vanilla
1 cup flour, sifted three times. Measure after first sifting
Optional:
  1 cup chopped walnuts or pecans

Preheat the oven to 325° F.

Cream the butter and sugar until fluffy. Beat in the eggs, and add the salt. Stir in the melted chocolate and vanilla. Gradually blend in the flour, mixing well after each addition. If you wish, add the nuts, blending thoroughly.

Butter a 7½-by-11½-inch (or 7-by-11-inch) pan. Pour the brownie mixture into the pan.

Bake for about 30 to 35 minutes, or until a toothpick inserted into the center comes out clean. Cut the brownies while they are warm and let them cool in the pan.

Yield: about 40 brownies

Southern pecan pie

Prominent among the dessert classics that are always appreciated at a church picnic is Pecan Pie, that southern specialty. This recipe came to me from the mother of a student of mine, Mrs. Dorothy McCraney. It is wonderful!

1 cup white sugar
1 cup dark brown sugar
4 tablespoons flour
6 eggs
2 cups light corn syrup
4 tablespoons melted butter
2 cups chopped pecans
2 teaspoons vanilla
3 nine-inch unbaked pie crusts
¼ cup pecan halves (optional)

Preheat the oven to 450° F.

In a large bowl, mix thoroughly with a fork the white and brown sugars and the flour. Stir in the eggs, corn syrup, melted butter, chopped pecans, and vanilla. (At this point the mixture can be refrigerated and used later; just remix it before pouring it into pie shells.)

Pour mixture into the pie shells. If you wish, distribute pecan halves in attractive patterns over the tops of the pies.

Bake for 10 minutes; lower the temperature to 350° and bake for 25–35 minutes more. The pie is done if it does not jiggle when shaken from side to side.

Yield: 3 pies

Marble cake

This is a fine old recipe adapted from the Mennonite Community Cookbook *by M. Emma Showalter.*

½ cup butter
1 cup sugar
2½ cups cake flour
2 teaspoons baking powder
¼ teaspoon salt
⅔ cup milk
1 teaspoon vanilla
4 egg whites

½ cup butter
1 cup brown sugar
½ cup molasses
4 egg yolks
2½ cups cake flour
1 teaspoon baking soda
¼ teaspoon salt
1 teaspoon cinnamon
1 teaspoon cloves
½ teaspoon nutmeg
1 cup buttermilk

WHITE BATTER
Cream the butter with the sugar and beat until fluffy.

Sift the flour with the baking powder and salt. Add the dry ingredients to the butter-sugar mixture, alternately with the milk and the vanilla. Beat thoroughly after each addition.

Beat the egg whites until stiff but not dry. Fold them into the batter.

DARK BATTER
Preheat the oven to 350° F. Grease a large tube pan.

Cream the butter. Add the sugar gradually and beat until fluffy. Add the molasses and egg yolks. Beat until thoroughly blended.

Sift the flour with the soda, salt, and spices. Add the dry ingredients to the butter-sugar mixture, alternately with the buttermilk. Beat thoroughly after each addition.

THE CAKE
Into the greased tube pan, drop alternate spoonfuls of each batter. When baked this will give a marbled effect.

Bake for 1 hour. Allow the cake to cool before removing from the pan.

This cake can be iced or can just be given a glaze, made from sifted confectioners' sugar and lemon juice. Mix about 1 cup sugar with just enough lemon juice so that you can drizzle it over the cake.

Yield: 1 very large cake

The discovery of a new dish does more for the happiness of the human race than the discovery of a star.

Brillat-Savarin, *The Physiology of Taste*

NAMEDAYS

In many parts of Europe, the birthday is hardly observed at all, and what is celebrated is a person's "nameday"—the feast of the saint for whom he or she is named.

These practices, while generally quite foreign to Americans, have much to recommend them, especially today. We often hear it said there are no heroes, no heroines for children today, no figures of real value for them to admire, on whom to model themselves. But surely one fact about the great Old and New Testament figures, the early followers of Christ, and the many saints in the Western and Eastern traditions, is that they provide models of moral strength: of charity, of courage, of faithfulness—of heroism.

So if your child bears, as many children do, the name of a great saint or other impressive Biblical figure or Christian, why not celebrate the "nameday"? And if your child doesn't have such a name, let him or her choose one. For example, let your Jason pick David, or the apostle James, or Paul; your Jennifer or Maya, Rebecca or Judith, or one of the several Marys of the New Testament.

So celebrate the nameday as an intimate family gathering in honor of the person God made your child to be. Light a candle, read a Psalm (let your child choose one), pray together. Helen McLoughlin's *My Nameday, Come for Dessert* is full of charming suggestions for things to do—and to cook.

Your whole family might consider the possibility of doing as the Serbs do: consecrating the whole family to the patronage of one of the saints.

To find out when your child's (or your own) nameday falls, you can easily consult one of the various paperback dictionaries of saints.

Kugelhopf

The Kugelhopf is the traditional European nameday cake. Here is a particularly delicious version.

½ pound (2 sticks) sweet
butter
1½ cups sugar
6 egg yolks
Rind of 1 orange
Rind of ½ lemon
1 cup raisins, half golden,
half dark
3 tablespoons Cointreau or
other orange liqueur, or
rum
2 cups flour
2 teaspoons baking powder
Pinch of salt
½ cup milk
6 egg whites
Optional:
⅛ cup whole or sliced
blanched almonds

Preheat the oven to 350° F. Generously butter a large bundt pan.

Cream the butter, and add the sugar gradually. Cream until very fluffy. One at a time add the egg yolks, beating well after each addition. Stir in the orange and lemon rinds, the raisins, and the Cointreau.

Sift the flour with the baking powder and the salt. Add the flour and the milk alternately to the butter mixture, stirring constantly. Beat the egg whites until stiff but not dry. Fold them gently but thoroughly into the batter.

If you are using almonds, place them around the bottom of the bundt pan. Pour the batter into the pan.

Bake for about 1 hour, or until a straw inserted in the cake comes out clean. Cool the cake for 15–20 minutes in the pan. Loosen around the edges and the center of the pan, and turn out onto a platter.

Dust with confectioners' sugar

Yield: 1 large cake

Variations:

Replace the Cointreau with 1 teaspoon vanilla plus 2½ tablespoons orange juice. Non-raisin lovers can eliminate the raisins.

Russian nameday pretzel

KRENDL

In the Russian Orthodox tradition, the nameday is an important event. The person whose day it is first goes to church, as this is considered a holy day, then a party is held. At the feast, the guests may well eat Russian specialties such as pirogi *(little turnovers filled with meat or fish, etc.), preceded by* zakuski *(hors d'oeuvres). Toasts are drunk, the first three being offered to the guest of honor. The high point of the evening is the serving of the Krendl, a large beautiful sweet Pretzel, which all share.*

Prepare the dough for a Kulich (page 204), but do not work the almonds into the dough: they will be sprinkled on top later. You may include or omit the raisins and/or the chopped fruit.

After the dough has risen (once) to double its volume, punch it down. Place it on a large floured surface and form it into a long rope, about 1 inch thick in the middle, thinner at the ends.

Transfer the rope to a large buttered baking sheet. Form it into a large pretzel (see illustration). Tuck the ends of the rope into the fatter part of the pretzel. Cover the pretzel lightly and let it rise again in a draft-free spot until almost doubled in volume—about 20 to 30 minutes.

Sprinkle the finely chopped almonds over the surface.

Bake at 400° F. for 15 minutes. Reduce the heat to 350° and bake for another 30 to 45 minutes, or until the top is a golden brown. Sprinkle with confectioners' sugar.

Cool on a wire rack.

Yield: 6 servings

BIRTHDAYS

One of the best ways I know of for enhancing and deepening the bonds of family love and loyalty is to have a family party for each child's birthday. Include grandparents, if possible, and maybe one or two of the family's or the child's very dearest friends. But what matters most is the presence of the child's parents, brothers, and sisters.

During the party, go around the table and have each person there tell the birthday child what they especially love about him or her. We focus all the family's love and appreciation on that child. To know, to *hear,* how you are loved and admired by your whole family, isn't this a wonderful experience for a child of any age? This is the kind of moment that throws a warm and lasting glow over family life.

As to the menu for such a party, you will want to include some of the birthday child's favorite foods. There are many recipes for cake in this book; you can choose among them. You might enjoy making a homemade ice-cream cake, with two or three or more of your child's favorite flavors. Follow the directions given for the Molded Ice-Cream Dessert, page 151. You can unmold the dessert ahead of time. Place it on a freezer-proof platter. Make flowers or other decorations and write your child's name with icing or decorettes. Return the cake to the freezer until you are ready to serve it.

BAPTISM

Baptism is, in all branches of Christianity, a great sacrament, a momentous occasion. If the baptism, or christening, of babies is so especially moving, it is perhaps because babies themselves are so moving. As Dickens put it: "I love these little people, and it is not a slight thing when they, who are so fresh from God, love us." But, of course, it is not only babies who are baptized: often adults make the conscious decision to receive this sacrament, which gives it a particular resonance.

There are, in various countries, traditional dishes served after baptisms. In some countries, such as Lithuania, particular foods are brought by particular members of the party: the godmother brings a cake or fruit bread, the midwife a porridge of buckwheat groats.

Many of the traditional baptismal foods tend to be white or light-colored sweetmeats. The whiteness symbolizes the innocence of the newly baptized; the sweetness expresses, no doubt, the wish for a sweet life. Here is one charming example.

> *Sons are a heritage from the Lord, children a reward from him.*
> Psalm 127:3 (NIV)

Maltese christening cookies

BISKUTTINI TAL-MAGHMUDIJA

This is slightly adapted from Recipes from Malta *by Anne and Helen Caruana Galizia.*

7 cups flour
3½ cups sugar (see note)
1 teaspoon cinnamon
½ teaspoon ground cloves
Pinch of salt
1 teaspoon baking soda
8 eggs
2 ounces candied lemon
  peel, finely chopped
Optional:
  Pink and white icing

Preheat the oven to 400° F.

Place the flour in a large bowl. Stir in the sugar, cinnamon, cloves, salt, and baking soda. Mix thoroughly.

Separate the eggs. Add the yolks, one at a time, into the flour-sugar mixture, mixing well after each addition. Stir in the chopped lemon peel. Beat the egg whites until stiff but not dry. Fold them thoroughly but gently into the flour mixture.

Cover a large baking sheet with waxed paper, oil it lightly, and sprinkle it with a little flour and white sugar.

Flour your hands lightly. Taking a heaping tablespoon of the batter, roll it in your hands to form a round or oblong shape. Place the cookies about 2½ inches apart on the prepared baking sheet.

Bake for 7 to 10 minutes, or until the cookies are firm. Do not let them brown.

Optional:
Decorate with curlicues of pink and white icing.

Note: A mixture of white and brown sugar is traditional, but to accentuate the whiteness of the biscuit, you can use all white sugar.

FIRST COMMUNION AND CONFIRMATION

Many Christians are baptized as infants or little children, and thus have no memory of the occasion. But the taking of communion for the first time and confirmation can be deeply moving and memorable events for children and adolescents. One can reinforce the specialness of the occasion by having a party, composed of family, godparents, and special friends. The party could either be a simple reception or a whole meal, but it certainly should feature a beautiful cake. A Cassata is a specialty for such occasions. Or a large sheet cake may be decorated in honor of the event.

Italian cheesecake

CASSATA ALLA SICILIANA

1 pound of pound or sponge cake
1 pound ricotta cheese
¼ cup sugar
¼ cup heavy cream, whipped
¼ cup brandy, rum, orange-flavored or maraschino liqueur
2 ounces semisweet, bitter, or sweet chocolate, grated
¼ cup mixed candied fruit (optional)
Whipped Cream Icing (below) or any white icing
1 ounce bittersweet or sweet chocolate
Maraschino cherries and/or pistachio nuts

Trim off the crusts of the pound or sponge cake. Cut the cake into slices about ½ inch thick.

Using a spoon, force the ricotta through a sieve into a bowl. Stir in the sugar, cream, brandy (or other liqueur), grated chocolate, and candied fruits.

Oil a glass or ceramic loaf pan. (If you use a metal pan, the Cassata may pick up a metallic flavor.)

Place in the pan a layer of pound cake. Then spoon a layer of the ricotta mixture generously on top. Repeat the procedure, alternating cake and ricotta, and ending with a layer of cake. You should have about 4 layers of cake and 3 of ricotta.

Cover lightly and refrigerate for at least 3 or 4 hours (or overnight). When you are ready to ice the Cassata, turn it out onto a serving platter.

Coat the Cassata generously with the icing. Grate the chocolate over the top of the Cassata, and decorate it with cherries and/or pistachios, in a pretty design.

continued

Italian cheesecake, continued

WHIPPED CREAM ICING

½ pint heavy cream, whipped
3 tablespoons confectioners' sugar (or to taste)
½ teaspoon vanilla extract

Mix together the whipped cream, confectioners' sugar, and vanilla· extract.

Yield: about 8 servings

Variation:

You can replace the brandy or liqueur with 1 teaspoon of vanilla extract, 1 teaspoon lemon juice, and some maraschino-cherry liquid, or more cream, unwhipped.

Note: Not all children like candied fruit; leave it out if your young guest of honor doesn't like it.

Four-egg cake

For this occasion—and for many others that will occur in the pages of this book—here is a basic, flavorful cake. This recipe makes three 9-inch layers, or an 8-by-12-inch sheet cake. Several delicious (and simple) icing recipes are below.

1 cup butter, at room temperature
2 cups sugar
4 eggs at room temperature, separated
2⅔ cups sifted flour
2½ teaspoons baking powder
½ teaspoon salt
1 cup milk
2½ teaspoons vanilla extract (or, 1½ teaspoons vanilla, plus 1 teaspoon almond extract)

Preheat the oven to 350° F. Grease the baking pan or pans with butter or shortening. Sprinkle flour around in the pan, shake the pan from side to side, then discard excess flour.

Cream the butter, then add the sugar, beating until fluffy. Beat the egg yolks until lemon-colored, then stir them into the butter mixture, mixing thoroughly.

Resift the flour with the baking powder and salt. Add a little of the flour mixture to the butter mixture, mix well, then add a little milk; mix thoroughly. Continue adding the flour and the milk alternately to the butter mixture, until all are thoroughly incorporated. Stir in the vanilla.

Beat the egg whites until stiff but not dry. Fold them gently but thoroughly into the batter. Pour into the pan or pans.

Bake for 30 minutes for the 9-inch pans, 40 minutes for the larger pan—or until a toothpick inserted into the center comes out clean.

Let the cake cool for about 10 minutes in the pan on a cooling rack. Then loosen the sides of the cake with a spatula, and turn it out onto a wire cake rack. Frost when *fully cool.*

BUTTER-CREAM ICING

¼ cup butter, softened
4 cups confectioners' sugar, sifted
1 pinch salt
¼ cup heavy cream
1 teaspoon or more vanilla extract, or 1 tablespoon instant coffee and/or 1 tablespoon cognac or rum

This delicious and simple recipe makes enough icing for the tops and sides of any standard cake. The flavor can be varied in several ways: see below.

Cream the butter with a fork; add the sugar gradually, mixing well. Stir in the salt, cream, and desired flavoring. Mix thoroughly. If too thin, add more sugar; if too thick, add more cream.

Yield: about 2¼ cups of icing

DECORATIVE ICING

This icing, under several different names, is one of the basic decorating icings and certainly is one of the simplest. Keep it covered, once it is ready; it gets hard fast.

2 egg whites
2½ cups confectioners' sugar
1 teaspoon vanilla extract
1 teaspoon lemon juice
¼ teaspoon cream of tartar
Optional:
Food coloring (one or more colors)

Beat the egg whites until stiff but not dry, adding gradually during the beating the confectioners' sugar, vanilla, lemon juice, and cream of tartar. If you wish, add food coloring: you can divide the icing into several batches and make several different colors if you want.

To make the icing stiffer, add more sugar; thinner, add more lemon juice or water—*a little at a time.*

Yield: about 2 cups of icing

Decorated sheet cake

You can also prepare for a first communion or confirmation a large flat white cake (or any kind of cake), with a white icing. It can be decorated in any of the following ways (among others).

- With the words "Happy (or Blessed) First Communion (or Confirmation)," plus the child's name.
- With a short quotation from Scripture, such as "Blessed are the pure in heart; they shall see God" or another of the Beatitudes (Matthew 5), or from Psalms, perhaps.
- With the image of a dove, often a symbol for the soul.
- With an image of a chalice and a paten (the flat dish holding the sacred Host).
- With the image of a standing person praying with arms outstretched (from early Christian art).
- With an early Christian image of two angels carrying a "sacred monogram" that is, the letters chi and rho (χ and ρ), which are the first two letters of the Greek word for Christ.

Chaldean coconut cookies

AKRAS JOUZ AL-HIND

These triangular coconut cookies are served at First Communion parties among Christians in such countries as Iraq. According to their tradition, St. Thomas the Apostle on his way to India brought the Gospel to the Chaldeans of Babylon and Assyria.

This recipe is adapted from Babylonian Cuisine: Chaldean Cookbook from the Middle East *by Julia Najor.*

1½ cups sugar
½ cup water
2 eggs
4 cups flaked coconut
1 teaspoon cardamom
1 teaspoon almond extract
2 tablespoons cornstarch
½ teaspoon baking powder

In a small heavy saucepan mix the sugar and water. Stir over medium heat until the sugar is dissolved. Let the mixture come to a boil and skim off the foam. Let cook, stirring constantly, until the mixture registers 240° F. on a candy thermometer. Let cool.

In a bowl beat the eggs lightly, and add the remaining ingredients. Stir in the sugar syrup. Knead the dough gently in the bowl with the palm of the hand and the fingers for about 5 to 7 minutes.

Refrigerate for 2 hours.

Preheat oven to 300° F.

Take balls of dough a little larger than a walnut. Using a spoon or your fingers, form each ball into a flattish triangle about ¼ inch thick.

Place the cookies on greased baking sheets. Bake them for 35 to 40 minutes, or until they are a very light brown.

Yield: about 2 dozen cookies

Blessed are all who fear the Lord, who walk in his ways.
You will eat the fruit of your labor; blessings and prosperity will be
* yours.*
Your wife will be like a fruitful vine within your house;
your children will be like olive shoots around your table.
Psalm 128:1–3 (NIV)

MARRIAGE

A marriage is one of the greatest traditional causes for rejoicing and feasting. Almost every culture has found reason to rejoice, and to express good wishes, at weddings. The Judeo-Christian tradition has gone beyond these natural and universal motives, and has honored marriage as a sacred institution—for Catholics and Orthodox it is a sacrament. The very regulations concerning marriage in the Old Testament (and they are numerous) show the deep importance of this bond. There are in the Old Testament several beautiful and deeply religious relationships between husband and wife, such as that between Isaac and Rebecca, and between Tobit and Sarah—blessed, indeed "destined," by God. These are, truly, marriages made in heaven.

Jesus honored marriage by performing his first miracle at a wedding feast, at Cana. Reaffirming the law, he condemned adultery—and he even went beyond Jewish tradition in his condemnation of divorce. St. Paul, in his Letter to the Ephesians, compared the relationship of man and wife to that of Christ and the Church: a man must love his wife just as Christ loves his Church; no lesser love is enough.

Thus, intermingled with all the festivity and rejoicing at a Christian wedding feast is the nobility, the majesty, of the Christian view of marriage.

The dishes associated traditionally with wedding feasts tend to be spectacular: large, elaborately decorated breads and extraordinary cakes—such as the American wedding cake—accompanying a great plethora of meats and other festive dishes. (After all, this has been, in the lives of most wedding couples over the centuries, not merely a special occasion, but a unique, once-in-a-lifetime, event.) Many of these dishes picked up themes of sweetness, richness, fertility: the Armenians make a "wedding pilaf," to which raisins and nuts are added. Several kinds of fruitcake are traditionally made, such as the Dundee Cake given below. The themes of separateness and union are also stressed: in some places, the husband has "his" cake (often a dark, rich fruitcake), and the wife "hers" (often white, no doubt symbolizing virginity)—but each must eat of the other's cake: they must, henceforth, share.

Dundee cake

This light fruit cake, in which raisins and currants predominate, is made for weddings—with a piece reserved for the first christening. It can also be made for Christmas. A Dundee Cake can receive a milk-and-sugar glaze, or, if you prefer, an almond paste icing.

¾ cup each dark raisins,
  golden raisins, currants
⅓ cup each mixed candied
  fruit peel, chopped, and
  glacé cherries, halved
Flour for dredging fruits
1 cup sweet butter, softened
1 cup sugar
4 eggs
2 cups sifted flour
1 teaspoon baking powder
½ teaspoon cinnamon
¼ teaspoon nutmeg
Pinch of salt
¼ cup blanched almonds,
  ground
Grated rind of 1 orange
Grated rind of 1 lemon
Juice of ½ lemon
1 tablespoon brandy or rum
½ cup blanched almonds,
  slivered

GLAZE:
2 tablespoons milk
1 tablespoon sugar
Or Almond Paste Icing
  (page 185)

Preheat the oven to 325° F. Grease an 8- or 9-inch cake pan, line with waxed paper, and grease the paper.

Dredge the raisins and currants, fruit peel and cherries with flour. Shake off excess flour.

Cream the butter, and work in the sugar until the mixture is creamy. Add the eggs one at a time. Sift the flour with the baking powder, spices, and salt. Add the flour mixture to the butter mixture gradually, stirring well between additions. Stir in the ground almonds, the dredged fruit peel, the grated orange and lemon rinds, the lemon juice, and the brandy or rum. Turn the batter into the pan, and sprinkle with slivered almonds.

Bake for 1¼ to 1½ hours, or until the cake has shrunk from the sides of the pan and a toothpick inserted into the center comes out clean. Cool in the pan on a rack.

For the glaze: Heat the milk and stir in the sugar until dissolved. Pour over the cake. Or ice with the Almond Paste Icing.

Yield: 1 eight- or nine-inch cake

I sing of brooks, of blossoms, birds, and bowers:
Of April, May, of June, and July flowers.
I sing of Maypoles, Hock-carts, wassails, wakes,
Of bridegrooms, brides, and of their bridal cakes.

Robert Herrick, *Hesperides*

MORE FOOD FOR THOUGHT ON OCCASIONS OF FEASTING

Some festive foods are associated with particular feasts, such as turkey with Thanksgiving, particular breads with Christmas or Easter. But many dishes are just *generally* festive: they have traditionally been served or might well be served at any happy occasion.

You will find an assortment of them in this section of the book.

French pastry ring, flavored with Swiss cheese
GOUGÈRE

No festive occasion in France—especially in Burgundy—would be complete without a Gougère: this is a beautiful (and easy-to-prepare) pastry, flavored with Swiss cheese. It is delicious as an appetizer or first course. Try serving it with red wine. Or serve with a Kir. This now-famous French drink—a mixture of white wine or white vermouth, with a dash or two of crème de cassis—was named for a French priest, active in the Résistance to the Nazis in World War II, and mayor of the city of Lyon. He is said to have loved this light mixture of wine and cassis. It makes a nice substitute for heavy (and highly alcoholic) American cocktails.

1 cup milk
⅓ cup sweet butter
½ teaspoon salt
1 cup flour
4 large eggs
1 cup Gruyère or other good-quality Swiss cheese, grated
¼ cup the same cheese, diced
1 egg, beaten

Preheat the oven to 375°F. Butter a cookie sheet.

Put the milk, butter, and salt in a saucepan. When the milk is hot and the butter has melted, remove the pan from the heat, and add the flour *all at once*. Beat until all the flour is incorporated.

Return the pan to moderate heat and beat constantly with a wooden spoon until the mixture leaves the sides of the pan.

Remove from the heat, and add the eggs, one at a time, beating hard. Be sure to incorporate each egg thoroughly before adding the next. Gradually beat in the grated cheese.

Form the dough into a ring on the cookie sheet. Sprinkle the top with the diced cheese, and brush on the beaten egg.

Bake for 25 minutes. Lower the heat to 350° F. and bake for another 10 minutes, or until the Gougère is puffed and golden brown.

Yield: 4 to 6 servings

Shrimp mold

The fish being of such importance in our tradition, this dish makes a symbolically meaningful first course for any feast. Fish molds are available in many department and cookware stores.

1½ cups (about 1 pound) cooked shrimp
1 package unflavored gelatin
¼ cup cold water
½ cup hot water
2 tablespoons chili sauce
2 tablespoons grated onion
2 tablespoons lemon juice
1 cup mayonnaise
½ cup finely chopped celery
Optional:
  A dash of Tabasco

Peel and devein the shrimp. Chop coarsely.

Sprinkle the gelatin into the cold water in a large bowl. Let sit until softened. Stir in the hot water until the gelatin is dissolved. Add the chili sauce, grated onion, lemon juice, mayonnaise, celery, and chopped shrimp. Add the tabasco, if you like. Adjust seasoning.

Oil a fish mold lightly. Pour the shrimp mixture into the mold and refrigerate for several hours or until set.

Yield: 4 to 6 servings

Steamed artichokes

An artichoke makes a splendid first course or vegetable dish for any feast.

4 artichokes
1 bay leaf
6–8 peppercorns
Optional:
    Lemon juice

Trim off the stems of the artichokes so that they can stand flat. If you like, trim off the top ½ inch or so of each large leaf, using kitchen scissors. Trim off the top inch or more of the artichoke itself so that the top is flat. Rub the cut surfaces with lemon juice.

Place the artichokes on a vegetable steamer in a large pot with a tight-fitting lid. Toss in the bay leaf and peppercorns. Pour in about 1 inch of water. Bring to a boil. Cover the pot, reduce heat, and steam the artichokes for about 1 hour, or until done. Test by pulling off a large leaf for tasting: the fleshy part should be soft. Check occasionally to be sure the water has not boiled away.

Serve hot, with Hollandaise Sauce (page 41) or melted butter to which a little lemon juice, salt, and pepper have been added. Or serve cold with a vinaigrette to which you can add a little chopped onion and parsley and a few capers; or with mayonnaise flavored with lemon juice, salt, and pepper.

Yield: serves 4

Roast suckling pig

Perhaps the most traditional meat for festive occasions throughout much of the world—from Croatia to Peru—is Roast Suckling Pig. Served with a beautiful red apple or a large yellow lemon in its mouth, and perhaps with a garland of flowers or leaves around its neck, a golden roast pig is truly a triumphant spectacle. Delicious, too! You will need a large roasting pan.

Serve this with spiced apples (below).

1 suckling pig, about 10 to
    12 pounds, cleaned and
    oven ready
Salt
Freshly ground pepper
Sage and/or thyme

Sprinkle the inside of the pig with salt, pepper, sage and/or thyme.

For the stuffing: Sauté the onions in the butter until soft and translucent but not brown. Add the remaining ingredients and mix thoroughly but lightly. Taste for seasoning.

STUFFING:
4 cups chopped onions
¾ cup butter
6 cups dry breadcrumbs
2 eggs, beaten
Salt and freshly ground
pepper to taste
½ teaspoon sage and/or
thyme
½ teaspoon paprika
1 or 2 tart apples, finely
chopped or grated
Stock, white wine, or
slivovitz to moisten
lightly

FOR BASTING:
olive oil, cooking oil, butter,
or lard
or a Hungarian version: ½
cup melted lard to 3
tablespoons wine vinegar
or a Croatian specialty:
equal parts melted butter
and beer

Cherries or grapes, for the
eyes
An apple or lemon, for the
mouth
Optional:
Leaves or flowers for the
garland

Fill the pig with the stuffing. Close with skewers and string. Place an apple-sized ball of aluminum foil (or a block of wood, or a large potato) in the pig's mouth.

Place in a roasting pan, if possible on a rack. Place the hind legs under the rump, the front legs forward (as best you can). If need be, prop the legs up on an aluminum-foil "extender" to your roasting pan. Rub the pig with oil, butter, lard, or a basting mixture. Stick a meat thermometer into the thickest part of the thigh.

Roast at 450° F. for 30 minutes, then reduce the heat to 350° F. Roast for about 20 minutes per pound, or approximately 3½ to 4 hours. (When the internal temperature has reached 185° F. and the legs move easily, the pig is done.) Baste frequently with oil, butter, lard, or one of the basting mixtures.

When it is done, remove the pig to a hot platter. Remove the skewers, lacings, and aluminum-foil coverings. Place an apple (or lemon) in the mouth; cherries or grapes in the eyes. Optional: Make a garland of leaves or flowers to place around the neck.

For a sauce, skim the fat from the pan drippings and serve with the roast.

To carve: first remove the forelegs and hind legs. Cut down the center of the back, and remove the rib chops.

Yield: 10 to 12 servings

Note: A suckling pig is prepared at least in large part for show: because it is such a spectacular-looking dish. But there is not an enormous amount of meat on it. If you are serving a large group, you might want to prepare a pork roast, such as a loin, as well, and have it all sliced and ready to serve when you bring out the pig. You can combine the two on the plates as you serve them.

3 large cooking apples
3 tablespoons butter
Confectioners' sugar
2 tablespoons water
1 teaspoon white vinegar
⅛ teaspoon ground cloves
¼ teaspoon cinnamon
Currant jelly

SPICED APPLES
Core the apples, and cut crosswise into slices.

In a large frying pan heat the butter and place the apples in the pan in a single layer. Sprinkle lightly with the confectioners' sugar. Add the water, vinegar, cloves, and cinnamon. Cover the skillet and simmer the apple slices, gently, until just tender. Remove the cover, and brown the apples on both sides.

Arrange the slices on a serving platter. Fill the centers with currant jelly.

Mock venison

One of the great festive dishes has traditionally been venison—but for centuries it was accessible only to the nobility; and today not many of us have deer hunters in our families. But here is our consolation, a marvelous Mock Venison: a leg of lamb marinated so that it tastes a great deal like venison.

1 six-pound leg of lamb, fell and excess fat removed
2 cups dry red wine, dark beer, or dark ale
1 cup vinegar
6–8 peppercorns
2 bay leaves
12–15 juniper berries, lightly crushed
1 sprig parsley
2 sprigs thyme or rosemary
2 crushed cloves garlic
2 sliced onions
1 teaspoon nutmeg
½ teaspoon mace
2 teaspoons salt
Optional:
   10 to 15 whole cloves
   1 cup heavy cream

In a nonreactive bowl (enamel, glass, pottery, or stainless steel) cover the meat with the wine and vinegar. Add the remaining ingredients, except the cloves. Refrigerate for 2 or 3 days (or longer). Turn the meat occasionally.

Dry off the meat, reserving the marinade. Optional: stud it with the cloves. Place the meat on a rack in a roasting pan. Roast it at 400° F. for 30 minutes. Then reduce the heat to 350° and continue roasting for another 30 minutes for rare meat, or longer if you like your lamb well done. Baste frequently with the marinade. Optional: In the last 5 to 10 minutes of cooking, baste the lamb with the cream.

Remove the lamb to a serving platter. Degrease the juices, if necessary. Scrape the pan, and blend the remaining juices into a smooth sauce. Strain and serve with the roast.

Yield: 6 to 8 servings

Variations:

There are many different versions of this dish. The blend of herbs and spices can be modified a good deal, according to your tastes. The one unusual but essential ingredient is juniper berries.

Haitian pork in spicy lime sauce

GRIOT

1½ pounds boneless pork loin cut into 1-inch chunks

MARINADE:
Juice of 3 limes
¾ teaspoon coarse salt
¼ teaspoon thyme
2 scallions, chopped
1 whole hot red or green pepper
Olive or corn oil

GARNISH:
Sliced limes, sliced hot pepper, chopped parsley

Here is an extraordinarily festive dish from Haiti. Try serving it with Marinated Raw Cabbage, Fried Plantains, and Spicy Tomato Sauce (recipes below).

Marinate the meat overnight or for several hours in a mixture of the lime juice, salt, thyme, scallions, and hot pepper.

Simmer the meat in the marinade until it is no longer pink on the inside. Drain the meat and fry it in a little olive or corn oil, until nicely browned.

Serve with slices of hot pepper and lime, and sprinkle with chopped parsley.

Yield: 4 servings

MARINATED RAW CABBAGE
Grate a small green cabbage into a bowl. Marinate for several hours in a mixture of chopped hot red or green pepper, salt, and a little warm water. Drain before serving.

FRIED PLANTAINS
Plantains are large, nonsweet relatives of the banana.

1 large green plantain
2 cups water
Salt
About ¼ cup peanut oil

Peel the plantain and cut it into diagonal slices about 1½ inches thick. Soak the slices in the water, to which 1 tablespoon salt has been added, for about 1 hour. Drain well.

Fry the slices in the oil over medium heat for about 5 minutes. Remove from the oil and drain on paper towels. Reserve the oil.

Place the plantain slices on a flat surface and mash them slightly with a small cutting board—or, when they are sufficiently cooled, with your palm.

Fry the slices again until nicely browned on each side. Drain thoroughly on paper towels and sprinkle with salt.

Yield: 4 servings

½ teaspoon thyme
¾ teaspoon chopped
    shallots
1½ teaspoons chopped
    onions
Chopped hot red or green
    pepper, to taste

SPICY TOMATO SAUCE
Make 1½ cups Basic Delicious Tomato Sauce (page 60). Add to it the ingredients listed here.

> The Creator, while forcing men to eat in order to live, tempts him to do so with appetite and then rewards him with pleasure.
>
> Brillat-Savarin, *The Physiology of Taste*

Baked carrots

3 cups grated or julienned
    carrots
4 tablespoons butter, melted
1 teaspoon salt
½ teaspoon freshly ground
    pepper
1 teaspoon powdered ginger
1 tablespoon brown sugar

This dish is slightly adapted from a specialty of Enfield Shaker Village, Connecticut, as reprinted in The Best of Shaker Cooking, *by Amy Bess Miller and Persis Fuller.*

Place the carrots in a casserole. Combine with the remaining ingredients. Cover and bake at 350° F. for ½ hour.

Yield: 4 to 6 servings

Heaven and earth

HIMMEL UND ERDE

Here is a fine accompaniment to Roast Suckling Pig, Mock Venison or any rich meat. Heaven and Earth (what a wonderful name!) is a traditional peasant dish, composed of mashed or puréed potatoes, turnips, and apples. It can be varied in numerous ways, according to taste.

1 pound yellow or white
   turnips
1 pound potatoes
½ pound apples
6–8 tablespoons butter
A few tablespoons milk or
   cream
Salt
Freshly ground pepper
   (black or white)
Nutmeg, preferably freshly
   grated
Optional:
   1 or 2 teaspoons sugar

Peel and quarter the turnips, potatoes, and apples. Cook the turnips and potatoes in boiling salted water until tender. Cook the apple quarters in a little water until soft.

Mash together the turnips, potatoes, and apples. Stir in the butter and slowly add enough milk or cream to produce the consistency of mashed potatoes. Stir in salt, pepper, and nutmeg to taste. Add sugar if you like.

Serve hot with meat.

Yield: 8 to 10 servings

Variations:

Modify the proportions in any way you wish. You can also eliminate the apples: a mixture of puréed potatoes and turnips is delicious. Or you can replace the apples with cooked, mashed carrots.

Other ways of flavoring the mixture include a little paprika, some caraway seeds, or some sour cream.

Bavarian-style cabbage

4 tablespoons diced bacon
6–8 tablespoons chopped
   onion
1 clove garlic, finely
   chopped (optional)
4 tablespoons bacon fat
1 pound cabbage, shredded
1 tablespoon sugar
2 tablespoons vinegar
1 small onion, studded with
   4 cloves
1 bay leaf
4 tablespoons chicken or
   beef stock
1 tablespoon caraway seeds
¼ cup white wine

This is a delicious and traditional accompaniment to all the rich holiday meats.

Sauté the bacon, chopped onion, and garlic, if used, in the bacon fat. Stir in the cabbage, sugar, and vinegar. Add the whole onion, bay leaf, stock, and caraway seeds. Cover and simmer very gently about 15 minutes, until tender. Stir in the white wine and simmer for 2 or 3 more minutes.

Yield: 4 to 6 servings

Whole cauliflower

A whole head of cauliflower is an impressive sight. It can be served hot with Herbed Breadcrumbs (see below) or with Hollandaise Sauce (page 41); or cold with Mustard Vinaigrette (below).

1 whole cauliflower: choose as handsome and perfect a head as possible
1 teaspoon salt

Trim off the leaves and cut off the stem. Shave off any imperfections in the cauliflower's surface.

Place in a large pot of boiling salted water to cover and boil uncovered for about 20 minutes, or until just tender when pierced with a fork. Drain thoroughly. (You can also steam the cauliflower: place it on a steamer rack in a large pot with a tight-fitting cover. Pour in about 1 inch water. Bring the water to a boil, cover the pot, and reduce the heat. Steam the cauliflower until just tender.)

Serve hot or at room temperature.

HERBED BREADCRUMBS

6 tablespoons sweet butter
¾ cup breadcrumbs
1–2 teaspoons chopped fresh parsley, tarragon, or dill
2 teaspoons lemon juice
Salt and freshly ground pepper to taste

Melt the butter in a skillet. When it begins to bubble, stir in the breadcrumbs. Sauté for 2 to 3 minutes, or until the crumbs are golden brown. Add the chopped herbs, lemon juice, and salt and pepper to taste.

Variations:

Sauté ½ to 1 clove garlic, pressed, *or* sliced or slivered almonds along with the breadcrumbs.

Vary the herbs: use chives, chervil, or basil.

MUSTARD VINAIGRETTE

6 tablespoons olive oil
2 tablespoons lemon juice
1 teaspoon tarragon or chervil
1 teaspoon dry mustard
2 tablespoons chopped fresh parsley
1 clove garlic, pressed (optional)
Salt
Freshly ground black pepper
12 black olives, preferably oil-cured (optional)
Sprigs of parsley

Combine thoroughly the oil, lemon juice, tarragon, mustard, parsley, and garlic. (You can whirl them in your blender.) Add salt and pepper to taste.

Pour the vinaigrette over the cauliflower and let it marinate for several hours or longer.

Serve it in a large flat bowl or on a platter, surrounded by black olives, if you like, and sprigs of parsley.

Yield: 4 to 6 servings

Vegetables baked in a mold

One of the handsomest ways of serving vegetables such as broccoli, cauliflower, spinach, and asparagus (and many others) is what the French call a timbale, *the Italians a* sformato. *The vegetables are first cooked, then mixed with a béchamel sauce and often grated cheese, and turned into a mold. The mold is placed in a* bain-marie: *that is, in a large pan of boiling water in the oven. The term* bain-marie *(Mary's bath) derives from a curious legend. In the Middle Ages Moses was thought to have had a sister Mary who was an alchemist and used this cooking device in her preparations.*

The dish is unmolded onto a platter and is often served with a delicious sauce such as Hollandaise or Béarnaise, both given opposite.

1 pound (about 2⅓ cups) cooked broccoli, cauliflower, spinach, or asparagus
6 tablespoons butter
8 tablespoons flour
1¾ cups milk
3 eggs
4–6 tablespoons freshly grated Parmesan cheese
½ teaspoon salt
Freshly ground black pepper
⅛–¼ teaspoon freshly grated nutmeg
1 to 2 teaspoons lemon juice (optional)
2 tablespoons grated onion (optional)
Butter for the mold
Hollandaise or Béarnaise Sauce (optional)

Preheat oven to 400° F.

Chop the vegetables fine, put through a food mill, or chop in a processor.

Melt the butter in a heavy saucepan over low heat. When it is beginning to bubble, mix in the flour and, stirring frequently, let cook over low heat for 2 to 3 minutes. Remove from heat.

Heat the milk until almost boiling. Pour it all at once into the butter-flour mixture, stirring constantly with a whisk or a wooden spoon. Return the saucepan to medium heat and, still stirring constantly, cook the sauce until it is thick and smooth. Let cool.

Stir in the eggs, Parmesan cheese, salt, pepper, nutmeg, and if you wish, the lemon juice and grated onion. Add the vegetables. Mix thoroughly. Adjust seasoning.

Butter a mold generously. Pour the vegetable mixture into the mold. Set the mold in a fairly large, high-sided ovenproof pan. Pour in enough boiling water to come several inches up the sides of the mold.

Place the pan in the oven and cook for 60 to 70 minutes, or until a knife inserted in the center comes out clean and the vegetable mixture begins to pull away a little from the sides of the mold. If during cooking the top surface of the vegetable mixture begins to get too dark, cover with aluminum foil.

Remove the mold from the pan and let cool for about 10 minutes. Turn out onto a serving platter. Serve hot or at room temperature. (This dish can also be reheated successfully.) It is good by itself, or with a Hollandaise or Béarnaise Sauce (following recipes).

Yield: 6 to 8 servings

HOLLANDAISE SAUCE
This sauce, like the following, is one of the classics of French cuisine. It is delicious with almost any hot vegetable, and with many fish and meat dishes as well.

3 egg yolks
1 tablespoon water
1 stick (¼ pound) sweet butter, cut in pieces
Pinch of salt
1½ teaspoons lemon juice
Optional:
    Pinch of cayenne pepper or a little ground white pepper

Place the yolks in the top of a double boiler. Beat with a wire whisk for 1 minute. Add the water and beat for 1 minute. Place the top of the double boiler over 1 or 2 inches of hot but *not boiling* water.

Beating constantly with the whisk, gradually add the butter, one piece at a time. Beat until the sauce is thickened. If the sauce gets too thick, it can be thinned out with a little water. If it curdles try adding up to a teaspoonful of boiling water.

Add the salt, lemon juice, and if you like, the pepper. Adjust seasonings.

Variations:
You can add as additional flavoring a little mustard, or a little chopped or dried tarragon.

BÉARNAISE SAUCE
Superlative with the molded vegetables opposite, and with almost any grilled meat or fish.

¼ cup wine vinegar
2 teaspoons shallots or scallions, finely chopped
2 teaspoons chopped fresh tarragon or 1 teaspoon dried
Pinch of salt
Freshly ground pepper
Plus: Ingredients for Hollandaise Sauce

Combine the vinegar, shallots, and flavorings in a saucepan. Boil down until reduced almost to a glaze: only a few teaspoons will be left.

Add this to the yolks and proceed as for Hollandaise Sauce.

Béarnaise can be flavored with more chopped herbs if you wish: add at the end chopped parsley, chervil, or more tarragon; more lemon juice or vinegar.

Baked acorn squash

We really should give a place of honor to the squash, or gourd: in some of the very earliest paintings in Christian art, the gourd is shown as a symbol of redemption. This is because, in the Book of Jonah, God delivered Jonah from the whale, and made a plant grow over him as "shade for his head." This plant becomes very important in the story. (Reread Jonah, and see why.) In the early Christian era, the gourd plant, which is how the Hebrew text was translated (now we find "castor oil plant"), came to represent divine mercy and salvation. Sometimes the "gourds" in question look like our winter squashes, sometimes more like cucumbers or zucchini. Serve these dishes with any roast.

4 acorn squash
4 tablespoons brown sugar
  or honey
8 tablespoons butter
Salt and freshly ground
  black pepper

Cut the squash in halves and discard the seeds. Arrange the halves, cut side up, on a baking sheet.

Place ½ tablespoon brown sugar and 1 tablespoon butter in each half, and season to taste with salt and pepper. Bake at 350° F. for 45 minutes, or until the squash is tender.

Yield: 8 servings

Variations:

Place applesauce in the cavities, along with the butter and sugar, or fill with the apple and prune stuffing found on page 221.

Stuffed zucchini

4 zucchini
About 4 tablespoons olive
  or peanut oil
1 clove garlic, pressed or
  minced
½ medium onion, finely
  chopped
¾ cup breadcrumbs
½ teaspoon oregano, basil,
  or mint
2 tablespoons finely
  chopped fresh parsley
4 tablespoons freshly grated
  Parmesan cheese
1 to 2 tablespoons stock,
  wine, or tomato juice
Salt and freshly ground
  pepper to taste

Preheat oven to 350° F.

Cook the zucchini in boiling water to cover for about 15 minutes, or until just tender when pierced with a fork. Halve lengthwise. With a sharp paring or grapefruit knife, carefully remove most of the pulp, leaving the shells intact.

Chop the zucchini pulp and sauté it in the oil with the garlic and onion. Mix in the breadcrumbs, and add the oregano, parsley, Parmesan cheese, and a little liquid: just enough to moisten the mixture slightly. Add salt and pepper to taste.

Lay the zucchini halves on a greased baking sheet and fill with the stuffing. Bake for 20 minutes. To brown tops, run briefly under the broiler.

Yield: 8 servings

Variations:

There are many ways of varying the flavoring in the stuffing. You can add crushed canned or chopped fresh tomatoes to the mixture, or change the herbs; add a little lemon juice or chopped nuts.

Here, as well, is a Middle Eastern version: With the zucchini pulp, garlic, and onion, brown ¾ cup ground lamb or beef. Stir in ¾ cup cooked rice and add ½ teaspoon dried mint, ¼ teaspoon ground allspice, and 2 tablespoons chopped fresh parsley. Add liquid to moisten, and salt and pepper. Stuff the zucchini and proceed as above.

Serve with tomato sauce.

Note: Eggplant also lends itself admirably well to the same treatments. As with zucchini, begin by boiling the eggplant in water to cover for about 12 to 15 minutes, or until just tender. Proceed as for zucchini, but of course you will need more of everything as eggplants are substantially larger.

Oyster-and-wild-rice casserole

2 cups raw wild rice (or a wild-rice and white-rice mixture)
1 stick butter at room temperature
1 cup thick white sauce (see Note)
1 cup half-and-half
2 tablespoons chopped onion
¾ teaspoon tarragon or thyme
Salt
Freshly ground pepper
3 pints oysters (preferably small oysters)
¼ cup chopped fresh parsley

Cook the rice until soft (follow directions on the package). Drain thoroughly. Add the butter and stir until the mixture is well blended.

Preheat the oven to 325° F.

Butter a large shallow casserole or baking dish and pour in the rice mixture, spreading it evenly.

Combine the white sauce with the half-and-half. Stir in the onion, tarragon, and salt and pepper to taste. Mix in the oysters. Pour this mixture evenly over the rice. Bake for about 45 minutes.

Sprinkle with parsley before serving.

Yield: 8 to 10 servings

Note: To make a thick white or béchamel sauce: Melt 2 tablespoons butter in a saucepan. Stir in 2 tablespoons flour and cook, stirring, for 2 or 3 minutes. Gradually add ¾ cup hot milk and cook over medium heat, stirring constantly, until thickened. Season to taste with salt, pepper, nutmeg, and lemon juice. If you are in a rush, you can substitute canned cream of celery or cream of mushroom soup for the white sauce.

An oyster, that marvel of delicacy, that concentration of sapid excellence, that mouthful before all other mouthfuls, who first had faith to believe it, and courage to execute? The exterior is not persuasive.

Henry Ward Beecher, *Eyes and Ears*

FIVE CLASSIC POTATO DISHES

Let's face it: many of our near and dear would rather have potatoes than anything else along with their meat, on festive or any occasions. Here are five all-time favorite potato dishes: Pan-Fried, Scalloped, homemade French Fries, Potato Puffs and Stuffed Baked Potatoes.

Pan-fried potatoes

4 large potatoes
4–6 tablespoons butter, bacon fat, beef drippings, or olive oil
Salt
Freshly ground black pepper

Wash and peel the potatoes. Cut them in thin slices and place them in a bowl of cold water for 10 to 20 minutes. Dry thoroughly.

Melt the fat in a heavy skillet. Add the potato slices and cook over medium heat, turning often so that they brown evenly. Season them with some salt and pepper as they are cooking.

The potatoes are done when golden brown and tender. Adjust seasoning.

Yield: 4 servings

Scalloped potatoes

4 large potatoes, peeled, sliced thin
½ cup onions, finely chopped or sliced thin
About 1½ teaspoons salt
Freshly ground black pepper
4–6 tablespoons butter
Milk

Preheat oven to 375° F.

Butter a baking dish or casserole about 10 inches square. Lay in it a layer of potatoes, sprinkle it with onions, season with a little salt and pepper and dot it with butter. Continue this procedure until all the potatoes are used up. Pour in the milk so that it is just even with the top layer of potatoes. Sprinkle with salt and pepper.

Cover and bake for 30 minutes. Remove the cover and bake until the potatoes are nicely browned, and are tender when pierced with a fork: 30 to 45 minutes.

Yield: 4 to 6 servings

Variations:

Substitute chopped scallions or chives for the onions, or eliminate the onions.

Sprinkle grated Parmesan cheese in with or instead of the onions between layers. Sprinkle some on top as well. Before serving, dot the top with butter and run the dish briefly under the broiler.

Sprinkle chopped or whole anchovy fillets or crumbled fried bacon between layers. In this case, reduce salt.

Use heavy cream and/or chicken broth in place of all or part of the milk.

French fries

What can match a homemade French fry?

6 mature baking potatoes
1½ to 2 quarts vegetable oil
   or rendered suet (beef
   kidney fat) or a
   combination of both
Salt
Freshly ground black pepper

Peel the potatoes and slice them into strips about ½ inch thick. (First cut them into ½-inch slices, then cut the slices into ½-inch strips.) Soak the potato strips in cold water for 20 to 30 minutes. Dry thoroughly.

Heat the oil in a large pot or deep-fat fryer until it registers 350° F. on a deep-frying thermometer.

Place about a cup of the potatoes in a metal basket and fry them in the oil until they are golden brown but not yet crisp, about 3 to 4 minutes. Remove and drain thoroughly on paper towels or brown paper bags. Continue until all the potatoes are cooked. Let sit for 5 minutes, or until just before you are planning to serve the potatoes.

Heat the oil to 375°. Return the potatoes to the basket: this time you can put them all in at once. Fry them until crisp and brown, about 2 to 3 minutes.

Drain thoroughly. Season to taste with salt and pepper

Yield: 4 servings

Variations:

To make shoestring potatoes, make the potato strips thinner: about $3/16$ of an inch; to make potato chips, cut the potatoes into slices as thin as possible. For either, reduce the first cooking time to 1 minute.

Potato puffs

½ cup flour
1 teaspoon baking powder
¼ teaspoon salt
1 cup mashed potatoes, at
   room temperature
1 egg, lightly beaten
2 teaspoons finely chopped
   fresh parsley
Pinch of paprika
About 1 quart vegetable oil
   for deep-fat frying

Combine the flour, baking powder, and salt in a bowl. Mix in the mashed potatoes. Add the egg, parsley, and paprika. Adjust seasoning.

Heat the oil to 375° F.

Drop the potato mixture by teaspoonfuls into the hot fat. Fry until golden brown. Drain thoroughly on paper towels or brown paper bags.

Yield: 4 servings

What I say is that, if a man really likes potatoes, he must be a pretty decent sort of fellow.

A. A. Milne, *Not That It Matters*

Stuffed baked potatoes

4 large, mature Idaho
  baking potatoes
1 tablespoon butter or
  vegetable oil
3 tablespoons butter
3 tablespoons heavy cream,
  or sour cream
½ teaspoon salt
1 tablespoon grated onion
  and/or ¼ cup freshly
  grated Parmesan cheese
  (optional)
Paprika

Preheat oven to 400° F.

Wash and scrub the potatoes. With a sharp knife make a slit about ½ inch long on the top of each potato. Dry them and rub with the 1 tablespoon butter or vegetable oil. Place on a baking sheet.

Bake for 40 minutes to 1 hour or until the potatoes are soft when pierced with a fork. Remove the potatoes from the oven. Cut them in half lengthwise. Scoop out pulp.

Preheat broiler.

In a bowl, mix the pulp with the butter, heavy or sour cream, and salt. Stir in the grated onion or Parmesan cheese, if you like, or both. Adjust seasoning.

Fill the potato shells with the mixture. Sprinkle with more Parmesan cheese, if you like, and with paprika.

Run the potatoes under the broiler until nicely browned.

Yield: 8 servings

Variations:

You can substitute chopped chives for the onions; add crumbled fried bacon; use grated sharp Cheddar cheese instead of the Parmesan.

Pray for peace and grace and spiritual food,
For wisdom and guidance, for all these are good,
But don't forget the potatoes.
    J. T. Pettee, *Prayer and Potatoes,* from M. F. K. Fisher,
        How to Cook a Wolf

Day by day

The greater part of this book is concerned with special days—Sundays, picnics, and feasts in honor of some particular occasion or holy day on the Christian calendar. But the most important day, the day on which our true appreciation of all the others depends, is still "every day." We must find how to live so that each day is somehow consecrated, for each day sets the tone for how we live out the year.

One practice we can introduce that will unquestionably enhance the quality of our family life is to eat our meals together as often as possible. Nowadays, a great many people eat all their meals alone, and on the run. Supper may consist of a bite grabbed at a pizza parlor or a drive-in burger joint, or scrounged out of the refrigerator. Nutritionally speaking, this is a disaster. Such snacking is not the stuff of which balanced meals are made. What is also serious is the long-term impact of such eating patterns on the family.

When we sit down to a meal with other people, we share the pleasure of having our hunger satisfied. We share the pleasure of eating good food and we share the pleasure of conversation. We reveal ourselves to each other; we really get to know each other.

Conversation occurs at other times as well, of course, but there is simply no better, no more natural, no more pleasant setting for it than a meal. Table conversation is particularly important to family life. All intimate relationships have their tensions, their strains; this is true even in the most loving of families. To talk at mealtimes keeps the channels of communication open; it ensures that members of the family who may otherwise be having a hard time getting along keep talking to each other. The structures and pleasures of the meal itself, and the presence of other family members, serve as a neutralizer for feelings of anger. (This is, of course, why enemies who can manage to eat together often stop being enemies.)

Spread the table and contention will cease.

English Proverb

48

There is a spiritual dimension to this issue as well. Eating together has particular importance in Christianity. Just think of the number of shared meals in the New Testament—the miraculous loaves and fishes, the Last Supper, Christ cooking breakfast on the beach for his disciples, the agape meals of the early Christians. All shared meals are, in a sense, sacred in Christianity. Eating together should remind us that we are all members together, of one Body.

We simply cannot allow family life to disintegrate, with respect to the breaking of bread together. But it's a real problem! Here are a few practical suggestions.

Try to reschedule activities for other times. Say "no" more often to early-evening meetings, classes, and so on. Struggle to keep your work at the office from interfering with family life. Turn off—unplug! *dismantle!*—the TV if it gets in the way of preparing and eating dinner. If the whole family can't sit down together at the table, see to it that those who can, share the meal. For example, if the father comes home late, at least have the children eat together—with Mom present—and then she can eat later with Dad.

Try to make sure that the meal is pleasant for all concerned. This means that everyone should have an opportunity to talk; no one or two persons should be allowed to monopolize the conversation. And rudeness or unpleasantness or ridicule should not be present. This does not mean that controversial topics cannot be discussed at all, but certain rules of courtesy must be respected. (You'll probably have to work on table manners too.) Parents should make this a time to pass out deserved compliments, and to encourage each child to talk about his or her interests and activities. Every shared meal should work toward an increase of unity and harmony within the family.

A second suggestion is to say grace before dinner. In my family, asking God's blessing over food has encouraged us all to think about the sacredness of food, about the fact that things have grown, that animals have died, that we might eat. Saying a blessing over food brings up—in all our minds—the big questions of life, such as the relationship between what we eat and what we are supposed to do with our lives. As the old blessing says, "Bless, O Lord, this food to our use, and our lives to your service. Give us grateful hearts, and keep us ever mindful of the needs and feelings of others."

Blessings: a few traditional and otherwise lovely graces, from various sources

Bless, O Lord, this food to our use, and our lives to your (loving) service. Give us grateful hearts, and keep us ever mindful of the needs (and feelings) of others. Amen.

Bless us, O Lord, and these thy gifts, which we are about to receive, from thy bounty, through Christ, Our Lord. Amen. (This is the basic old Latin grace that Christians throughout the world have said for centuries: *"Benedic, Domine, nos et haec tua dona, quae de tua largitate sumus sumpturi, per Christum dominum nostrum. Amen."*)

Our heavenly Father, thou has provided us with all good things, so fill our hearts with thy love and grace that we may use every gift to thy glory. Amen.

Eastern Orthodox blessing: Blessed be God, who in his mercy nourishes us from his bounteous gifts by his grace and compassion. O Christ, our God, bless the meat and drink of which we are about to partake, for you are holy forever. Amen.

Jewish blessing: Lift up your hands toward the sanctuary and bless the Lord. Blessed are you, O Lord our God, King of the universe, who brings forth bread from the earth. Amen.

Another Latin grace, this one inscribed on a sixteenth-century knife, today in the Louvre. The knife also bears a musical notation, but perhaps one of your children could make up a new melody to go with it: *Quae sumpturi benedicat trinus & unus* (May the three and one bless those things which we are about to eat).

When the children are eating together, I encourage them to take turns saying the blessing. We generally say one of a number of traditional blessings that the children know by heart, and they each feel free to add an extra prayer for a particular person, or about a special occasion, or in honor of a visitor. You can also, of course, make up your own blessings.

A third suggestion is to encourage each child to contribute to the meal in some way. Whether it be by actually helping with the cooking or by planning the menu, doing the shopping, setting or clearing the table, helping with the dishes, each child should have a share in the preparation of as many meals as possible. And I have found that even very small children are eager to be helpful in the kitchen. (I will offer some recipes below to make good use of their enthusiasm.) If you're tempted, as I sometimes am, to say, "Don't bother me! Go away!" just ask yourself, "Do I really want to dampen this enthusiasm, this desire to be with me, to help me—and to learn how to do things in the kitchen?" It's true: often it takes longer when children are helping you. But who cares? What matters more—doing it *fast,* or doing it together and lovingly?

Not all children are going to take to cooking. But encourage them to cooperate in some way. If they are truly resistant, let them find some "alternative service" to perform for the family, on a regular basis. The point is to share in keeping the family enterprise afloat. Remember that all experiences mean more when we have worked, offered our time and skill to produce them.

And play down the spirit of competition among the children. Let this be something we do together, for—not against—each other. Encourage children to think of dishes they can prepare to surprise and please each other, or perhaps their father or mother or a friend. We need to think of all cooking—not just fruitcakes at Christmas—as gift giving.

And let's remember to thank each other, in particular, to thank each child for his or her contribution to the meal. Being appreciative is so important.

Let's try to bring the members of the family home—out of their own rooms (where each does his own thing), out of the TV room (where each person watches alone), back to the center of the home: back to the kitchen, back to the table, back to the celebration of our lives together.

Food in the New Testament

I have always meant to go through the New Testament to see how many times food is mentioned, how many times Christ dined, supped, picnicked with His disciples. He healed St. Peter's mother-in-law and she rose to serve them. He brought the little girl back to life and said, "Give her to eat." He broiled fish on the seashore for His apostles. Could it possibly be that Mary was less solicitous for the happiness and comfort and refreshment of others?

It is part of a woman's life to be preoccupied with food. She nurses her child; she has nourished him for nine long months in her womb; it is her grief if her breasts fail her; she weeps if her child refuses to eat. Her work as food provider is her pleasure and her pain, pain because of the monotony and because right now the cost of food has gone up one hundred percent.

Dorothy Day, *On Pilgrimage*

THOUGHTS AND RECIPES FOR
FAMILY MEALS

Life, within doors, has few pleasanter prospects than a neatly
arranged and well-provisioned breakfast-table.

Nathaniel Hawthorne, *The House of the Seven Gables*

Granola

*One of the great problems that almost all of us have is getting
our children—ourselves as well—off for the day with a good breakfast.
Granola cereal is one of the answers. One of the advantages to making
your own Granola is that you can concoct it just the way you like it:
if you love coconut, go heavy on it; if you and your children don't
care for it—just leave it out. The same goes for the nuts and fruits;
choose what you like, in your favorite proportions. (You may want to
make several different batches, to please the different family tastes.)
Granola is fun for children to help cook. Once they have made their
own, and seen not only how good it tastes but understood how
healthy it is, they will be less inclined to want to eat the
oversweetened-marshmallow-chocolate-artificially-colored-and-flavored
junk that passes for breakfast food in the supermarkets.*

4 cups rolled oats
½ cup flaked, unsweetened coconut
½ cup sesame seeds
½ cup sunflower seeds
½ cup raw wheat germ
1 cup chopped nuts
½ teaspoon cinnamon (or a mixture of cinnamon and nutmeg)
½ teaspoon salt (optional)
½ cup honey, molasses, or corn syrup
¼ cup peanut butter
⅛ cup vegetable oil or melted butter
⅛ cup water
¼ to ½ cup dried fruits: raisins, chopped dates, etc.

In a large bowl combine the dry ingredients, including salt if you
wish.

In a saucepan, combine the remaining ingredients, except
fruit. Heat, stirring, until the mixture is well blended.

Pour the liquid ingredients over the dry ingredients, and mix
thoroughly. Turn the mixture out into large greased baking pans.
Spread out in a thin layer.

Bake at 350° F. for 20 to 25 minutes, or until golden and
crunchy. During baking, stir every few minutes.

Let the mixture cool in the pans. Then mix in the dried fruits.

Variations:

For the coconut, substitute more of the seeds or nuts, or some
whole-wheat flour or cornmeal. For the peanut butter, you can
substitute milk or cream or water. Try adding a teaspoon or two
of vanilla, as an added flavor booster.

Yield: about 8 cups

Cinnamon-nutmeg muffins

One of the little treats my family really appreciate is a fresh, hot batch of muffins for breakfast. It's quickly done—only 20 minutes to ½ hour in all. Here are our two favorite muffin recipes.

1¾ cups sifted flour
2½ teaspoons baking powder
⅓–½ cup sugar
½ teaspoon cinnamon
¼ teaspoon nutmeg
½ teaspoon salt
1 large egg
⅔ cup milk
5 tablespoons butter, melted

OPTIONAL TOPPING:
5 tablespoons butter, melted
⅓ cup sugar
½ teaspoon cinnamon
½ teaspoon nutmeg

Preheat the oven to 425° F.

In a large bowl, resift the flour with the baking powder, sugar, cinnamon, nutmeg, and salt.

In a bowl, beat the egg; stir in the milk and the melted butter. Stir the liquid ingredients into the dry with a minimum of strokes—just make sure the dry ingredients are thoroughly moistened. The batter will be lumpy.

Spoon the batter into well-greased muffin pans, filling each cup about two-thirds full.

Bake for 12 to 15 minutes, or until lightly browned.

Optional topping: Melt the butter, stir in the sugar, cinnamon, and nutmeg, stirring until well blended. With a pastry brush, coat the top of each muffin with the topping.

Yield: 12 muffins

Variation:

For Sunday morning, make Muffin Jewels. (I learned about these from M. M. O'Brien's *Bible Cookbook.*) Fill each muffin cup about ½ full. Then put in about a teaspoon of jam. Then pour in a little more batter, filling the cups two-thirds full. Omit the optional topping.

1 cup flour
½ cup whole-wheat flour
¼ cup sugar
2½ teaspoons baking powder
¼ teaspoon baking soda
1½ teaspoons cinnamon
¾ teaspoons salt
¼ cup wheat germ
¼ cup sunflower seeds, chopped walnuts, or pecans (optional)
⅓ cup milk
⅓ cup oil or melted butter
¼ cup honey
1 egg
2 medium bananas, mashed

Banana muffins

This is a particularly nutritious muffin

Preheat the oven to 400° F. Grease muffin pans well.

In a large bowl, mix well the flours, sugar, baking powder, baking soda, cinnamon, and salt. Stir in the wheat germ, and the sunflower seeds or nuts, if you wish.

Mix the milk, oil, honey, egg, and bananas in a bowl. Add the wet ingredients to the dry with a minimum of strokes—just make sure the dry ingredients are thoroughly moistened.

Spoon the batter into muffin pans, filling each cup about two-thirds full. Bake for 15 to 20 minutes, or until golden brown.

Yield: about 15 muffins

Homemade graham crackers

Finding wholesome snacks for children—another big problem. Here is a nice solution: Homemade Graham Crackers, slightly adapted from a wonderful cookbook for children: Loaves and Fishes, a "Love Your Neighbor" Cookbook, *by Linda Hunt, Marianne Frase, and Doris Liebert. These crackers go well with a glass of milk or a cup of hot chocolate.*

½ cup softened butter or
  margarine
⅔ cup brown sugar
½ cup water
2¾ cups whole-wheat flour
½ teaspoon salt
½ teaspoon baking powder
1 teaspoon (or more)
  cinnamon
½ teaspoon freshly grated
  nutmeg

In a large bowl, put the softened butter or margarine and the sugar. Beat until smooth and creamy. Add the remaining ingredients to the butter-sugar mixture and mix well. Let the mixture sit for 30 to 45 minutes.

Turn the dough out onto a floured surface and roll it to about ⅛-inch thickness. Cut into squares or long rectangles, or with cookie cutters cut into whatever shapes you like. Place on a greased cookie sheet.

Bake at 350° F. for 20 minutes, until lightly browned.

Chicken soup

Good chicken soup—this is what memories of home cooking are made of! And there are many evenings when a hearty soup—served perhaps with a salad, some good bread and cheese, and fruit—is just what we need. Try making it with herbs (and perhaps vegetables) you have grown yourself.

1 three- to four-pound
  chicken
2½ quarts (10 cups) water
2 teaspoons salt
8 peppercorns
4 cloves
1 bay leaf
1 sprig fresh thyme or a
  little dried thyme
2 sprigs parsley
1 onion, finely chopped
1 rib celery (with leaves),
  finely chopped
Vegetables, such as:
  4 or 5 potatoes,
    quartered, or raw rice or
    noodles
  4–6 carrots, cut in large
    chunks
  1–2 cups peas
Optional:
  2 tablespoons butter

Cut the chicken into serving pieces. Place them in a large pot with the water and salt, and bring to a boil. Skim off the scum on top.

Place the spices in a tea ball or tie in cheesecloth, and add them to the pot with the onion and celery.

Simmer partly covered until the chicken is tender and falling off the bones: generally 1 to 2 hours. Remove the pot from the heat and take out the chicken. When it is cool enough to handle, remove the bones and return the meat to the pot. Add the desired vegetables, and simmer for another 20 minutes or until the vegetables are tender. If you are using peas, add them only for the last few minutes of cooking.

Remove the spice bag. Taste for seasoning. Stir in butter, if you wish.

Yield: 6 servings

Variations:

For an interesting Pennsylvania Dutch flavor, put in the spice bag 3 or 4 small pieces of anise and a 1-inch stick of cinnamon.

Brown-rice-and-spinach casserole

A number of recent cookbooks and nutrition books have pointed out the importance of introducing into our diet more nonmeat protein. It is not only vegetarians who have this concern. Many are disturbed at the ways in which we in America squander the earth's capacity to produce protein: such is the essential message of Frances Moore Lappé's Diet for a Small Planet. *After all, the idea of "stewardship"—that man was created to be not the master and consumer of nature but its steward and caretaker—is a great Christian theme.*

Even those of us who enjoy meat cannot always afford it, or afford very much of it. It is useful for us to know how to offer our families the most healthful meals we can at the minimum cost and with the maximum of pleasure.

Let's also remember that the great traditional holiday menus, often heavy with meat and rich in butter, sugar, etc., drew their effect partly by contrast with these simpler, everyday dishes, in which basic nutrition is of the essence.

This casserole is delicious as a main dish, served with a salad or contrasting vegetable, and a good, nutritious bread. Or it may be served as a side dish with meat. The recipe is inspired by Diet for a Small Planet.

1½ cups cooked brown rice
¾ cup grated Cheddar cheese
¼ pound fresh spinach (more if desired), chopped (or 1 package frozen spinach, defrosted, well drained)
2 eggs, lightly beaten
2 tablespoons parsley, chopped
1 tablespoon lemon juice
About ¼ cup chicken stock or water
½ teaspoon salt
¼ teaspoon freshly ground pepper
2 tablespoons wheat germ
1–2 tablespoons butter, melted

Combine the rice, cheese, spinach, eggs, and parsley. Pour into an oiled casserole. Add the lemon juice and enough stock to moisten the mixture slightly. Stir in the salt and pepper. Mix the wheat germ with the melted butter, and sprinkle over the casserole.

Bake at 350° F. for 30 minutes.

Yield: 4 to 6 servings

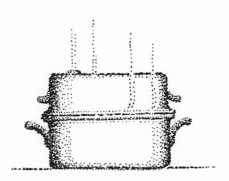

Indonesian fritters

All of us who cook on a daily basis need recipes that aren't too complicated or too expensive, that help us to make sure our families get the necessary nutrients, and that they enjoy. A tall order! But here is a recipe that I recommend highly. In these fritters, my children will eat vegetables that otherwise they would hardly touch with their forks.

Try letting your young children grate the carrots, chop the celery and peppers—with a dull knife! (Never a very sharp knife: children are always falling off a stool, etc!) They can also do the measuring of the ingredients. (Another tip: don't ever let them measure ingredients over the mixing bowl but do it over a plate; that way, if they spill or get carried away, there is no harm done.) They can also do the mixing.

Serve the fritters with rice (white or brown) and soy sauce. Chinese plum and duck sauces can be used as condiments.

1 cup flour
1 egg, lightly beaten
¾ cup bean sprouts, fresh or canned, drained
½ cup chopped celery
½ cup coarsely grated (unpeeled) zucchini (squeeze out moisture, pat dry)
½ cup coarsely chopped Bermuda onion
¼ cup coarsely grated carrot
¼ cup chopped green pepper
1 or 2 cloves garlic, pressed
½ teaspoon salt
A few grindings of pepper
1–2 tablespoons soy sauce
About 3–4 tablespoons water
Cooking oil

Mix all the ingredients. The mixture should be thick and just moist—not runny. Add flour or water as necessary.

In a frying pan or wok heat ½ to 1 inch cooking oil. Drop the mixture in cakes about 3 to 4 inches across, and fry until crisp on both sides. (If you prefer, you can make smaller cakes.)

Drain thoroughly on paper towels.

Yield: about 6 servings

Variations:

You can vary—eliminate, add to, substitute—the vegetables used. You can also add ½ cup or more chopped, cooked shrimp or some crabmeat.

When a man's stomach is full it makes no difference whether he is rich or poor.

Euripides, *Electra*

Brazilian beans-and-rice dinner

Beans are, of course, one of the most economical dishes you can serve, and very nutritious. This Brazilian version of beans and rice, made with black beans, is a national festive dish. It can make a splendid dish for company, or a more simple but still very tasty family dinner. You can vary it in many ways; see below.

2 cups black (turtle) beans
1 orange (whole or halved)
3 large onions, chopped
3 cloves garlic, chopped
2 bay leaves
½ teaspoon freshly ground pepper
4 ribs celery, chopped
3 tomatoes, chopped
2 green peppers, chopped (optional)
2 teaspoons cilantro (optional)
About 1 teaspoon salt
⅛ teaspoon Tabasco
Garnish: Orange slices

Let the beans soak in water to cover overnight, or use the quick method: Put the beans in a large pot with water to cover. Bring to a boil and cook for 2 minutes. Remove the pot from the heat. Cover, and let sit for 1 hour.

Return the beans and water to the heat. Add the orange, onions, garlic, bay leaves, pepper, celery, tomatoes, and optional green peppers and cilantro. Simmer, partly covered, until the beans are soft; add more water if necessary. This should take about 3 hours.

In the last few minutes of cooking, taste for seasoning. Add more chopped onion and/or garlic, salt and Tabasco to taste. Remove a cup or more of the beans and mash them, returning them to the pot; the mashed beans will thicken the dish. The mixture should be quite thick and soupy. Remove and discard the cooked orange.

Serve over rice. Garnish with orange slices.

Yield: 6 to 8 servings

Variations:

Use red kidney beans instead of black beans.

For the last ½ hour or so add cooked pigs' ears, tails, feet, or chopped ham, sausage, or tongue.

Over the cooked dish sprinkle toasted bread crumbs or sesame seeds. (In Brazil, they sprinkle it with *farofa*—cassava meal. The Cuban way is to sprinkle black beans and rice with chopped raw onion, and olive oil and vinegar. I love it that way!)

LIME SAUCE
1 cup lime juice
1 large onion, chopped
1 or 2 cloves garlic, chopped
4 or 5 hot red or green peppers, seeded; or 2 ounces canned green chilies, seeded; or 1 teaspoon canned jalapeño sauce
Salt

Or make this spicy lime sauce for the rice.

Blend all ingredients except salt in the blender until smooth. Add salt to taste. (Add the hot peppers or jalapeño sauce to the blender a little at a time and taste as you go.)

West African stew

One of the cookbooks that I have grown to love is the More with Less Cookbook (Suggestions by Mennonites on How to Eat Better and Consume Less of the World's Limited Food Resources). *Aside from the many practical suggestions that it offers on how to eat more wisely and how to waste less food (by "gathering up the fragments" in imaginative ways) this book includes wonderful recipes sent in by Mennonite missionaries and other Mennonites from all parts of the world. Everyone in my family loves this recipe. (Don't be alarmed by the peanut butter: It just gives a subtle peanut flavor.)*

3 tablespoons oil
2 pounds beef cubes, 1 inch or smaller, rolled in salted flour
½ teaspoon nutmeg
1 tablespoon chili powder
4 medium-sized onions, sliced
1 clove garlic, minced
¾ cup tomato paste
6 cups water
Red pepper to taste (optional)
½ cup chunky peanut butter
2 tablespoons oil

In a large heavy kettle, heat the cooking oil. Add the beef cubes and brown in the oil. While they are browning, sprinkle on the nutmeg and chili powder.

When the meat is brown, add the onions, garlic, tomato paste, water, and red pepper, if desired. Simmer until the meat is tender.

A half hour before serving, heat in a small saucepan the peanut butter and 2 tablespoons of oil. Stir over medium heat for 5 minutes. Add the peanut-butter mixture slowly to the beef stew, and simmer over low heat for 20 minutes. Taste for seasoning. Serve over rice.

This may be accompanied by small dishes of condiments, such as any kind of chutney; peanuts, sunflower seeds, grated coconut; chopped scallions, onions, tomatoes, or green pepper; pineapple tidbits; diced apples; raisins; banana slices; chopped hard-cooked eggs.

Variations:

Use chicken pieces in place of beef. To use leftover cooked meat, begin by sautéing onion and garlic, then add meat with tomato paste, spices, and water.

Yield: 8 servings

Meat loaf

One of the basic recipes that we all need in our repertoire is meat loaf. Here's one that's first-rate, along with some variations. This is, incidentally, a good project to hand over to a teenager, or even a somewhat younger child.

1 pound ground round beef
1 egg, lightly beaten
4 tablespoons chopped
  parsley
½ cup soft, fresh
  breadcrumbs
⅓ cup milk
1 teaspoon lemon juice
1 clove garlic, minced
½ teaspoon oregano or
  thyme
½ teaspoon basil
1 teaspoon salt
½ teaspoon freshly ground
  pepper
⅓ cup chopped onion
2 tablespoons chopped
  celery

Mix all the ingredients lightly but thoroughly with a fork or your hands. Form into a loaf on a rimmed baking pan or dish. Bake at 350° F. for 1 hour. Baste occasionally with the cooking juices.

This is delicious served hot, at room temperature or cold. Try it with a good tomato sauce.

Yield: 4 servings

Variations:

For a marvelous Italian flavor, add ¼ teaspoon fennel seeds.

Use 3 parts beef to 1 part lean pork; or a blend of beef, pork, and veal.

Use wheat germ in place of part or all of the breadcrumbs, for added nutrition.

Insert halved hard-cooked eggs inside the loaf. (Form the bottom part of the loaf, arrange the eggs end to end on top, then add the top part of the loaf.)

You can also make the loaf in a greased loaf pan. Or make it in a greased ring mold; this makes a handsome dish. Turn it out onto a platter, and serve a green vegetable (such as peas or artichoke hearts) in the center of the mold.

If you cook the meat loaf in a bread pan, you can pour a little ketchup into the pan before adding the meat mixture, or pour some ketchup or chili sauce over the top before cooking. This gives a nice flavor and crust.

You can add chopped green pepper, or grated carrot, or more celery.

Boiled new potatoes

When I think of boiled potatoes, I always remember the lady I knew of who—with a large family—was too busy to set aside much time for prayer or meditation. But, whenever she boiled potatoes, she would say a little prayer for someone she knew and loved (or someone she just wanted to pray for) as she threw each potato into the water. She boiled potatoes "for the intentions" of all these people; that is, she prayed for them and all their needs. A lovely custom, I think. Using new potatoes will allow you to pray for many people!

New potatoes, washed but
  not peeled (allow 4 to 6
  new potatoes per person)
Butter
Chopped parsley

Boil the potatoes in a large pan of salted water until just tender: 10 to 15 minutes. Drain well and serve with butter and chopped parsley.

Basic delicious tomato sauce

3 tablespoons olive oil
2 medium-sized onions,
   chopped
1 or 2 cloves garlic, finely
   minced
1 stalk celery, finely
   chopped (optional)
1 one-pound-12-ounce can
   Italian plum tomatoes,
   drained, seeded, coarsely
   chopped
4 tablespoons tomato paste
½ cup water (or the juice
   the tomatoes were packed
   in)
1 teaspoon sugar
½ teaspoon salt
Freshly ground pepper
1 bay leaf
1 teaspoon oregano
1 teaspoon dry basil, or a
   handful of fresh basil
   leaves

There are so many dishes that are good with tomato sauce, from spaghetti to meat loaf to Italian sausages to various fish dishes. The aroma of tomato sauce cooking will bring your family to the table early, sniffing in anticipation. Here is a fine basic recipe. You can make a lot, and freeze some.

Heat the olive oil in a large saucepan. Sauté the onions and garlic until they are soft and transparent but not brown.

Add the remaining ingredients and simmer, partly covered, for about 1 hour. Stir occasionally. Optional: Press through a sieve, or purée. Taste for seasoning.

Yield: about 4 cups

The minister's bride set her luncheon casserole down with a flourish, and waited for grace. "It seems to me," murmured her husband, "that I have blessed a good deal of this material before."

Irma Rombauer, *The Joy of Cooking*

Shepherd's pie

Chopped or ground cooked
   meat and vegetables
Any of the following:
   gravy, tomato sauce,
   cream sauce, cream, a
   little dry white vermouth
Any of the following:
   sautéed onion, celery,
   garlic; a sprinkling of
   fresh or dry herbs
Leftover or fresh mashed
   potatoes, moistened with
   milk
Butter

One of the many traditional ways of serving up leftovers attractively is Shepherd's Pie. This dish has the advantage of being exceedingly variable: almost any cooked bits of meat (and vegetables) can be accommodated. From our point of view, this pie has the added benefit of bringing up the ancient theme of the Shepherd. One of the very earliest ways in which Christ is represented in art is as the Good Shepherd.

Spread the meat and vegetables in a baking dish. Stir in the gravy or other liquid and the sautéed onion and/or other flavorings. Taste for seasoning.

Soften the potatoes (if necessary) with milk. Make a layer of mashed potatoes over the meat and vegetables. (For extra attractiveness—and this is fun for a child to do—lay on the mashed potatoes with a pastry tube in decorative swirls.) Dot with butter.

Bake at 350° F. until the potatoes are nicely browned.

Turnovers

Here is an inventive and appealing way of dealing with leftovers: bake them into turnovers. The cream-cheese pastry is delicious and easy to make. Try handing over this job to a teenager.

2 sticks sweet butter, at room temperature
8 ounces Philadelphia cream cheese, at room temperature
1 teaspoon salt
2 cups flour

FILLING:
Cooked, crumbled hamburger or other very finely chopped cooked meat. Mix with a little chopped onion and some fresh chopped (or dried) dill. Or try using deviled ham.
Cooked chopped vegetables, such as broccoli or asparagus. Mix with a little grated Parmesan cheese and a sprinkling of tarragon or chervil.
Preserves or cooked fruit, with a little cinnamon or nutmeg

In a mixing bowl cream the butter and cream cheese with a fork until fluffy. Add the salt.

Add the flour gradually, blending well after each addition. Form the dough into a ball. Wrap it in plastic wrap and chill it in the refrigerator for at least 1 hour. (This dough can be frozen. Defrost in the refrigerator.)

Preheat the oven to 400° F. Butter baking sheets.

On a lightly floured surface, roll the dough out to about $\frac{1}{8}$ inch thick. Cut it out with round cutters about 3 inches in diameter—or larger, 5 inches, if you prefer.

Place a heaping teaspoon of filling in the center of each round. (If you made larger rounds, a heaping tablespoon.) Lightly moisten the edges. You can either fold the dough over to make flat, somewhat crescent-shaped turnovers, or you can pick up three sides and pinch them toward the center, to make pointed, three-sided turnovers. Seal the edges with your fingertips.

Place the turnovers on baking sheets. Bake for 20 to 35 minutes, or until golden brown.

Yield: about 4 dozen small or $1\frac{1}{2}$ dozen large turnovers

---

And because I am a woman involved in practical cares, I cannot give the first half of the day to these things, but must meditate when I can, early in the morning and on the fly during the day. Not in the privacy of a study—but here, there and everywhere—at the kitchen table, on the train, on the ferry, on my way to and from appointments and even while making supper or putting Teresa to bed.

Dorothy Day, *House of Hospitality*

Basic bread

If you haven't learned how to bake bread yet this is the time to learn. Baking your own bread has to be one of life's most satisfying experiences. In the Middle Ages one of the English words for yeast was "goddisgoode" because "it cometh of the grete grace of God."
Let's bake it and break it together.

1¼ cups warm water (100°– 110° F.)
1 package dry yeast
2 tablespoons sugar
1 cup milk
2 tablespoons butter
2 teaspoons salt
6 to 7 cups flour, preferably unbleached
Optional:
  2 tablespoons melted butter

The water should be just slightly warm to the touch. Water any hotter will kill the yeast. Remember that yeast is alive: it is a plant that in a warm environment, with water and a little sugar, grows rapidly and causes fermentation. This fermentation process releases alcohol and carbon dioxide, which raises the dough.

Sprinkle the yeast onto the warm water in a large mixing bowl. Stir in the sugar and let the mixture sit until it is frothy: about 10 minutes.

Scald the milk (that is, heat it until bubbles form around the edge) in a saucepan. Stir in the butter and salt, mixing with a wooden spoon until the butter is melted. Cool to lukewarm. (Again, you don't want to kill the yeast.) Stir into the yeast.

Add the flour very gradually to the yeast mixture, at first beating it in with a wooden spoon, then finally working it in with your hands. (You can also use the dough hook of a food mixer or processor.) Blend well between additions. Add enough flour to make a dough that isn't sticky to your fingers.

Turn the dough out onto a lightly floured surface. Knead the dough for 5 to 10 minutes, until it is smooth and elastic. To knead, place the heel of one hand in the middle of the dough and push it toward the edge of the dough. With the other hand, turn the dough slightly. Keep repeating these movements. The point is to press and stretch the dough. Working the dough releases the gluten in the wheat flour. Toward the end of the kneading, you can also throw the dough down on the table a few times. If as you are kneading the dough seems too sticky, add a little more flour.

Place the dough in a greased bowl, turning the dough to grease the top. Cover with a towel or plastic wrap. Place the bowl in a draft-free spot. (Dough rises fastest in a warm place, but a slower rising produces a slightly better taste. The dough needs to be protected from drafts, which inhibit yeast cell growth.) Let the dough rise until it is doubled in bulk; when you stick in a finger, the hole should remain. This will take *about* 1½ hours (but the time can vary).

Preheat oven to 450° F.

Punch the dough down with your fist. Knead it for a minute or two. Divide the dough in two by cutting it with a sharp knife.

Form each piece into a ball, then stretch each ball slightly to form a cylinder. Place each piece in a buttered loaf pan, seam side down.

If time permits, let the bread rise again until almost doubled in bulk (this will produce a more finely textured bread), but this second rising is not necessary if you are in a rush: just let the dough sit in the pans for 5 to 10 minutes. If you like, brush the tops of the loaves with melted butter.

Bake at 450° for 15 minutes. Reduce the heat to 400° and bake for another 15 minutes, until the top is golden brown. Remove the bread from the pans with a clean dish towel or large hot pad. If the bottom sounds hollow when you rap it with your knuckles, it is done. If not, return the loaf (without the pan) to the oven and let it bake for another 5 to 10 minutes, or until it does sound hollow.

Cool on a rack. For a hard crust, let cool fully before wrapping. For a softer crust, wrap in foil or plastic wrap while still slightly warm.

Yield: 2 loaves

Variations:

You can vary the milk-to-water ratio, or use all one or the other. (All milk makes an enriched but rather crumbly bread. Water gives a crisper crust.)

You can substitute 1 or 2 cups of whole-wheat flour for the white (all-purpose) flour.

Try replacing the sugar with honey.

Try adding up to ¼ cup wheat germ while you are kneading.

Instead of baking the bread in loaf pans, you can form the dough into round loaves and bake them on greased baking sheets. In this case, make a slightly stiffer dough by adding a little more flour. If the dough is too soft, it will flatten out too much on the baking sheet.

You can slash the loaves with a razor blade or a very sharp knife just before putting them in the oven. If you are using loaf pans, give the dough one long slash 1 inch deep along the middle of the top surface. If you have made round loaves, you can make one large cross cut, or several intersecting cuts.

For a crustier bread, put a pan of boiling water on the floor of the oven a few minutes before you put the bread in the oven. And use water in your dough, rather than milk.

The smel of new breade is comfortable to the heade and to the herte.

Anonymous, From *Notes from a Country Kitchen* by Jocasta Innes

Pizza

Try making your own pizza; you'll see what fun it is—and how good the pizza is.

1 package dry yeast
½ cup warm water
    (100–110° F.)
1¾ cups flour
¾ teaspoon salt
4 teaspoons olive oil
1¼ to 1½ cups thick tomato
    sauce. (You can use any
    tomato sauce, thickened if
    necessary with a little
    tomato paste. See Basic
    Delicious Tomato Sauce,
    page 60. A special tomato
    sauce for pizza is given
    below.)
About 1 cup (½ pound)
    diced or coarsely grated
    mozzarella cheese

Sprinkle the yeast into the warm water. Let it stand for about 10 minutes. Combine the flour and salt in a bowl. Stir in the yeast and oil. Mix thoroughly.

Turn the dough out onto a lightly floured surface. Knead for about 10 minutes, until the dough is smooth and elastic.

Place the dough in an oiled bowl, turning the dough to oil the top. Cover and let the dough rise in a draft-free spot until doubled in bulk, about 1 hour.

Punch the dough down and knead it briefly. Return it to the oiled bowl and let rise again until doubled, about 1 hour.

Preheat the oven to 425° F.

On a lightly floured surface, roll the dough out to a large circle. Transfer the circle to an oiled 12-inch pizza pan. With oiled fingers, stretch the dough toward the edge of the pan, pinching it to make a ½-inch rim all around.

Spread the pizza with a layer of tomato sauce.

Bake the pizza for 15 minutes, then sprinkle it with about 1 cup mozzarella. Arrange the toppings attractively over the surface. Sprinkle the Parmesan cheese on top. Return to the oven and bake for another 10 to 15 minutes, or until the rim is crusty and brown.

Yield: one 12-inch pizza

TOMATO SAUCE FOR PIZZA

4 tablespoons olive oil
¼ cup chopped onion
1¼ cups Italian plum
    tomatoes, chopped
1½ teaspoons basil
1½ teaspoons oregano
1 garlic clove, pressed
Freshly ground black pepper

Heat the oil. Sauté the onions until golden. Add the remaining ingredients and simmer uncovered for about 1 hour. Cool before using on pizza dough.

TOPPINGS

About ¼ cup freshly grated
    Parmesan or Romano
    cheese

Use any combination of the following: anchovy fillets; thin slices of hard sausage such as pepperoni; thin strips of prosciutto; cooked, crumbled, drained Italian sausage or hamburger meat (seasoned with salt, pepper, garlic, and oregano or basil); fresh sautéed mushrooms; thin strips of bell pepper; chopped onions or scallions; chopped green or black olives; oregano or basil.

Variations:

Instead of the sauce and toppings discussed above, try this: Mix 4 seeded, chopped Italian plum tomatoes with 1 clove pressed garlic, 3 tablespoons olive oil, a little salt, and basil or oregano to taste. Spread over the pizza. Bake for 20 minutes. Sprinkle over the top about ½ cup crumbled goat cheese. Bake for another 5 to 10 minutes.

CALZONE

Roll the pizza dough out into 2 or 3 circles. Fill with cooked, crumbled, drained sausage or hamburger seasoned with salt, pepper, garlic, and oregano or basil; or use whatever filling you prefer (see pizza toppings for inspiration). Fold the dough over as for a large turn-over. Seal edges with your fingers, then with the tines of a fork.

Bake at 425° F. for about 10 minutes.

Brush the tops with olive oil. Bake for another 10 minutes or until the top is golden brown.

The great thing about baking with yeast is the difficulty of failure.

George and Cecilia Scurfield, *Home Baked*

Apple crisp

For dessert, it's good to serve fresh fruit: peaches, pears, plums, grapes, oranges, watermelon—whatever is in season. But we all like to be able to offer our families a special treat sometimes. Here is one of my family's favorites.

6 large tart apples, peeled, sliced
½ cup brown sugar
½ cup white sugar
¼ teaspoon ground cloves
1 teaspoon cinnamon
1 tablespoon lemon juice
¾ cup flour
Pinch salt
6 tablespoons butter
⅓ to ½ cup chopped pecans or walnuts

Place the apples in a bowl. Mix in ¼ cup of the brown sugar and ¼ cup of the white sugar. Stir in the cloves, cinnamon, and lemon juice. Put the mixture into a buttered casserole or baking pan.

Mix the rest of the brown and white sugars with the flour and salt, and cut in the butter until crumbly. Add the nuts. Spread over the top of the casserole.

Bake at 350° F. for about 45 minutes, or until the crust is nicely browned.

Variation:

For extra nutrition, substitute rolled oats for part or all of the flour; sprinkle a little wheat germ in with the topping mixture.

Yield: 6 to 8 servings

French cherry dessert
CLAFOUTI

When a French mother wants to make an economical but delicious dessert treat for her family, she is very apt to whip up a clafouti. Try it and you'll see why.

3 to 3½ cups black cherries (washed, pitted, dried) or canned Bing cherries, drained
1 cup flour
Pinch of salt
3 eggs
½ cup sugar
1½ cups milk
1 tablespoon vanilla
2 tablespoons melted butter
Optional:
  ¼ cup confectioners' sugar

Preheat the oven to 350° F. You will need an 8- or 9-inch square baking pan or a 9- or 10-inch round one.
Prepare the cherries.
Mix the flour and salt. Beat in the eggs, one at a time, mixing thoroughly after each addition. Beat in the sugar. Gradually add the milk and vanilla, stirring until the batter is smooth.
Pour the butter into the pan. Tip the pan to spread the butter. Pour in enough batter to make about a ¼-inch layer.
Bake at 350° F. for 5 minutes or until lightly set. Remove the pan from the oven. Spread the cherries over the surface, and cover with the remaining batter. Return to the oven, and bake for about 70 minutes or until puffed and brown. If you like, sprinkle with confectioners' sugar.

Yield: 4 to 6 servings

Variations:
You can use sliced apples, peaches, or pears instead of the cherries: use 3 to 3½ cups peeled, sliced fruit.

Flavored ices

You don't have to have an ice-cream machine to make these ices, which are such a welcome taste in the summertime.

LEMON ICE
2 cups water
1 cup sugar
Grated rind of ½ lemon
1 cup lemon juice

STRAWBERRY, RASPBERRY, OR PEACH ICE
1 cup water
½ cup sugar
2 cups puréed fruit (wash, peel, pit, hull fruit, and put it through a food mill or processor)
2 tablespoons lemon juice

For each ice, combine the water and sugar in a saucepan. Stir until the sugar is dissolved. Boil for 5 minutes. Let cool to lukewarm.
Stir in the remaining ingredients.
Pour the mixture into an ice-cube tray (without the divider). Freeze for about 4 hours. If you prefer a finely textured ice, stir the mixture every 20 to 30 minutes, to reduce the size of the ice crystals. If you like a coarser, mushier ice, stir less frequently and thoroughly.

Yield: about 1½ pints of each ice

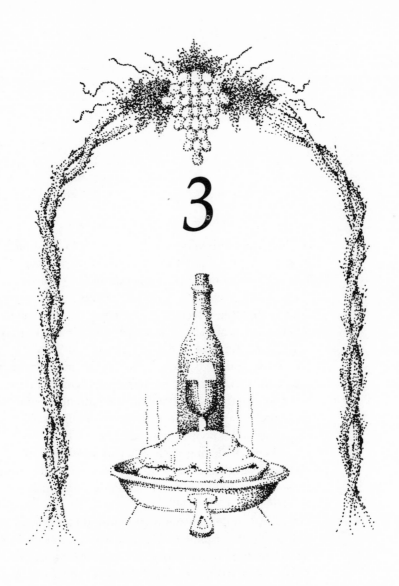

3

Traditions of
Christian hospitality

A Polish proverb says it well: "A guest in the home is God in the home." We need to try, and it isn't always easy, to make room at our tables—in our homes, in our hearts—for unexpected guests. Even when the place is messy, or one more person at the table means that the silverware and china won't match, never mind! That extra guest may be an angel; that person, hungry for food, for a welcome, for love, is Christ himself.

What could go back further or be more fundamental in our tradition than the call to hospitality and charity? Already in Genesis we find Abraham entertaining three strangers who turn out to be the Lord Himself in the form of three angels. The importance of kindness to the poor is stressed.

"Keep on loving each other as brothers," St. Paul urges the Hebrews, and he adds, "Do not forget to entertain strangers, for by so doing some people have entertained angels without knowing it" (Hebrews 13:1–2, NIV).

Christ added an important new dimension to the traditional obligation of hospitality. He said that whatever we do, or do not do, to the least of our brothers, we are doing, or not doing, to *Him.* This passage from the Gospels has been, over the centuries, a major impetus for Christians in their treatment of the poor and oppressed. Many religious orders and other religious communities have been established precisely in order to be able to respond to the letter to Christ's call to see *Him* in every stranger, every hungry or thirsty or homeless or sick or poor person, every prisoner. Families are of course more limited than monasteries in their ability to welcome strangers into their midst. (Prudence is, after all, one of the great virtues.) But families too, individuals as well, have always felt the obligation to feed the hungry, either directly, at their table or door, or indirectly through donations to charity.

EMERGENCY RECIPES FOR ENTERTAINING (POSSIBLY) ANGELIC VISITORS

Generally, when we have guests for supper, we know well in advance that they are coming. We invite company for a particular day, a particular hour; they accept and appear. But the guests that we are dealing with in the concept of Christian hospitality are often unexpected; they turn up at the last minute—perhaps they come into town unannounced or come along to dinner with someone who *was* invited—and often at a rather inconvenient moment. (In fact, they almost invariably appear at an inconvenient moment.) Rather than turn them away ("I'm terribly sorry, but this is a very busy day/week/month/year for me/us"), we need to have emergency procedures for dealing with these "angelic" visitors.

First, some basic hints for extending a meal that has been planned for a smaller group, then a few dishes you can whip up easily in an emergency—dishes that call only for ingredients that you can make a point of always having on hand, and/or that call for little preparation and attention.

Before supper serve cheese and crackers with whatever sort of drinks you prefer: try using one of the various "spicy" cheeses (soft cheeses mixed with garlic or spices) and a harder cheese such as Swiss, with a couple of different kinds of crackers (rye, sesame, etc.).

Serve good bread (bakery or homemade) with the meal.

Add a first course, such as an omelet (see below).

Add an extra vegetable or a salad.

Serve fresh fruit as a separate course, before dessert.

Serve smaller portions.

Ask the members of your family not to request seconds tonight—perhaps even to expect small firsts. This is a small sacrifice being asked of them in the name of hospitality.

The first unit of society is the family. The family should look after its own and, in addition, as the early Fathers said, "Every home should have a Christ room in it, so that hospitality may be practiced." "The coat that hangs in your closet belongs to the poor." "If your brother is hungry, it is your responsibility."

Dorothy Day

An omelet—with infinite variations

An omelet is very quick to prepare and can function as a first or main course or be served for brunch or as a dessert, depending on its size, and on what it is filled or flavored with. This basic omelet recipe is for 1 person. A few of the possible variations are given below.

2 eggs
¼ to ½ teaspoon salt
Freshly ground pepper
1–2 tablespoons sweet
    butter
Optional:
    A prepared filling (see
    Variations)

Beat the eggs lightly. Add the salt and pepper. Heat the butter in the pan over high heat. As the butter is bubbling, and just as it is beginning to turn brown, pour in the eggs. Shake the pan back and forth on the burner, stirring the egg with a fork held horizontally. Keep lifting up the edges with a fork or spatula to let the soft part run down underneath. When the omelet is done, spread the prepared filling (if you are using one) over half the omelet. Fold the omelet in two with a spatula before you slide it onto a plate.

Variations:
    Fill each omelet with a few tablespoons of any of these concoctions, or with a mixture of several:
    Mushrooms sautéed in butter, with a little lemon juice added. Optional: Add a little heavy cream and parsley, and boil down until the mixture is thick.
    Gruyère or Cheddar cheese, chopped; or perhaps some Amish Swiss; or some goat cheese, such as St. Maure (he was a sixth-century French abbot).
    Fresh herbs, such as basil or tarragon, or some parsley. Mix them perhaps with a little sour cream.
    Some chopped ham, chopped tomatoes, or diced cooked potatoes—sautéed, perhaps with a little garlic.
    Alternatively, add to the eggs themselves any fresh herb, finely chopped, ½ to 1 tablespoon grated Parmesan or Romano cheese, and/or finely chopped baked or boiled ham, or crumbled cooked bacon.

A DESSERT OMELET
Follow the preceding recipe but reduce the salt to a mere pinch. Add, if you like, a little sugar and/or grated lemon rind to the egg batter.
    Fill the omelet with any of the following: jam or preserves or marmalade, a few tablespoons honey, a little fresh fruit (such as apples, bananas, peaches, plums) cooked and (optional) slightly sweetened.
    Sprinkle the top with confectioners' sugar, or garnish with whipped cream sweetened with a little confectioners' sugar.

Baked chicken

This main dish receives a high score on my "Culinary Rating Scale"—a scale on which you divide how good a dish tastes by the number of steps required to produce it. It is very good indeed, and requires very little effort. This dish consists of pieces of chicken (I generally make it with just breasts) baked with thick slices of Bermuda onion, Parmesan cheese, and heavy cream. It practically prepares itself—which leaves you free to talk, or to do whatever else needs to be done. It is delicious with rice or noodles and a green salad.

Salt
Freshly ground pepper
6 chicken breast halves (or
  1 cut-up chicken)
2 large Bermuda onions,
  sliced about ¾ inch thick
1 cup heavy cream
½–¾ cup Parmesan cheese

Salt and pepper the chicken, and place in a baking dish or casserole. Lay 1 slice of onion on each piece of chicken. Pour the cream over the chicken. Sprinkle the Parmesan cheese on top. Bake at 350° F. for 50 minutes to 1 hour.

Yield: 6 servings

Baked bananas

A quick and marvelous treat, using things we commonly have on hand.

6 bananas, peeled
4–6 tablespoons sweet
  butter, cut into pieces
About ¼ cup dark-brown
  sugar
Optional:
  ¼ teaspoon ground ginger
  ⅓ cup rum, to flambé the
  bananas

Arrange the peeled bananas in a lightly buttered baking dish. Dot with the butter and sprinkle with brown sugar; if you like, sprinkle the bananas with ginger.

Bake at 350° F. for about 10 minutes, or until the bananas seem soft and the butter and brown sugar are bubbly.

If you wish to flambé the bananas, warm the rum gently in a saucepan or large ladle. Averting your face, carefully ignite rum with a match. When the flame subsides, pour it over the bananas.

Yield: 6 or more servings

OTHER SUGGESTIONS FOR A WARM WELCOME

You might welcome a visitor—expected or unexpected—with a hot cup of tea. As for recommendations on how to brew it: here's how a sixteenth-century missionary to the Orient explained to a friend in Europe the way in which this strange new substance, tea, was prepared. You steep, he said, the leaves in boiling water "long enough to recite the 'Miserere' Psalm" (Psalm 51).

Accompany the tea, perhaps, with Lace Cookies (below) or a Madeleine or two, baked in that cockle-shell shape which has long symbolized pilgrimage (see page 258).

Lace cookies

I always associate lace cookies with my mother, who has taught me so many things (and not just about cooking). This is one of her specialties. These cookies keep very well in a tightly covered tin.

½ cup (1 stick) sweet butter
½ cup light corn syrup
½ cup brown sugar
1 cup flour
Pinch of salt
1 cup chopped pecans
1 teaspoon vanilla extract

Preheat the oven to 350° F.

Combine the butter, corn syrup, and brown sugar in a saucepan. Heat to boiling. Stir until thoroughly blended.

Stir in the flour, salt, pecans, and vanilla. Mix thoroughly. Drop by heaping teaspoonfuls several inches apart on buttered baking sheets.

Bake for about 8 minutes, or until golden brown and bubbly.

The only tricky part is getting the cookies off the pan. Wait about 1 minute—but not much longer—before removing them gently with a spatula. Cool on a rack.

Yield: about 5 dozen cookies

TAKING FOOD TO OTHERS

We often don't realize how much people appreciate certain thoughtful things we can do for them until someone has done them for *us:* I still remember how moved I was, twenty-five years ago when, after my father died suddenly, a friend of my parents' brought food to tide us over those first hard days. And recently, when our youngest was born, a kind neighbor brought us a big bowl of fresh fruit salad the day I came home from the hospital with the baby. We were all so touched by the thoughtfulness of the gesture—and enjoyed the salad all the more.

These are things that you can do for people that they never forget. Such gifts are part of hospitality; they are certainly at the very heart of kindness and charity.

Casseroles are often ideal in such circumstances. Many are delicious. They are a meal in one, often combining meat and rice (or potatoes) and a vegetable or two. They can be heated and reheated; frozen, if need be. You can even present them in throw-away metal containers, so that you don't leave your friends with the burden of getting a pan back to you.

Some basic possibilities include a roast chicken or small turkey, a basket of fruit, a fruit salad, homemade applesauce; almost any kind of cake or a coffeecake; or a pie.

Greek beef or lamb stew

STIFATHO

Here is a casserole that I have loved and frequently prepared for many years. It is slightly adapted from a book I highly recommend: Myra Waldo's The Casserole Cookbook: 170 Ingenious One-Dish Dinners. *Not only will this dish feed your friends—it will, by its attractive and unusual flavor, cheer their hearts. Incidentally, it is popular with both children and adults. You might deliver, with the casserole, a loaf of French bread, and herbed soft white cheese.*

3 pounds beef (eye round, chuck, or other) or lamb (leg or shoulder), cut in 1-inch cubes
1 tablespoon salt
½ teaspoon freshly ground pepper
1 teaspoon cinnamon
⅓ cup olive oil—more if necessary
12 small white onions
1 cup canned or homemade tomato sauce
2 cups beef or chicken broth
3 cups diced eggplant
2 carrots, sliced
½ cup raw rice

Season the meat with the salt, pepper, and cinnamon. Heat ¼ cup of the oil in a skillet; brown the meat in it a little at a time. Transfer to a casserole.

In the oil remaining in the skillet, sauté the onions until golden. Add them to the casserole with the tomato sauce and broth. Cover and cook over low heat for about 1¼ hours.

In the meantime, place the diced eggplant in a colander. Sprinkle it with salt. Let it sit for 20 minutes or so (to let the bitter juices seep out). Pat dry. Heat the remaining oil in the skillet. Sauté the eggplant until nicely browned on all sides. (Add more oil if necessary.)

Add the sautéed eggplant, carrots, and rice to the casserole. Cover and cook gently for 30 minutes longer.

Yield: 6 to 8 servings

Blueberry pie

Needless to say, you can make this for your family as well as for others—charity does begin at home!

Pastry for a 2-crust pie
3-4 cups fresh blueberries, or frozen, defrosted
Grated rind of ½ lemon
1 tablespoon lemon juice
¼ teaspoon cinnamon
½ cup sugar
1 to 2 tablespoons flour
About 2 tablespoons butter

Preheat the oven to 450° F.

Prepare the crusts. Lay one in the bottom of the pie pan.

Mix the blueberries lightly with the grated rind, lemon juice, cinnamon, and sugar. Place them in the crust. Sprinkle them lightly with flour. Dot with butter.

Lay the top crust over the berries. Seal the edges with your fingers, or, gently, with the tines of a fork. Trim the edges (not too close) and make cuts—decorative ones, if you wish—in the top crust.

Bake for 20 minutes. Reduce the heat to 350° F. and bake for 40 minutes longer, or until the top crust is nicely browned.

Yield: 1 pie, about 6 servings

SOUP KITCHEN

Catch-as-catch-can soup

For the many who work as volunteer cooks in soup kitchens one difficulty is knowing how to help prepare soups and stews that are at once economical, nutritious, and tasty—and that no one person is quite in charge of organizing. It isn't easy!

Here are some tips and ideas from a friend who works regularly in the kitchen of Mother Teresa's Missionaries of Charity, in New York's South Bronx. The recipe is organized in two parts: One is what to do to get the soup started. Part Two is what to do if you arrive in the kitchen toward the end, when the soup is nearly done.

PART ONE
Starting the soup, some basic ingredients and how to use them:
1. *Bones.* Ham or any kind of bones add flavor to soups. Try bringing your own bones. You can generally get them cheap or even free from butchers. Place whatever bones you have in a large pan.
2. *Meat.* This can be fresh or leftover cooked meat. If the meat is fresh, cut it into pieces about ¾ to 1 inch square; place the meat in the pan with the bones. *If you are using fresh meat,* add a little cooking oil to the pan and brown the meat (and bones) in the oil. Save leftover cooked meat to put in later.
3. *Garlic* and *onion.* Fresh pressed garlic and fresh sliced onion are best. If you wish, you can brown them with the meat in the oil; or add them after browning the meat. If (as is often the case) you do not have fresh garlic and onion available, use garlic and onion salt or powder. Sprinkle them in the pot.
4. *Water.* The amount of water you use will of course depend on how many people you are planning to feed. Calculate about 1 pint (2 cups) water per person. If you are not using bones or meat, you may want to add bouillon cubes to the water.
5. *Seasonings.* To the water add salt and pepper to taste. See what herbs are available, or bring your own: try oregano and basil for good strong flavor, but thyme, dill, and other herbs are nice too. Curry powder is a possibility, as well. But do try to find some way of adding seasoning to the soup!
6. *Tomatoes.* Canned tomatoes add flavor and color to any soup.
7. *Coarsely chopped celery and carrots.* Almost a must.

8. *Dried beans.* Beans, such as white and red, are cheap and full of protein. Many beans, however, take a long time to cook—longer perhaps than the time available. Be sure to check on the package. What you can do is use the "quick method": Cover beans with water in a pot. Bring to a boil and let boil for 2 minutes. Remove from heat and let sit for 1 hour. Then drain and add to the soup; this will speed things up. Also try lentils: they are fairly quick cooking and have great taste.

Bring the soup to a boil, reduce heat and let simmer for 2 to 3 hours, or until the meat and beans, if you used them, are done.

PART TWO
If you arrive on the scene toward the end of the soup making, how can you add nutrition, color, and flavor? In the last ½ hour or so of cooking, you can add to the pot:

1. *Rice* or *pasta.* You can use either white or brown rice. If you are adding pasta, try using (bring your own?) something with body, that won't get too soft, such as twists or shells.
2. *Canned beans;* more *tomatoes;* more fresh chopped *carrots* and *celery.*
3. *Frozen vegetables,* such as peas or chopped broccoli or cauliflower.
4. *Leftover meat,* of any sort. Cut into bite-sized pieces.
5. *More seasoning.* More garlic or onion (fresh chopped, or salt or powder). More oregano or other spices. Taste again for salt and pepper.

Bread pudding

Here is a recipe inspired by one the Missionaries of Charity have devised to put stale doughnuts and bread to good use.

Stale doughnuts, crullers, or other sweet breads (see note)
Milk
3 or 4 eggs per quart of milk
Pinches of salt
1 teaspoon vanilla per quart of milk, and/or some cinnamon, nutmeg
Raisins (optional)

Chop the doughnuts and other breads coarsely and lay the pieces in a pan. Mix the milk with the eggs, salt, vanilla, and raisins, and pour over barely to cover. Mash the mixture a little so that it is semi-liquid. Sprinkle on cinnamon and/or nutmeg.
Bake at 350° F. for about 30 minutes.

Note: Jelly doughnuts add a nice touch of color. You can also use some stale white or whole-wheat bread. If you are using a large proportion of bread to sweet-rolls you may wish to add sugar.

The Sheep and the Goats

When the Son of Man comes in his glory, and all the angels with him, he will sit on his throne in heavenly glory. All the nations will be gathered before him, and he will separate the people one from another as a shepherd separates the sheep from the goats. He will put the sheep on his right and the goats on his left.

"Then the King will say to those on his right, 'Come, you who are blessed by my Father; take your inheritance, the kingdom prepared for you since the creation of the world. For I was hungry and you gave me something to eat, I was thirsty and you gave me something to drink, I was a stranger and you invited me in, I needed clothes and you clothed me, I was sick and you looked after me, I was in prison and you came to visit me.'

"Then the righteous will answer him, 'Lord, when did we see you hungry and feed you, or thirsty and give you something to drink? When did we see you a stranger and invite you in, or needing clothes and clothe you? When did we see you sick or in prison and go to visit you?'

The King will reply, 'I tell you the truth, whatever you did for one of the least of these brothers of mine, you did for me.'

"Then he will say to those on his left, 'Depart from me, you who are cursed, into the eternal fire prepared for the devil and his angels. For I was hungry and you gave me nothing to eat, I was thirsty and you gave me nothing to drink, I was a stranger and you did not invite me in, I needed clothes and you did not clothe me, I was sick and in prison and you did not look after me.'

"They also will answer, 'Lord, when did we see you hungry or thirsty or a stranger or needing clothes or sick or in prison, and did not help you?"

"He will reply, 'I tell you the truth, whatever you did not do for one of the least of these, you did not do for me.'

"Then they will go away to eternal punishment, but the righteous to eternal life."

Matthew 25:31–46 (NIV)

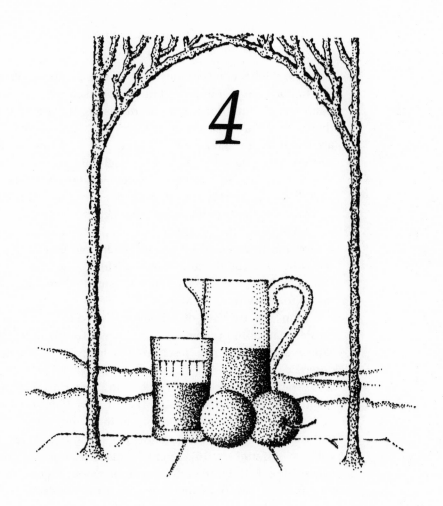

4

Fasting

Thus far we have looked mostly at all the delights of eating and at the importance of nutrition. But interspersed with all the feasting is an ancient and deep tradition of fasting. In the Old Testament there are many references to fasting, which is almost always accompanied by mourning, weeping, the "wearing of sackcloth," supplication—the prostration of oneself physically and spiritually before God. In fact, fasting is more a disposition of the will, the soul, than a mere afflicting of the body. It is a sign of humility, and a prayer for divine pardon and guidance.

Sometimes the entire people fasted, as when some great misfortune threatened, or actually overcame them: they implored the Lord to rescue them. It was, and still is, the practice of Jews to fast completely on the Day of Atonement (Yom Kippur). Moses fasted for forty days on Mount Sinai.

John the Baptist—of whom Christ said that there was no greater man born of woman—was known for his fasts: he ate only locusts and wild honey. Jesus himself fasted for forty days in the desert.

When the criticism was made to Jesus that his disciples did not fast (unlike other Jews), he said that at a wedding feast the guests do not fast while the bridegroom is there, but added: "The time will come when the bridegroom will be taken from them; then they will fast" (Matthew 9:15). Later Christians reading the Gospels took Christ himself to be the bridegroom of whom he had spoken, and they fasted in honor of him, gone from their midst.

Throughout the centuries, fasting continued to be a major Christian practice. Paul and the other early leaders fasted before undertaking major tasks and making important decisions. The early Christians fasted each Good Friday and Holy Saturday, through to Easter morning. The ancient hermits in the deserts of Egypt ate next to nothing, ever. The Eastern Orthodox and Catholic Christians kept and still keep major and minor seasonal fasts, as well as a fast before partaking of the Eucharist. And Protestant groups, such as the Puritans (and numerous other Christians as well), have kept fasts of supplication. All these practices are still alive in Christendom.

It is to two aspects of the tradition that the following pages are devoted. First, how to fast. That is, if, as part of your prayer life, you want to carry out a "radical," almost total, fast, how do you do it? Second, how does one observe the traditional days of abstinence of the Orthodox and Catholic traditions?

TIPS ON FASTING

Do not undertake major fasts (lasting more than a day or two) without the advice and counsel of someone whose judgment you respect, and who is experienced in fasting. Fasting can be spiritually (and physically) healthful, but, like eating, it can also be harmful if done imprudently.

Do not try to "beat the record" of any other faster; that is pride, not humility and supplication. Be careful about discussing your fasting with other people (other than your one or two advisors); again, pride.

Remember that the basic purpose of fasting is to be an aid—a "wing"—to prayer. It is a form of supplication to God. (And remember that prayer's *other* wing, according to Augustine, is "almsgiving": charity to the poor.)

If you intend to fast for several days, it is advisable to give up coffee and tea a few days before beginning.

While fasting, be sure to drink plenty of water (hot or warm—not cold).

When breaking your fast, begin by taking small amounts of fruit juice; then add milk and yogurt. Only gradually add solids, beginning with cooked fruits and vegetables, eggs and cheese, working up last to meats and starchy foods.

Do not undertake long fasts until you have had some experience with shorter ones.

Fasting is a medicine.

St. John Chrysostom

DAYS OF ABSTINENCE

Christians, throughout the centuries, have "fasted" and have practiced "abstinence." To fast is, simply defined, not to eat—or to eat as little and as late in the day as possible. (Normally a faster continues to drink water, which is absolutely essential to the body.) We can distinguish between a *full* or total fast (such as the early Christians kept from Good Friday through to Easter morning) and a *partial* fast, in which during the day only one full meal is eaten, often late.

Abstinence is a narrower concept, and refers to the avoidance of particular *kinds* of foods. Most commonly the abstainer avoids the flesh of animals, though other foodstuffs may be refused as well, such as all dairy products, oil and wine, and fish. The renunciation of meat is clearly symbolic of a renunciation of the desires of the flesh, of "carnality." Oil and wine and fish were simply other "good things" of life to be given up for God.

Fasting and abstinence do not necessarily go together. Sometimes a person is only fasting: cutting down on the *amount* of food eaten; for example, eating only one meal a day. Sometimes he or she may just be abstaining from certain *kinds* of food: most commonly, avoiding meat. But the two, fasting and abstinence, are often combined: on such solemn holy days as Ash Wednesday and Good Friday many Christians eat very little and also avoid meat.

The Christian custom of weekly fasting goes back to the Judaic tradition. Many Jews at the time of Christ fasted (apparently a partial fast) twice a week, on Tuesdays and Thursdays. The early Christians—most of them of Jewish origin—wished to maintain their old practices of piety, but to convert them as well. So they continued the tradition of biweekly fasting, but shifted the days— from Tuesday and Thursday to Wednesday (the day on which Judas betrayed Christ) and Friday (the day of the Crucifixion).

Over the centuries the tradition of fasting on Wednesdays and Fridays was mitigated by a requirement only to abstain from certain foods. (The Orthodox restrictions are far more extensive than the Catholic.) And in Catholic countries eventually only Friday remained a day of abstinence. In the Orthodox groups, on ordinary Wednesdays and Fridays no meat, olive oil, wine, or fish can be consumed; among Catholics, only meat is forbidden and only on Friday. More accurately, American Catholics are required to abstain from meat on Fridays, *unless* they replace that abstinence with some other form of penance or good work. (Many Catholics, curiously enough, do not know this rule; it is one, nonetheless.)

In the Protestant tradition, weekly abstinence was eliminated by the early reformers. Later on, it was reintroduced, to some degree. In particular, the Wesley brothers, founders of Methodism in the eighteenth century, and fathers of the Protestant "Great

Awakening," favored some form of Wednesday and Friday fasting or abstinence, while stressing the voluntary nature of the practice. Thus many Protestants, as well as Eastern Orthodox and Catholic Christians, have long abstained from meat on Fridays.

There is a great deal of similarity between Lenten dishes and those for Friday (in the Orthodox world, Wednesday as well). Most "abstinence" dishes in this book are to be found under "Lent," but here is just a little handful of Friday favorites from different countries.

When the stomach is full, it is easy to talk of fasting.

St. Jerome

FRIDAY

Greek bean soup

This delicious soup is a favorite in villages throughout Greece. When prepared on a Wednesday or Friday, or during Lent, the olive oil is not used by the serious Orthodox, because of fasting regulations.

1 pound dried white beans, such as Great Northern, or navy or pea beans; or lima beans, or chickpeas
12 cups (3 quarts) water
3 large onions, chopped
3 cloves garlic, minced
½ cup olive oil or vegetable oil
1 pound can Italian peeled tomatoes, drained, liquid reserved
Freshly ground pepper to taste
2 bay leaves
1 tablespoon fresh mint, chopped, or 1 teaspoon dried
Salt to taste

Pick over the beans, removing pebbles, etc. Rinse. Bring the water to a boil, add the beans, and boil for 2 minutes. Remove them from the heat and let them sit for 1 hour.

In the meantime, sauté the onions and garlic gently in the oil until translucent and golden.

After the beans have soaked for an hour, add the onions, garlic, and oil to the bean pot, along with the drained tomatoes, the pepper, the bay leaves, and half of the mint.

Simmer, partly covered, until the beans are soft. You may wish to purée part or all of the soup in the blender. Thin it, if necessary, with juice from the tomato can, or water.

Add the salt and the rest of the mint.

Yield: 8 to 10 servings

Variations:
You can eliminate the tomatoes; use oregano or basil instead of the mint; add chopped parsley at the end; or you can sauté some chopped celery along with the onion and garlic.

Swiss onion and cheese tart

ZWIEBELWÄHE

This "tart" is really the Swiss answer to the pizza, and it rather resembles a quiche as well. It is a Friday favorite in Switzerland. It is made here with a yeast dough—but it can be made with a pie dough, and it can also receive other fillings, such as spinach.

DOUGH:

2 packages yeast
½ cup lukewarm water
   (about 100–110° F.)
½ cup milk, scalded and
   cooled to room
   temperature
3½ cups flour
1 teaspoon salt
6 tablespoons (¾ stick)
   sweet butter, softened

FILLING:

3 cups chopped onion
4 tablespoons butter
4 tablespoons flour
1 cup heavy cream
2 eggs
¼ teaspoon ground nutmeg
½ pound Gruyère (or other
   Swiss cheese), coarsely
   grated
2–3 tablespoons grated
   onion (optional)
Paprika or caraway seeds

Stir the yeast into the lukewarm water. Let stand for 10 minutes. Stir in the milk.

In a large mixing bowl, combine the flour and the salt. Blend in the softened butter thoroughly with a fork. Make a well, and pour in the yeast mixture. Mix well. Turn the dough onto a floured surface and knead vigorously for about 15 minutes, or until the dough is smooth and elastic. If it is sticky, add a little more flour.

Place the dough in a greased bowl, turning it to grease the top. Cover, and let it rise in a draft-free place for about 1 hour, or until doubled in bulk. Punch the dough down. Knead briefly on a floured surface. Return to the bowl, cover and let rise again for about 1 hour.

In the meantime, prepare the filling:

Sauté the onions in 4 tablespoons of butter until soft and transparent but not brown. Stir in the flour and cook for a minute or two. Remove from the heat. Cool to lukewarm. Add the cream, and stir in the eggs. Sprinkle in the nutmeg.

When the dough is ready, roll it out to a rectangle about 12 by 18 inches. Lay it on a large greased baking sheet, turning up about 1 inch around the edges. If you prefer a thinner crust, you can roll the dough thinner and line a pie or tart pan with it. Reserve the rest for another tart, another occasion.

Sprinkle half of the grated cheese on the crust. Pour in the onion mixture. Then sprinkle the remaining cheese on top. If you like a strong onion flavor, sprinkle a little grated onion on top. Sprinkle with paprika or caraway seeds.

Bake the tart at 425° F. for 30 to 40 minutes, or until the top is brown and bubbly. Good hot, cold, or at room temperature.

Try serving the *Zwiebelwähe* with a tomato salad and cold beer.

Yield: 4 to 6 servings

Pasta shells stuffed with cheese

Ada Boni in her Italian Regional Cooking *explains that Italian pasta was first made in Sicily, and says, "There are references to* maccaruni, *the name given to the original pasta, in records dating from as far back as 1250. A legend concerning William the Hermit tells how he was invited to a meal by a Sicilian nobleman, who served him* maccaruni. *But instead of being stuffed with Ricotta cheese, the noodles were filled with pure earth. Undaunted, William blessed the food and by a miracle the earth became Ricotta as prescribed in the recipe." The dish still exists: Italian stuffed pasta.*

This makes a nice Friday dish, served with salad or a green vegetable.

1 pound jumbo pasta shells
1½ pounds ricotta cheese
½ pound mozzarella cheese, diced
¾ cup grated Parmesan or Romano cheese
2 eggs
¾ teaspoon salt, or to taste
Freshly ground pepper
Nutmeg
3 tablespoons finely chopped parsley
3 tablespoons (or more) pine nuts or chopped walnuts (optional)
4–5 cups tomato sauce
Additional grated Parmesan or Romano cheese

Cook the pasta shells in a large pot of boiling salted water, until they are partly but not completely done. (If you cook them completely, they will get *too* soft during the baking.) Drain thoroughly.

Mix the ricotta, mozzarella, and Parmesan (or Romano) cheeses with the eggs. Add salt, pepper, and nutmeg to taste. Stir in the parsley, and nuts if you wish.

While the pasta shells are still hot, stuff them with the cheese mixture, using a teaspoon or little spatula.

Cover the surface of a baking pan with a layer of the tomato sauce. Lay the shells in a single layer over the surface of the pan, packing them together fairly closely. Pour the rest of the sauce over the shells. Bake at 350° F. for 30 minutes. Serve with more grated cheese.

Yield: about 8 servings

EMBER DAYS OF ADVENT

Ember Days occur in the Catholic tradition four times a year, at the beginning of each of the four seasons of the year. (The word "Ember" apparently derives from an Anglo-Saxon word meaning "circuit.") They are the Wednesday, Friday, and Saturday following the Feast of St. Lucy on December 13 (for winter); following the first Sunday of Lent (for spring); following Pentecost (for summer); and following the Feast of the Holy Cross, September 14 (for fall).

These three days are set apart for some degree of fasting, for abstinence from meat, and for prayer, to sanctify each of the seasons. Ember Days have been observed since ancient times; we know they were already customary at the time of St. Augustine (A.D. 354–430), and it is said that they go back to the time of the Apostles. They may well, in fact, derive from the Jewish tradition, in which there were four yearly fast periods.

Japanese deep-fried seafood and vegetables

TEMPURA

Here is one of the most fascinating and unexpected of the traditional dishes: Japanese Tempura! The very word "Tempura" is supposed to come from the Latin name for the Ember Days: the Quattuor Tempora (Four Times). The earliest Christian missionaries to Japan, in the late 16th century, were Spanish and Portuguese. They brought with them, as Catholics, the commitment to abstain from meat and to pray at these moments of the year. From this need, on the one hand, and from the Japanese culinary traditions, on the other, was born this wonderful dish, now of course a favorite throughout the world. One note: this dish takes quite a while to prepare; it's more fun with a kitchen "collaborator." Here are some of the many things that can be prepared tempura-style.

Medium shrimp, shelled and deveined, but tails still attached. Make several shallow cuts across the underside of the shrimp to keep it from curling up when fried. *Note:* the shrimp should be fresh: do not use defrosted frozen shrimp for this recipe.

Bay or sea scallops (if the sea scallops are large, cut in two)

Raw squid, cut into squares about 1½ inches across

Small pieces of fish fillet

Slices of onion (put a toothpick through the sections to keep them from falling apart)

Slices of eggplant (¼ to ½ inch thick)

Slices of peeled raw sweet potato (⅛ inch thick)

Slices of green pepper

Slices of carrot (⅛ inch thick), or long thin carrot sticks

Green beans (ends removed)

Shiitake mushrooms or ordinary mushrooms, washed and trimmed

THE BATTER

The key to doing the batter right is that it should not be well mixed: it should be lumpy and floury looking. So do not stir it thoroughly. Here are the basic proportions. It is better to make several batches up fresh as you use it than to make a lot and let it sit.

1 egg yolk
1 cup ice water
1 cup sifted flour

Beat the egg yolk lightly in a bowl. Pour in the ice water and give it a couple of stirs with a fork or chopstick. Add the flour all at once and stir just until the ingredients are pretty well mixed. (Don't worry if there are still portions of unblended or even unmoistened flour.)

FRYING INSTRUCTIONS

Flour
Batter
Vegetable oil, or 3 parts
  vegetable oil to 1 part
  sesame oil

Heat the oil to 360° F.

Dry the shrimp, fish, and vegetables thoroughly. Begin with the shrimp: pick them up by the tails. Coat them lightly with flour, then dip them in the batter. Drop them, one by one, into the hot oil. Fry for 1 to 3 minutes, turning once or twice with a slotted spoon, until golden brown on all sides. Continue in the same fashion with the other seafood and the vegetables.

As you remove the foods from the oil, lay them on paper towels to drain. Keep hot.

Serve with Tempura Sauce.

TEMPURA SAUCE

If you have difficulty getting the ingredients for this sauce (which are available in many stores that sell Oriental food products), you can also buy it ready-made, or you can serve the Tempura with soy sauce and hot mustard.

1 cup water
2 tablespoons dried bonito
  flakes
⅓ cup mirin (or ½ cup sake
  mixed with 1 teaspoon
  sugar)
⅓ cup soy sauce
A few teaspoons freshly
  grated ginger, or a little
  ground ginger
Optional:
  Freshly grated Japanese
  white radish

In a saucepan, bring the water to a boil. Stir in the bonito flakes. Simmer for 3 minutes and strain the liquid (discard the flakes). This stock is called "dashi." Combine the dashi with the remaining ingredients. (Or you can let each person add ginger and radish to taste.)

Serve the Tempura with rice, and with the sauce in little bowls next to each plate.

Ember Day mouthfuls

BOUCHÉES QUATRE-TEMPS

1 cup diced cooked fish
½ cup diced cooked shrimp
½ cup diced cooked mussels
1 cup diced mushrooms
   sautéed in butter
1 small truffle, finely diced
   (optional)
1¼ cups Béchamel Sauce
   (see below)
Salt and freshly ground
   pepper to taste
8 baked puff-pastry patty
   shells

This recipe provides a characteristically—and amusingly—French way of handling religious restrictions on the diet: for the French cook such limitations are the very mother of invention. You just can't keep a good French cook from making a delectable meal!

This exquisite recipe is borrowed from Henri-Paul Pellaprat's classic Modern French Culinary Art.

Combine the fish, shrimp, mussels, mushrooms, truffle, and Béchamel Sauce. Adjust the seasonings. Heat.

Fill the patty shells, and top with the caps removed from the centers of the patty shells.

BÉCHAMEL SAUCE (FOR FISH DISHES)

4 tablespoons butter
4 tablespoons flour
½ cup fish broth
1 cup milk
½ cup heavy cream
Salt and white pepper to
   taste
Grated nutmeg to taste

Melt the butter, add the flour, and cook until slightly colored, stirring frequently. Add the fish broth, and stir until smooth. Gradually add the milk and cream and stir constantly until thickened. Cook 5 minutes over a low flame. Season to taste with salt, pepper, and nutmeg.

Ember Day tart

TART IN YMBRE DAY

2 tablespoons butter
1 large onion, finely
   chopped
3 tablespoons fresh
   breadcrumbs
4 eggs, lightly beaten
Pinch of saffron
½ teaspoon salt
⅛ teaspoon sugar
Pinch each: mace (or
   nutmeg), allspice,
   cinnamon
3 tablespoons dried currants
1 nine-inch pie crust,
   partially prebaked

This tart, clearly a forerunner of our quiche, is delicious and perhaps rather more in the spirit of abstinence than the preceding dish. The recipe is adapted from a fourteenth-century cookbook called Forme of Cury, *or way of cookery.*

Preheat the oven to 350° F.

Melt the butter in a skillet and cook the onion until soft and transparent.

Combine the crumbs in a bowl with the eggs, saffron, salt, sugar, spices, and currants. Add the onion and butter, and stir until the mixture is well blended. Pour into the pie crust and bake for about 30 minutes, or until golden brown; a knife inserted into the center should come out clean.

As the *Forme of Cury* invites: "Serve it forth."

Yield: about 6 servings

PART TWO *The Christian year*

*T*he Christian year, or calendar, is a marvelous, complex texture of fasts and feasts, vigils and celebrations. It is based primarily, of course, on the commemoration of certain great events in Christian history: Easter (the Resurrection of Christ), Pentecost (the Descent of the Holy Spirit), the Nativity of Christ, and his Epiphany (or Showing Forth, as to the Magi). These are generally considered to be the great Christian feasts. Early on, Christians began to observe, before Easter and then before Christmas, seasons of prayer and fasting, in order to prepare themselves to appreciate the joy of the feast. These seasons of prayer are Lent (before Easter) and Advent (before Christmas).

So far, very simple. Except that of these four great holy days two (Christmas and Epiphany) have fixed dates and two are "movable feasts." That is, the dates of Easter and of Pentecost can vary quite considerably from year to year, since these dates are determined by a lunar, not a solar, calendar. The Jewish calendar is lunar, and the Crucifixion and Resurrection occurred at the time of the great Jewish feast of Pesach, or Passover. So when the early Christians, many of whom were Jewish, wanted to commemorate the Resurrection, Easter, they quite naturally calculated its date in reference to Passover. And the dates of Lent, and of the Ascension of Christ and Pentecost (also originally a Jewish festival) are determined by that of Easter. Thus a major portion of the Christian calendar is "movable."

The dates of Christmas and Epiphany—and of all later established feasts, all the saints days—are determined by the solar calendar. The early Christians lived, increasingly, in a Roman culture (especially after the destruction of the Temple in Jerusalem, in A.D. 70). Their way of marking dates became Roman, and solar. They came to determine dates with reference to the months as we know them: using the so-called Julian calendar.

There is yet another variability, indeed an open-endedness, to the Christian calendar, which is a great strength of the tradition.

Any given country, region, parish, monastery has, over the centuries, felt quite free to pay particular honor to aspects of the divinity or of our relation to God, or to moments in the life of Christ or his Mother, or to saints, to which it had a particular devotion. Our American Thanksgiving Day is very much in this tradition. Many a saint is honored only nationally, or even just locally. The Greek Orthodox Church celebrates such feasts as those of the Holy Fathers of the Ecumenical Councils, the Holy Patriarchs, and All the Ancestors of Christ.

There is a time for everything, and a season for every activity under heaven:
a time to be born and a time to die,
a time to plant and a time to uproot,
a time to kill and a time to heal,
a time to tear down and a time to build,
a time to weep and a time to laugh,
a time to mourn and a time to dance,
a time to scatter stones and a time to gather them,
a time to embrace and a time to refrain,
a time to search and a time to give up,
a time to keep and a time to throw away,
a time to tear and a time to mend,
a time to be silent and a time to speak,
a time to love and a time to hate,
a time for war and a time for peace.

Ecclesiastes 3:1–8 (NIV)

Advent

We all live within several time frames, several notions of the year. The secular year, with its worldly hopes and resolutions, begins in January; the school year in September; the fiscal year, with its hard logic, begins whenever the entity in question so decrees. The Christian year, like the Christian era, begins with the coming of Christ. The liturgical year does not begin with Christmas itself, however, but rather with a season called Advent, whose purpose it is to help Christians prepare themselves—their hearts, their souls—for the coming of Christ. (The word "Advent" means, in fact, "the coming.")

Advent has had this function for about fifteen hundred years now; it is almost as old as the celebration of Christmas itself (which began in the fourth century). Christians apparently felt that, just as Lent preceded the great feast of Easter, Christmas should have a season of spiritual preparation and it extends from the fourth Sunday before Christmas through Christmas Eve.

Advent is not well known as a season: I am sure that many good Christians have never even heard of it. In any case Advent tends nowadays to be swallowed up in the general jollity and confusion of the increasingly secular holiday season. It is a hard season to observe. All the more reason to reflect on it carefully.

The season of Advent carries a double meaning. On the one hand, people feel a desire to prepare themselves for the coming of Christ into the world, into their lives. And, looking ahead to the Second Coming, the Last Judgment, they attempt to examine their consciences, to repent. Advent, then, has always been, like Lent, a period of prayer and fasting.

But Christians everywhere have felt that there was a great difference between Lent and Advent. Lent is a very somber period, leading to the Cross. Advent is intrinsically more joyful: after all, what it leads up to is Christ's birth. So if Advent is a period of spiritual preparation, of prayer, works of mercy, frequent visits to church, it is nonetheless suffused with Christmas joy.

How are we to observe this season of happy yet prayer-filled anticipation? How can we keep Advent from being swallowed up in the worldly Christmas season? Many people find that abstaining from meat, wine, sweets, or other food that they care about for two or three (or more) days a week is most helpful in reminding them that it isn't Christmas yet, that this is a time to prepare the heart. Some focus on the needs of the poor, even greater at this season than usual: not only is it cold out there (just think of the Holy Family, seeking shelter, so long ago), but poor families need money in order to have a Christmas dinner and to give their children gifts. Thinking about poor children can be very important for our children, most of them so amply endowed with possessions. Try letting each child pick out a toy, perhaps even contribute something from his or her allowance, for someone who has no toys. Such an experience can be a great builder of compassion. And, with your children, take cans or other unperishable foods to church to be distributed among those in need.

Advent has its authentic pleasures. These are anticipatory joys, such as the setting up of a crèche, one figure at a time perhaps. Day by day open the windows of an Advent calendar. Play and sing the music of Advent: "O Come, O Come, Emmanuel."

Maria von Trapp describes a beautiful Advent custom. On the first day of Advent, each member of the family picked out of a hat the name of some other member. From that day on, through Advent, that person became the secret "Christ child" for the one who had drawn his or her name: each day one tried to do something loving for that person. Many families, including my own, have found this a valued custom. One variation, especially nice for large families: try changing names each week so that each member focuses on several different people as the Christ child over the course of Advent. I will confess that I have on occasion "fixed" the hat, so that a child received the name of someone on whom I thought he or she especially needed to focus love.

Christmas is coming, the geese are getting fat,
Please to put a penny in the old man's hat;
If you haven't got a penny, a ha'penny will do,
If you haven't got a ha'penny, God bless you!

Beggar's rhyme

BAKING WITH CHILDREN

Advent is a wonderful time to bake with children. It's not just that it is fun—though it *is* fun. This baking picks up the themes of Advent: the preparing of gifts for others, to make *them* happy, and the waiting for Christmas before eating the good things we prepare.

I especially recommend cookie baking. Fruitcakes are more to adult tastes, and of course many of them are heavily laced with liquor; the batter is hence not suitable for tasting by little ones. Children may enjoy helping with Christmas breads, but cookies are certainly the most reliably enjoyable. And what is most fun is using cookie cutters and decorating the cookies (either before or after baking).

Here are a few tips on baking with children:

This is not the time to be a perfectionist. Don't expect the cookies to look like the ones in the magazines and cookbooks. What children bring to cookie baking (indeed, to all their cooking) is a wonderful inventiveness, and the willingness—which is sometimes really exhilarating—to experiment, to try daring new things. So have fun! Let *them* have fun! The only important consideration is: does the cookie look appealing, and edible? Don't let the children "gook" the cookies up so much that no one would want to eat them: these are, after all, gifts of *food*. Remember, most people get a real kick out of cookies made by children. To adults who are "not amused," give another sort of gift.

If you are going to be baking on several different occasions during the Advent-Christmas season, find ways to keep the enterprise exciting. For example, don't bring out all your cutters at once. You might begin with stars. Let them focus on the star cutters, on all the ways they can decorate stars—and on what the Christmas star means. A little later, or another day, introduce angels, perhaps. The point is, keep their attention by helping them to focus on one kind of shape, or one kind of technique, at a time. Not only is it more exciting; this way they can *master* the materials. Children can get really very good at (for example) painting cookie angels.

Incidentally, this introduction of the elements one or a few at a time also cuts down on the mess—not a trivial consideration! Bring out sprinkles only when you are ready for them, and only one or two kinds at a time (in hard-to-tip bowls). What a mess they can make!

If you are in a hurry, or to vary the pace of the baking enterprise, you can prepare and cut out the cookies yourself. Do it while the children are asleep or in school or otherwise occupied. Just bring them into the act for the decorating, either before or after baking the cookies.

For example, you can have the cookies all baked. Then set them out on the table, with pots of colored icing and paint brushes, and let the children go to town. There's hardly any mess (even spilled "paints" can't run very far).

The children can also join in wrapping the cookies as presents. They can pack the cookies in pretty tins, or lay them on pretty paper plates and wrap them with plastic wrap, or bright-colored cellophane, and a ribbon. Encourage them to make the cards that will accompany the gifts: let them draw the pictures, and (if they can write) do the text. The more the children have done themselves, the more the gifts will mean to them—and to the favorite friends or relatives or teachers to whom they give them.

Every belle, and every beau, the most renowned knight or the most rigid monk, welcomed alike the cinnamon, the nutmeg, the ginger, the pepper and the clove. All the manuscripts which remain of this period abound in praise of the spices. The facility of our intercourse with the East now has occasioned them to be treated with less veneration, although their loss would create a piercing outcry.

Anonymous, *The School for Good Living*

Old-fashioned white sugar cookies

1 cup (½ pound) sweet
  butter, at room
  temperature
1½ cups sugar
3 eggs
1 teaspoon vanilla extract
4 cups flour
1 teaspoon baking powder
½ teaspoon baking soda
½ teaspoon salt
1 teaspoon cinnamon
½ teaspoon nutmeg

Cream the butter with the sugar until fluffy. Stir in the eggs, one at a time, beating well after each addition. Beat until the mixture is fluffy. Stir in the vanilla extract.

Sift the flour with the baking powder, soda, salt, cinnamon, and nutmeg. Gradually stir the flour mixture into the butter mixture.

Optional: Wrap the dough in plastic wrap and let it rest for a few hours or overnight in the refrigerator.

On a lightly floured board, roll the dough out thin—about ⅛ inch (or ¼ inch, if you prefer), and cut into fancy shapes.

Bake on lightly buttered cookie sheets at 375° F. for 8 to 10 minutes, or until cookies are a light golden brown.

Yield: about 4 dozen cookies

Springerles

Springerles are among the most traditional of the German Christmas cookies. The word Springerle *refers to the vaulting or jumping horse that was an early motif on the molds used to make the cookies. (This motif is said to go back to pagan times.) Many German families have old Springerle molds; some of the most charming of them have a variety of motifs on them, for example a bishop, or a church, mixed in with birds and animals, hearts and flowers. Molds are available in many department and baking-goods stores.*

These cookies are wonderful with a cup of coffee or hot chocolate, or a glass of milk. They make particularly handsome Christmas presents. They can also be used as Christmas-tree ornaments: before you bake the Springerles, just make a little hole in the top of each for a thin ribbon to go through.

4 eggs
2 cups sugar
Pinch of salt
Grated rind of 1 lemon
¼ teaspoon baking powder
3½–4 cups flour
¾ cup anise seeds (or powdered anise, or anise oil; see Variations)

In a large bowl, beat the eggs well. Gradually add the sugar, and continue beating until the mixture is light and fluffy. Beat in the salt and lemon rind. Add the baking powder, and sift in the flour, 1 cup at a time, until the dough is fairly stiff and doesn't stick to your hands.

Turn the dough out onto a lightly floured surface. Knead until the dough is soft and shiny, 5 to 10 minutes. Roll the dough out to a thickness of ¼ inch. Let it stand for about 10 minutes. Flour the mold well. Press it down on the dough, pressing firmly all around.

Cut the cookies apart. Place them on a baking sheet that has been lightly buttered and sprinkled with anise seeds. Let the cookies sit, lightly covered with a clean dishtowel, overnight.

Bake at 300° F. for about 15 minutes, or until the cookies are set and a very pale golden color. Do not let them brown.

These cookies will keep for a long time—they just get harder. If you like them soft, pack with them in the cookie tin a piece of apple or rye bread, replacing the apple or bread from time to time.

Optional: If you want, you can paint the Springerles with tinted icing (see page 104) but they are beautiful just as they are.

Yield: about 5 dozen cookies

Variations:

Instead of anise seed, you can flavor the cookies with 2 teaspoons powdered anise or 3–4 drops anise oil: add along with the lemon rind.

If you do not care for the flavor of anise, you may replace it with more lemon rind—and perhaps a little orange rind as well— or with 1 teaspoon vanilla extract.

Peppernuts

PFEFFERNUSSE

Here is another traditional favorite in Germany and numerous other countries. There are hundreds—thousands—of variations on the Peppernut. (If you are a real Peppernut fancier you should see Norma Vost's Peppernuts, Plain and Fancy: a Christmas Tradition from Grandmother's Oven.)

Speculaas dough (page 103)
The rind of 1 orange or 2 lemons
½ to ¾ cup finely chopped walnuts, pecans, or almonds
Optional:
   Pinch of freshly ground white pepper
   2–3 drops of oil of anise

Before kneading the dough, add the rest of the ingredients listed here. Roll into thin ropes—½ to 1 inch thick, depending on what size you like your Peppernuts; the small ones make cookies the size of buttons. Let the dough rest in the refrigerator for several days. Cut the ropes into slices about ½ inch thick.

Place the "nuts" on a greased baking sheet. Bake at 350° F. for about 7 to 10 minutes, or until golden brown. The longer they bake, the harder they will be. (Some people like them as hard as nuts—some softer.) Small Peppernuts will cook faster, of course, than large ones. Cool on wire racks.

Optional: Dust with confectioners' sugar, before packing or before serving.

These cookies keep well in a tin. To keep them from getting too hard, pack in with them a piece of apple or of rye bread, replacing it from time to time.

Yield: about 10 dozen

Spritz cookies

Everyone loves these, and children enjoy helping to use the cookie gun. If you don't have one, use a pastry bag with a large star tip. You can decorate these cookies with bits of angelica or maraschino cherry, colored sugar or sprinkles.

2 sticks (½ pound) sweet butter, at room temperature
½ cup sugar
1 egg
2 teaspoons vanilla or almond extract, or finely grated orange or lemon rind, or 1–2 teaspoons rum
¼ teaspoon salt
2¼ cups sifted flour
Food coloring (optional)

Preheat the oven to 375° F.

Cream the butter with the sugar. Beat in the egg and the flavoring. Stir in the salt and flour. Add optional food coloring to all or part of the dough. Mix thoroughly until well blended.

Using a cookie gun, or a pastry bag fitted with a large star tip, form the cookies into desired shapes about 1 inch apart on a lightly buttered cookie sheet.

Bake for 8 to 10 minutes, until the cookies are just beginning to turn brown.

Yield: about 5 dozen cookies

Christmas roll cookies and cookies with delectable centers

⅔ cup sugar
2 sticks (½ pound) sweet
* butter, at room*
* temperature*
2 eggs
2 teaspoons vanilla extract
½ teaspoon salt
½ teaspoon baking soda
2¾ cups flour
Optional:
* Multicolored sprinkles,*
* finely chopped nuts, jam*
* Candied maraschino*
* cherries*
* Pecan halves*

Cream the sugar with the butter. Beat in the eggs, and add the vanilla extract. Stir in the salt, baking soda, and flour. Knead briefly until the dough is smooth and thoroughly blended. Form the dough into several rolls about 1 inch in diameter and 8 inches long.

Now you have several possibilities: You can coat these long rolls with sprinkles or with chopped nuts: put the sprinkles or nuts on a sheet of waxed paper and roll the long rolls back and forth until they are well coated; press the sprinkles or nuts in firmly. You can also leave the rolls plain and decorate them later (see below).

Wrap the rolls of dough in waxed paper or plastic wrap and refrigerate them for about 4 hours. If you are in a hurry, you can speed this chilling process by starting the dough in the freezer for 20 to 30 minutes. Slice the dough about ⅛ inch thick and place the slices on lightly buttered baking sheets.

Rolls that have been left plain should be sliced about ¼ inch thick. Place them on lightly buttered baking sheets. (Don't put both thin and thicker cookies on the same sheets, as the baking time will be different.) Make a little indentation in the center of each cookie with your finger, and place there a little jam, or a candied maraschino cherry, or a perfect pecan half.

Bake at 375° F. for about 8 to 12 minutes or until golden brown. The thicker cookies will take a little longer.

More variations:

You can omit all the decorations. In that case you might want to flavor the dough more intensely: add a little grated orange or lemon rind, or try substituting a tablespoon or more of kirsch (Swiss cherry brandy) for the vanilla extract.

O Wisdom, that proceedest from the mouth of the Most High, reaching from end to end mightily, and sweetly disposing all things: come and teach us the way of prudence.

Great Antiphon at Vespers on December 17th

Lithuanian jam squares

This delectable cookie is a favorite in Lithuania—and in my family too!

½ pound cream cheese
½ pound (2 sticks) sweet
  butter, at room
  temperature
Grated rind of 1 lemon
Pinch of salt
2 cups flour
Jam (2 or more kinds make
  a pretty contrast)
Confectioners' sugar

In a large bowl, cream the cream cheese with the butter until fluffy. Add the lemon rind. Stir in the salt and add the flour gradually, mixing well. Knead the dough for a minute or two, until it is smooth and thoroughly blended. Wrap in waxed paper or plastic wrap and refrigerate for several hours or overnight. (If you are in a hurry, start the chilling process in the freezer. Leave the dough in the freezer for about 20 minutes.)

On a lightly floured surface, roll the dough out thin, about ⅛ inch. Cut it into squares about 1½ inches across. (Or cut some or all of it into diamond shapes. For diamonds, make horizontal cuts 1 to 1¼ inches apart, then cut diagonally across them.) Smooth the jam generously over the entire surface of each square, using a pastry brush.

Place the squares on a lightly buttered baking sheet. Bake at 400° F. for about 10 minutes, or until the dough is lightly browned and the top is bubbly.

Remove cookies from the pan, and sprinkle with confectioners' sugar.

Yield: about 5 dozen cookies

Rum balls

My wonderful mother-in-law, Alda Vitz, faithfully prepares this treat every Christmas. Here is her recipe. As I have discovered, to my pleasure and surprise, Rum Balls are quick and easy to make.

1 cup finely crumbled
  vanilla wafers
1 cup confectioners' sugar
1 cup pecans, finely
  chopped
2 teaspoons cocoa
1½ teaspoons light corn
  syrup
¼ cup dark rum
Additional confectioners'
  sugar

Combine the vanilla wafers, 1 cup confectioners' sugar, pecans, and cocoa in a bowl. Stir in the light corn syrup and rum.

Mix thoroughly—with your hands is easiest. Roll into balls about ¾ inch in diameter. Roll the balls in confectioners' sugar.

Stored in a jar with a tight-fitting lid, in the refrigerator, rum balls will keep indefinitely.

Yield: about 2 dozen

Christ's diapers

GREEK DIPLES

Diples are "folds" in Greek. These cookies are sometimes shaped in bowknots or other fancy shapes, but for Christmas they are made in a shape suggestive of the swaddling clothes—or actually the diapers!—of the Infant Jesus.

6 eggs
3½ cups flour
¼ teaspoon salt
1 teaspoon baking powder
½ cup olive oil
Grated rind of 1 orange
Vegetable oil or shortening
    for deep frying
½ cup honey
½ cup water
1 teaspoon cinnamon
1 tablespoon lemon juice
Chopped pistachio nuts
Confectioners' sugar

With an electric beater, beat the eggs until light and fluffy.

Sift together the flour, salt, and baking powder. Gradually stir the flour into the eggs.

Turn the dough onto an unfloured board. Add the olive oil, a little at a time, and the grated orange rind. Knead the dough until it is smooth—about 10 minutes.

Roll the dough out paper thin on a well-floured board. Cut it into squares about 1½ inches across. Fold these into triangles, then join the ends to form diapers. Press the corners together gently but firmly. (If you don't press the corners well, the diapers will come undone!)

Drop the diapers, a few at a time, into hot fat (360–370° F. on a deep-fat-frying thermometer). Turn once or twice and fry until golden brown. Drain thoroughly on paper towels.

Bring the honey and water slowly to a boil in a saucepan. Stir in the cinnamon and lemon juice. Reduce heat and simmer for 1 or 2 minutes.

Dribble the honey syrup over the diapers, and sprinkle them with chopped pistachios, then with confectioners' sugar.

When the diapers are fully dry, pack them in a tin and cover tightly. These keep well, if well covered.

Yield: about 4 dozen

Almond or hazelnut crescents

These are so good! My dear friend, colleague, co-conspirator (in life), and fellow cook Kathryn Talarico taught me how to make them—as well as many other things.

2 cups unblanched almonds
    and/or hazelnuts
1¼ cups flour
¼ cup sugar
1 teaspoon vanilla extract
1 cup (½ pound) sweet
    butter, at room
    temperature
Confectioners' sugar

Grind 1⅔ cups nuts very fine. Chop fine the remaining ⅓ cup.

Mix the flour, sugar, and *ground* nuts in a bowl. Stir in the vanilla extract. With your fingers, work in the butter until thoroughly blended. Chill the dough for about 1 hour.

Roll the dough into balls about 1¼ inches in diameter. Form into rolls about 3½ inches long, then into crescents. Press the tops of the crescents into the chopped nuts.

Place them on ungreased cookie sheets and bake at 350° F. for 12 to 15 minutes, or until lightly browned. Cool on the pan for 7 minutes (*exactly!*), then remove to a rack.

While the crescents are still warm, roll them in confectioners' sugar.

Yield: 25 to 30 crescents

Variations:

Try mixing walnuts instead of hazelnuts in with the almonds. You can use ½ to 1 teaspoon cinnamon instead of the vanilla extract.

Inedible dough

Cookie Christmas ornaments are pretty, but as we all know, those that taste good disappear mysteriously from the tree. Try having your children make some ornaments each year out of inedible dough, to save. You can also make sets of ornaments, such as a crèche scene. Or try a Noah's ark. These figures make nice presents for children to give as gifts to godparents, favorite relatives, and friends.

2 cups flour
1 cup uniodized salt
About 1 cup water

Combine ingredients in a bowl. Knead until the mixture is smooth and well blended.

To form shapes, you can roll out the dough to ⅛- or ¼-inch thickness. Or you can mold figures by hand; do not make shapes thicker than about ½ inch. If you want to hang the ornament, make a little hole with a drinking straw or a toothpick at the top; or insert a wire loop or hairpin into the ornament.

You can add details—such as eyes, hair—to the surface of the ornament by using a toothpick or the instruments in a manicure set. You can add appliqués: roll out dough very thin, and cut out the desired shapes with a sharp knife; "cement" the shape in place with water. Try making hair with a garlic press.

Place the ornaments on a greased baking sheet. Bake at 225 to 250° F. for 2 hours or more, until completely dry and hard. When they are cool, smooth the ornaments with fine sandpaper or a fine emery board.

Paint front, sides, and back with poster or acrylic paints, or use marking pens. The metallic ones that are now available are great for adding highlights. Spray when dry with clear polyurethane, or paint with clear shellac. If pieces break, they can be easily and repeatedly repaired with Elmer's Glue-all.

THE FEAST OF ST. NICHOLAS
December 6

The traditional feast day of St. Nicholas is December 6. Honoring this saint on his day has, I believe, much to recommend it. First, it's nice just to remind our children (and ourselves) that Santa's real name is St. Nicholas. Santa Claus is *Saint* (Ni)Claus. So, behind the jolly fat man in the red suit, with the reindeer and the cute little helpers, stands a real person.

History and legend are almost inextricably intertwined in the story of Nicholas's life, but we do know that he really lived, in the fourth century, and that he was a holy bishop of the city of Myra, now in Turkey. He has been widely honored as a saint since the sixth century. Many stories are told about his great kindness, about his miraculous aid to those in distress. It is said that he threw three bags of gold through the window to three poor young girls for their dowries so that they could marry and avoid being given into prostitution. He is also supposed to have brought back to life three little boys who had been murdered and put into a vat of brine. He was famous for saving sailors from storms, and for many other miracles as well. At his shrine in Bari, Italy, a sweet smell is often reported. Because of these charming accounts, he is considered the patron saint of children, and of unmarried girls, of sailors, of perfumers—and many other groups as well.

St. Nicholas has been through the centuries among the most popular of the saints (he is the patron saint of Russia). Little children in Holland, Germany, Luxembourg, and elsewhere traditionally received a visit from their patron, St. Nicholas, on his feast day: to good children he gave candies, cookies, apples, nuts; naughty children were warned with a willow switch, or received pieces of coal. In Holland, the gifts were left in the children's wooden shoes.

You might consider the possibility of transferring "Santa's visit" to your house back to December 6, the feast of St. Nicholas. I'm all for anything that can free Christmas Day from the obsessive preoccupation with gifts. And whether or not we play along with the Santa story, we can at least tell our children who St. Nicholas *really* was—and call him by his real name.

We can find ways perhaps to use the saintly Nicholas to help us, gently but firmly, push the fat, bearded elf with the bag of toys (cute as he may be) from center stage—and to put the focus back on the Christ Child. I'm sure the good bishop would approve.

Speculaas cookies

These cookies, also called Speculatius, Speculaus, and Speculations, are claimed by various countries: they are traditional in Belgium, Holland, and the Rhineland, and are served especially on St. Nicholas Day. They are sometimes cut out into little men or animals; in Holland they are frequently pressed with a windmill motif. But they were also often cut out into the shape of St. Nicholas himself, dressed as a bishop, holding his bishop's staff. I have never been able to find such cookie cutters in this country; I finally resorted to cutting out St. Nicholas figures myself—and discovered, to my surprise, that it is really very easy to do. The shape is, after all, a simple one. You can also make cookies, with or without cutters, to recall other aspects of Nicholas's life and work: such as the three young girls to whom he threw the three bags of gold or the three little boys whom he brought back to life, or the sailors whom he saved from the storm. Lots of possibilities here.

You might find these delicious gingerbread cookies a nice way to begin your Advent-Christmas baking.

1 cup (2 sticks) sweet butter, at room temperature
2 cups dark brown sugar
2 eggs
Grated rind of 1 lemon
2 teaspoons cinnamon
1 teaspoon ground nutmeg or mace
½ teaspoon ground cloves
⅛ teaspoon ground ginger
⅛ teaspoon cardamom
⅛ teaspoon salt
4 cups flour
1 teaspoon baking powder
Optional:
  Icing (see page 104)

In a large bowl, cream the butter with the sugar until fluffy. Stir in the eggs one at a time, blending thoroughly after each addition. Stir in the lemon rind.

Sift the spices and salt with the flour and baking powder, and stir gradually into the butter mixture. Wrap in waxed paper or plastic wrap and chill for several hours or overnight. (If you are in a hurry, start the chilling process in the freezer: leave the dough in the freezer for about 20 minutes.)

On a floured surface, roll out the dough to about ⅛ inch. If you are going to make large figures—over about 6 inches—you might roll out the dough a little thicker, to about ¼ inch: the figures will be less fragile. Cut out with cookie cutters, or with a sharp knife. You can also just cut the dough in squares, if you prefer. This dough can also be used with a cookie mold, or can be molded by hand.

Place the cookies on lightly buttered baking sheets and bake at 350° F. for 10 to 12 minutes, or until set and lightly browned. Large or thick cookies will take somewhat longer. If you like your cookies soft, remove them from the oven when they are just set— the longer the baking time, the harder the gingerbread.

Optional: Paint when cool. These cookies—especially when baked in the form of St. Nicholas—are terrific fun to paint with colored icing.

continued

Speculaas cookies, continued

ICING

In little pots or plastic containers, mix confectioners' sugar with a little bit of water (or lightly beaten egg white, or lemon juice) and a few drops of food coloring, to produce the desired shades and the desired consistency for painting. Apply with small paintbrushes.

Yield: approximately 3 dozen cookies or fewer large figures

Variations:

This recipe makes a fairly mild gingerbread. If you like your gingerbread really spicy, you can increase slightly and proportionately the amounts of all the spices.

This recipe, with a few small additions, can also be used to make Peppernuts (page 97).

If cutting the dough into squares, you might like to sprinkle them with slivered almonds; this is traditional and delicious.

You can also press patterns into this dough using Springerle molds (page 96).

IDEAS FOR CHRISTMAS COOKIES

There are many beautiful cookie shapes for which there are no cutters. But, as with the St. Nicholas cookie, you will find that it is very easy to design and cut out figures yourself. The Madonna, below, is simple to make, and is a delight to paint, especially for older children—and for you. Such an ornament as this one, made out of Speculaas (page 103) or Swedish St. Lucy Ginger Snap dough (page 109) or any other sturdy cookie dough, makes an exquisite Christmas-tree ornament. If made of *in*edible dough and varnished, such a figure will last for many years.

Bishop, or bishop's wine

Traditionally served on the feast day of the saintly bishop of Myra, this drink can be a "loving cup" for a family gathering.

2 bottles full-bodied red
  wine
1 orange, studded with
  cloves and quartered
1 strip lemon peel
1 stick cinnamon
¼ teaspoon each: mace,
  allspice, ground ginger
2 to 4 tablespoons sugar, or
  to taste

Pour the wine into a saucepan. Add the orange, the lemon peel, stick of cinnamon, and the spices. Cover lightly and simmer for 5 to 10 minutes. Add sugar to taste, and simmer for another minute or two. Serve hot.

Yield: 8 to 10 servings

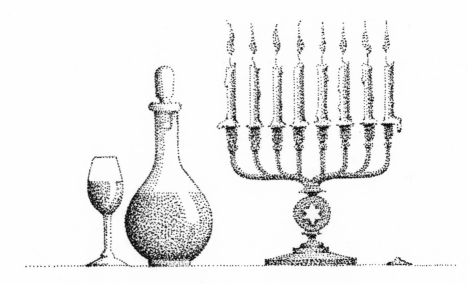

ADVENT—AND CHANUKAH

During the Christian season of Advent falls the Jewish Feast of Lights, or Chanukah. Since ours is, after all, the *Judeo*-Christian tradition, it is fitting to observe this feast along with our Jewish brothers and sisters.

The Feast of Lights commemorates what is in fact a fascinating piece of Jewish history. It is an extraordinary and moving story.

Early in the second century before Christ, Palestine fell into the hands of the Syrian emperors, and in 175 B.C. Antiochus IV came to power. Part of his program to consolidate his political control was the Hellenization (in fact, the *secularization*) of the Jews: he encouraged Greek dress and customs among the priesthood and upper class of Jerusalem's inhabitants. Finally he even decreed that the Temple should be rededicated as a temple to the Greek god Zeus, and he set up statues of Zeus, in his own likeness, bearing the inscription "Epiphanes": "God manifest."

At this point, a group of religious Jews, led by an aged high priest named Mattathias and his five sons, rose in armed rebellion. Under the leadership of Mattathias' son Judah, called the Maccabee, or "Hammer," the Jews were able to seize the Temple in Jerusalem and drive out the Syrian soldiers. They cleaned out the temple and rededicated it. (The word *Chanukah* means "dedication.") They relit the light that had always burned in the Temple, and although there was only enough oil to keep the light burning for one day, it burned—miraculously—for eight days and nights. That is why at Chanukah the candles of the Menorah (the traditional candelabrum), are lit, one each night for eight days, beginning on the 25th day of the lunar month of Kislev. (Kislev normally falls in our month of December, hence during the season of Advent.)

An inspiring story is it not? One of heroic faithfulness to God, that we all would do well to commemorate.

Potato pancakes

LATKES

There are several family traditions associated with Chanukah—aside from the relating of the story of the Maccabees and the lighting of the Menorah candles. One of them is the eating of delicious Potato Pancakes.

2 cups grated peeled, raw mature potatoes
1 small grated onion
1 teaspoon salt
Pinch of freshly ground pepper
½ cup flour
2 eggs
Shortening or oil

Extract the moisture from the potatoes by wringing them in a clean dish towel. Mix them in a bowl with the onion, salt, and pepper. Stir in the flour and eggs. Mix well.

Heat about a ¼-inch layer of shortening or oil in a frying pan. Drop the potato mixture, one heaping tablespoon per cake, into the hot shortening. Flatten a little with a spatula, to make flattish cakes about 2 inches across.

Fry, turning once or twice, until they are nicely browned and crisp on both sides. Drain thoroughly on paper towels.

Serve hot with applesauce and/or sour cream.

Yield: 4 to 6 servings

ST. LUCY'S DAY
December 13

St. Lucy's Day marks, in several different cultures, a moment of festivity in Advent. In Sweden, in particular, her feast is celebrated with beautiful customs hundreds of years old. The eldest daughter of a household, wearing a white dress with a crimson sash, and a whortleberry or lingonberry crown, set with lighted candles, wakes the members of the family, and serves them special buns or a cake and coffee. (The buns are often made in traditional X shapes, apparently suggestive of the sun, and presumably going back to pagan times; the cake is frequently made in the shape of Lucy's crown.)

What does this have to do with St. Lucy herself? She was a Christian martyr, killed around A.D. 304 at Syracuse, in Sicily, under Emperor Diocletian. In the legend a rejected suitor denounced her as a Christian. Her eyes figure prominently in the stories about her: according to some accounts, her eyes were plucked out during her torture, and God miraculously restored them. She was finally killed by a sword.

The feast of St. Lucy—whose very name means "light"—took on special meaning in Sweden, where December is most especially dark. So the elements of light, and sight, in her legend are picked up there and assimilated to the theme of the sun and the universal hope for the sun's return. (The crown also picks up the theme of martyrdom: the martyrs are said to wear crowns in heaven.) These themes—of light and waiting and hope—and the crown motif—indicating suffering and glory—are appropriate for the season of Advent.

St. Lucy's crown

I don't want to spoil anyone's fun, but I have to say that no daughter of mine is going to walk around with lit candles on her head, however worthy the cause! I do, nonetheless, eagerly await the day when Rebecca or Jessica will awaken me to ample slices of St. Lucy's Crown (a little butter on the side, please?) and a cup of steaming coffee. In the meantime, I find it lovely for us all to sit down together to so beautiful a crown, with its tapers lit. It is really an unforgettable sight.

continued

St. Lucy's crown, continued

¼–½ teaspoon saffron
  threads
1 cup lukewarm milk
2 packages dry yeast
¼ cup warm water (100–
  110° F.)
½ cup sugar
1 teaspoon salt
⅓ cup sweet butter
1 egg, lightly beaten
4 cups flour
Grated rind of 1 lemon
4–5 tablespoons blanched
  almonds, grated or finely
  chopped
4–5 tablespoons chopped
  candied citron (optional)
Confectioners' Sugar Glaze
  (see below)
Tapers or thin candles (see
  below) (optional)

Crush the saffron to a fine powder, and steep it in a tablespoon or two of the lukewarm milk for about 10 minutes. In a large bowl, dissolve the yeast in the lukewarm water. Stir in 1 tablespoon of the sugar. Set the mixture aside for 5 to 10 minutes, or until frothy.

Scald the remaining milk. Stir in the rest of the sugar, and the salt and butter. Stir until the butter is melted. Let cool to lukewarm. Stir into the yeast mixture. Add the saffron milk and lightly beaten egg. Stir in the flour gradually, mixing well. Add the lemon rind, almonds, and citron, if you like.

Turn the dough out onto a lightly floured surface. Knead for about 10 minutes, or until the dough is smooth and elastic. While you are kneading, add more flour if the dough is sticky.

Place the dough in a greased bowl, turning to grease the top. Cover and let rise in a draft-free spot until doubled in bulk, about 1 to 1½ hours.

Punch the dough down. Cut off one-third to make the top braid; set aside. Divide the remaining dough into three parts. Roll each part into a rope about 25 inches long. Place the three ropes close together on a buttered baking sheet and braid them together. (Try starting from the middle; you may find it easier.) Form the braid into a circle, pinching the ends to seal.

Divide the reserved dough into three parts. Roll each part into a rope about 24 inches long. Proceed as above: Place the three ropes close together on a buttered baking sheet and braid them together. Form the braid into a circle, pinching the ends to seal.

Cover both braids lightly and let the bread rise for 30 to 45 minutes, or until almost doubled in bulk.

Bake at 400° F. for 10 minutes. Reduce the heat to 350° F. and bake for about 40 minutes longer, or until the two braided rings are golden brown and sound hollow when tapped on the bottom.

Place the smaller braid on top of the larger. Drizzle over it the Confectioners' Sugar Glaze. Optional: stick thin tapers into the crown and light them. There is no fixed number of tapers; why not put in one for each member of your family?

Yield: 1 large double-braided St. Lucy's Crown

Variations:

You can eliminate the saffron, and flavor the crown with 2 teaspoons ground cardamom; add it along with the salt.

For a smaller crown, you can just halve this recipe; the baking time will be a little shorter.

CONFECTIONERS' SUGAR GLAZE

2–3 teaspoons lemon juice
   or milk or water
½–1 cup confectioners'
   sugar

Stir the lemon juice into the confectioners' sugar; mix well. Add more sugar or lemon juice as needed to produce a proper consistency for drizzling.

Swedish St. Lucy ginger snaps

LUCIAPEPPERKAKOR

Here is another delicious St. Lucy's Day treat, and a wonderful cookie to bake throughout Advent.

½ cup dark corn syrup
1½ cups dark or light
   brown sugar
¼ cup molasses
2 teaspoons ground ginger
Grated rind of 1 lemon
1 tablespoon baking soda
1 cup heavy cream
6–7 cups flour
Icing (see below)

Heat the corn syrup in a saucepan. Stir in the sugar, molasses, ginger, lemon rind, and baking soda.

In a large bowl, whip the cream until almost stiff.

Stir the syrup mixture gradually into the cream. Beat at low speed with an electric mixer for 4 to 5 minutes (about twice as long if you are beating by hand with a spoon or whisk). Add 4 cups of the flour, mixing well with a spoon. Then gradually add enough of the remaining flour to make a soft, pliable dough. Knead for 2 or 3 minutes.

Wrap the dough well in waxed paper or plastic wrap and refrigerate for several hours or overnight. (If you are in a hurry, you can start the chilling process in the freezer. Leave the dough in the freezer for about 20 minutes.)

On a lightly floured surface, roll the dough out about ¼ inch thick. Cut with fancy cutters, such as animals and people, hearts and flowers. Try making some pretty young girls—perhaps with crowns—like St. Lucy. If possible, do crèche scenes or other Christmas motifs, such as stars and angels. (Even in our baking, we can try to emphasize what matters about Christmas—the star, the baby, the angels singing—and play down Santa Claus and full stockings.)

Place the cookies on a lightly buttered cookie sheet. Bake at 275° F. for about 12 minutes or until the cookies are golden brown.

Ice when cold.

Yield: about 4 dozen cookies

ICING

Beat the white of an egg until frothy. Add 1 cup confectioners' sugar (and, optional, ½ teaspoon lemon juice). If the icing is too thick, add more lemon juice; too thin, more sugar. You can make several batches, adding food coloring as you wish. An even quicker icing is just a few drops of water mixed with confectioners' sugar and food coloring.

Swedish mulled wine

JULGLÖGG

Glögg is traditionally served in Sweden throughout the Christmas season, but it is often first served at a St. Lucy's Day party. It is a Swedish version of mulled wine (that is, a wine warmed and flavored with spices and fruit peel). Here is a basic recipe with a few of the many variations indicated.

2 bottles full-bodied red wine, such as Burgundy or Bordeaux
1 cup sugar, or to taste
12–15 bruised cardamom seeds
8 cloves
2 sticks cinnamon
2 tablespoons grated orange rind, or 3 strips orange peel
1 pint Swedish aquavit (or vodka)
1 cup whole blanched almonds
1 cup raisins or currants

Pour the wine into a saucepan. Add the sugar, spices, and orange rind. Let steep for several hours. Heat the wine slowly without boiling until the sugar is dissolved. If desired, pour it into a heavy ceramic or silver punch bowl.

Warm the aquavit slightly in a long-handled saucepan. Light with a match, and carefully pour into the wine.

Serve hot in mugs or cups with handles, with almonds and raisins sprinkled over the top.

Yield: about 12 to 15 servings

Variations:

You can vary the flavorings by adding nutmeg or lemon rind. In Sweden they often add 4–6 figs, along with the spices. You can float slices of orange or lemon on top in the punch bowl.

You can add as much—or as little—aquavit as you like. To reduce the alcohol content of the drink, you can simmer the wine a little in the pan.

To make the presentation of the punch even more dramatic, you can do as they do in Sweden. Do *not* add sugar to the original wine mixture. When you are ready to add the aquavit, lay a metal grill over the top of the punch bowl. Set on the grill about ½ pound of sugar cubes. As you light the warmed aquavit, pour it over the sugar cubes: they will melt into the Glögg. A handsome sight!

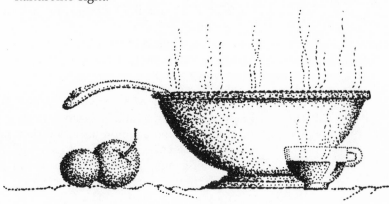

Eggnog

Eggnog is one of the drinks that we most associate with Christmas. It can be made either with or without liquor. (Without liquor, it is extremely popular with children—good for them too.)

6 eggs at room temperature, separated
½ cup sugar
2 cups heavy cream, well chilled
2 cups cold milk
1 pint any kind of whiskey or 1–2 more cups cold milk
2–4 ounces rum or vanilla extract to taste
Grated rind of 1 orange
Grated rind of 1 lemon
Freshly grated nutmeg
Optional:
  1 gallon block vanilla ice cream

In a large bowl, beat the egg whites until foamy. Gradually add the sugar and beat until the whites are very foamy and beginning to stiffen.

In another large bowl, beat the yolks until they drop from the spoon in a heavy ribbon. Beat the whites into the yolks until thoroughly blended.

In a large bowl, whip the cream until it begins to hold its shape. Beat the egg mixture gradually into the cream. Stir in milk.

Pour the mixture into the punch bowl. Gradually stir in the liquor, or the additional milk and the vanilla extract. Sprinkle the top with the grated rind and nutmeg. Chill if desired.

Optional: Before serving, set ice cream in the bowl.

Yield: approximately 20 cup servings

Rum pot

RUM TOPF

Strawberries, blueberries, raspberries, blackberries; also cherries. Sliced peaches are also nice, but do discolor; if this bothers you, avoid light-colored fruits and stick to the reddish-purplish.
Sugar: For every 2 pounds of fruit, use 1 pound of sugar.
115-proof dark rum: In Germany there is a rum made expressly for this purpose; in this country, you can mix 85 proof with 151 proof—half and half—to get the high degree of alcohol required. You will need enough rum to cover the fruit completely.

I got this fine recipe from my uncle (and godfather) and aunt, Mr. and Mrs. Walter W. Birge, Jr., who first tasted it in Hamburg. In Germany it is an Advent treat: the fruits are kept covered with rum in the cellar throughout the fall, to be brought out only at the beginning of the Advent season.

Serve with custard, whipped cream, or ice cream. Or add a little of the juice to white wine, champagne, or punch. Packed in a large jar or crock, with your own label, it makes an unusual and welcome Christmas present.

As the fruits come into season, wash them and pit them if necessary. Mix them with the sugar. Place them in a large nonmetallic container or crock. Pour the rum over them to cover. Keep the fruit weighted down with a plate so that it does not float. Keep the crock in a cool place: a basement is ideal.

Add fruit, sugar, and rum as the summer season passes and its fruits ripen.

Let the mixture sit throughout the fall, and bring it out at the beginning of Advent. You can just ladle out what you need, and leave the rest to sit in the crock, in its cool spot.

THE PARADISE TREE
December 24

There was a very old and charming European custom connected with the 24th of December. It involved the setting-up of a fir tree, which was then decorated with apples, wafers (or small breads or little cookies), and often pieces of candy. The origin of this custom is connected to the history of our Christmas tree.

In the Middle Ages, in about the eleventh century, religious theater was born. One of the most popular plays concerned Adam and Eve, their fall and expulsion from the Garden of Eden—from the Early Paradise. The play ended with the prophecy of a coming Savior, and for this reason, this particular play was often enacted during Advent.

The one piece of scenery—the Paradise Tree—became a popular object, and was often set up in churches, eventually in private homes as well. Since the tree represented not only Paradise, and man's fall, but also the promise of salvation, it was hung not merely with apples, but also with bread or wafers (representing the Eucharist), and often sweets (representing the sweetness of redemption).

This tradition can still be practiced today. You can either add these "ornaments" to an already decorated Christmas tree—just be sure to leave some room for them. Or you may want to set up a special small tree (real or made of cardboard) exclusively in honor of the Tree of Paradise and its fruits. (December 24 is also a day to celebrate if you have a little Adam or Eve: this has traditionally been the nameday for children bearing those names.)

CHRISTMAS GIFT GIVING

In the Advent section, I suggested a whole array of delicious cookies, most of which can be baked with the help of children, and all of which make fine Christmas presents.

But there are many other kinds of food that are welcome as gifts. And these gifts are especially meaningful because you made them yourself, and it is clear that you have given real thought to what to give to each person on your list. Some of the food gifts suggested below have particular meaning in the Christian tradition. So, all in all, these gifts will be not only delicious and beautiful, but meaningful as well: in a word, unforgettable.

And think of all you stand to gain from this change in Christmas strategy: you trade department store hysteria and jostling crowds for the company of help-mates in the kitchen and the wonderful aromas of Christmas baking.

TIPS ON THOUGHTFUL GIVING

To friends who are trying to lose weight give, perhaps, an herbed vinegar, or a set of homemade crèche ornaments. Or give a nonfattening kind of preserves, such as the one recommended on page 121 for diabetics. Do not give them sweets or other fattening foods. We need to let our friends know that in all life's challenges—and losing weight is certainly one—we are on their team.

To people who live alone give things that will keep well: cookies in tins, jams, mustards.

Perishables such as large breads and cakes are always welcome—and will be made short work of—in families with many children, or lots of company.

To people who do not approve of liquor, and to people who have a drinking problem, be sure to offer a gift that has been prepared without the addition of alcohol. This is an issue on which we all need to be careful to respect each other's convictions and needs! (The same thoughtfulness goes, of course, for what we serve to guests in our homes.)

You can give interesting combinations of gifts: for example, give to someone who loves to cook, or who is learning to cook, a Madeleine tin, along with the recipe for Madeleines, and a fresh batch of those exquisite cookies! Or a dozen perfect Springerles, along with a pretty new mold and the recipe. Such gifts are also very much appreciated for birthdays and wedding showers.

Here is yet another kind of combination. In a pretty basket (which is a well-liked gift in itself) or in a gift box, pack an assortment of good things to eat. Some can be store-bought, some made yourself. Possibilities are endless, but here are just a few: a handsome loaf of bread with some homemade jam or preserves, or some good sausage and mustard; a few pieces of choice fresh fruit, along with a small fruitcake or stollen; and perhaps a bottle of fresh cider or good wine. Who can resist such a Care Package!

One final sort of package. In Germany there is an old tradition of giving to loved ones, at Christmastime, baskets full of some of the necessities of life. Such baskets, called "Christ Bundles," might contain a new pair of mittens or gloves, a pair of slippers, some socks or stockings; sometimes (especially for students) new pens or pencils, perhaps some new paper. You get the idea.

German Christmas bread

CHRISTSTOLLEN

This bread has been baked at Christmastime in Germany since the Middle Ages, and was long a specialty of Dresden.

When you bake a Stollen, you fold the dough over so the folds show—you don't put the bread seams down (as you usually do with bread) on the baking sheet. You want those folds to show because they are meant to be reminiscent of the swaddling clothes of the Infant Jesus.

This slightly sweet, fruit-laden bread makes an especially meaningful present to give to a friend for Christmas. Wrapped tightly in foil, or in a plastic bag, it will keep for weeks.

½ cup mixed diced candied fruits
¼ cup golden raisins
¼ cup currants
¼ cup rum or other spirits or fruit juice
1 package active dry yeast
¼ cup warm water (100–110° F.)
⅓ cup plus 1 teaspoon sugar
⅓ cup milk
6 tablespoons (¾ stick) sweet butter
½ teaspoon salt
Grated rind of ½ lemon
Grated rind of ½ orange
½ teaspoon almond extract
2½–3 cups flour
1 egg plus 1 yolk, lightly beaten
⅓ cup chopped blanched almonds
4 tablespoons (½ stick) sweet butter, melted
2–3 tablespoons sugar
Confectioners' sugar

Place the candied fruits, raisins, and currants with the rum in a bowl. Mix well. Let stand for 1 hour, stirring occasionally. Drain thoroughly, and reserve the liquid.

Dissolve the yeast in the lukewarm water. Stir in 1 teaspoon of sugar, and set the yeast aside for 10 minutes or until foamy.

Combine in a saucepan the milk, 6 tablespoons of butter, ⅓ cup of sugar, and the salt. Heat, stirring occasionally, until the sugar is dissolved and the butter melted. Pour into a large bowl, and cool to lukewarm. Stir in the rinds and almond extract. Stir in the yeast and ¾ cup of the flour. Mix well. Cover lightly, and set in a warm spot for 30 minutes, or until the mixture is bubbly.

Stir in the eggs and the reserved rum, and work in just enough of the remaining flour (1¾ to 2¼ cups) to make a soft dough that does not stick to your hands.

Dredge the drained fruits and the chopped almonds with 1 to 2 tablespoons flour.

Turn the dough out onto a floured surface and knead until the dough is smooth and elastic—about 10 minutes. Work in the fruits and nuts a little at a time, just until they are well distributed through the dough. (Don't knead the dough any more than that once the fruits have been added, or they will discolor the dough.)

Place the dough in a large buttered bowl, and turn the dough to grease the top. Cover and let it rise for about 1 hour, or until doubled in bulk. Punch the dough down.

On a buttered baking sheet, roll the dough out into a large oval, about 12 by 16 inches. Brush the dough with 2 tablespoons of the melted butter. Sprinkle with 2 or 3 tablespoons of granulated sugar.

Fold one long side over so that it extends a little past the middle of the oval. Press down gently but firmly. Fold over the other side so that it overlaps for 2 or 3 inches. Press down gently but firmly.

Cover lightly. Let rise for 1 hour, or until almost doubled in bulk.

Bake at 400° F. for 10 minutes. Reduce the heat to 350° F. Bake for 25 to 30 minutes longer, or until the Stollen is nicely browned and sounds hollow when you tap it on the bottom. (If the bread gets brown too fast, cover it lightly with a sheet of aluminum foil.)

When you take it from the oven, brush it with the remaining melted butter. When cool, sprinkle with confectioners' sugar.

Yield: 1 large Stollen (about 12 inches long)

Variation:

You can also use the recipe to make 2 smaller Stollen. Baking time will be reduced.

Classic light fruitcake

Fruitcakes are perhaps the most traditional of all the Christmas food gifts. Here is an excellent recipe for a light fruitcake.

1 pound sweet butter, at room temperature
2 cups sugar
6 eggs
¼ cup rum, brandy, sherry, any kind of whiskey, or a mixture (see Note)
1 teaspoon vanilla
4 cups flour
2 teaspoons baking powder
2 teaspoons salt
2½ cups raisins (or half dark and half golden raisins)
2 cups currants
1½ cups mixed candied fruit peel

GLAZE:
Confectioners' sugar
Water or milk
Grated lemon rind
Whole glacé cherries and/or pecan halves

Cream the butter with the sugar until fluffy. Stir in the eggs, one at a time, blending thoroughly after each addition. Stir in the spirits and the vanilla.

Sift the flour with the baking powder and salt. Stir the flour into the butter mixture until thoroughly mixed. Add the raisins, currants, and candied fruits.

You can bake the cakes in large loaf pans or a large tube pan. You can also use small disposable foil pans, such as 6-by-3-by-2-inch ones. Butter the pans generously.

Pour the batter into the pans. Bake at 300° F. for 2 hours, or until a straw inserted into the center comes out clean. Small cakes will require shorter baking time than large ones. You may cover cakes with aluminum foil toward the end of the baking time if they are getting too brown on top.

Let the cake or cakes cool for 10 or 15 minutes, then remove them from the pans.

Make a thin glaze of confectioners' sugar mixed with a little water or milk, and a little grated lemon rind. Decorate the cakes with whole glacé cherries and/or pecans, and paint with the glaze.

Yield: 1 large tube cake, 2 large loaf cakes, or 6 small cakes

Note: You can substitute fruit juice for the spirits, but the fruitcake will not age as well, or have quite the same rich taste.

Black fruitcake

Here is a dark, spicy fruitcake, a specialty of Maryland and of much of the southern United States. Moist and rich, it is a favorite Christmas treat.

¾–1 cup dark rum or other spirits or a mixture, or fruit juice
1½ cups currants
1½ cups raisins
1½ cups golden raisins
1½ cups candied fruit peels
½ cup butter, at room temperature
1⅓ cups dark brown sugar
3 eggs
1¼ cups flour
¼ teaspoon salt
1 teaspoon baking powder
1 teaspoon cinnamon
1 teaspoon ground ginger
½ teaspoon ground allspice
½ teaspoon ground nutmeg
½ teaspoon ground cloves
¼ teaspoon ground mace
¼ cup dark molasses
Optional:
  ¼–½ cup chopped walnuts and/or ¼–½ cup grated or chopped blanched almonds

GLAZE:
About 1½ cups apricot jam
Whole glacé cherries and/or pecan halves

Pour ½ cup liquid over the fruits and let them steep overnight. Drain the fruits thoroughly, and pat them dry. Reserve the liquid, and add enough additional liquid to make ½ cup.

In a large bowl, cream the butter with the sugar until fluffy. Add the eggs one at a time, mixing thoroughly after each addition.

Dredge the fruits and fruit peels with ¼ cup of the flour. Sift the remaining flour with the salt, baking powder and spices. Stir the molasses, rum, and flour mixture alternately into the batter, mixing thoroughly. Stir in the fruits, and nuts if desired.

You can bake the cakes in loaf pans or tube pans: butter the pans, and line them with buttered brown paper. You can also use small disposable aluminum pans; butter them well.

Pour the batter into the pans. Press the batter down well with a spoon or your hand. Bake at 275° F. for about 4 hours, or until a straw inserted into the center of a cake comes out clean. Smaller cakes will take less time than larger ones.

Cool in the pans for 20 minutes. Turn the cakes out onto a rack. Remove the paper. Glaze when cool.

Glaze: Place the apricot jam in a saucepan along with 4 tablespoons of water. Boil down to half. Pour the jam through a sieve, forcing a few of the softest pieces through as well. Give the cakes one coat of glaze. Set the fruits and/or nuts in place and give the cakes another coat of glaze.

Yield: 1 large tube cake, 2 nine-inch loaf pans, or several smaller cakes; about 4½ pounds

Variation:

You can pour more spirits over the cakes before glazing: wrap them in cheesecloth and then in aluminum foil, and let them age for several weeks. Then glaze them and decorate.

Old-fashioned mincemeat

Mincemeat—or minced meat—is another one of those Christmas dishes that go back for hundreds of years, to well into the medieval period. A jar of homemade mincemeat is a real treat. (It's good served over ice cream or topped with whipped cream.) Or you can give it already baked up in a pie (see page 153). Mincemeat, if spirits are used, is best made ahead and aged for several weeks, or even longer.

1½ pounds lean beef brisket
 or rump
1 teaspoon salt
½ pound beef suet, very
 finely chopped or ground
1 cup dark raisins
1 cup golden raisins
1 cup currants
4 cups peeled, chopped
 apples
1 to 2 cups sour cherries
 with their juice (optional)
⅓ cup diced citron
⅓ cup diced orange peel
⅓ cup diced lemon peel
Juice and grated rind of 1
 lemon
2 cups brown sugar
½ cup molasses
2 cups cider or apple juice
1 teaspoon cinnamon
1 teaspoon ground nutmeg
½ teaspoon ground cloves
½ teaspoon coriander
½ teaspoon mace
½ to 1 cup chopped walnuts
 or almonds (optional)
½ cups brandy, or other
 spirits, or a little fruit
 juice

Place the meat in a saucepan and cover with water. Add the salt. Bring to a boil, reduce heat, and simmer for about 1 hour, or until the meat can be easily shredded. Drain and shred.

In a saucepan, combine the shredded beef and the suet. Stir in the raisins, currants, apples, (optional) cherries, citron, diced orange and lemon peel, lemon juice and grated rind, sugar, molasses, and cider. Simmer for 30 minutes, stirring frequently. Add the spices and continue simmering until the mixture is nicely thickened. Stir in the nuts, if you wish.

Turn the mixture into a large bowl or crock and pour the spirits over. If you are using spirits, the mixture can sit, covered, in the refrigerator for weeks—even months. (Some say years!) It is best when somewhat aged. Stir occasionally, and add more liquor as the spirits are absorbed.

If you choose not to cover the mixture with spirits, moisten lightly with fruit juice. The mincemeat can be used right away, or preserved in hot sterilized jars, and sealed with paraffin.

Yield: about 4 quarts

Variations:

There are many different versions of this dish. You can vary the dried and candied fruits in almost any way you choose. For example, you can add dried dates or figs, candied cherries, or pineapple instead of or along with those mentioned above. You can use beef tongue along with or instead of part of the lean beef.

Blueberry jam

If I leave this jam around unprotected for long, my children steal "finger sandwiches" of it (and I don't mean the kind they serve at fancy cocktail parties).

1 pound fresh blueberries,
 or frozen blueberries
 (without sugar), defrosted
1½ cups sugar
2 tablespoons lemon juice
1 teaspoon grated lemon
 rind
Optional:
 1 tablespoon or so crème
 de cassis

Place the blueberries in a saucepan, crushing them lightly. Simmer until soft, stirring occasionally. Stir in the sugar and lemon juice and simmer until the mixture is thickened, about 20 to 30 minutes. Remember that the jam will thicken a little more as it cools. Stir in the lemon rind and the optional crème de cassis.

Pour into hot sterilized jars and seal with paraffin or refrigerate.

Yield: 1½ to 2 pints

Strawberry preserves

One word: wonderful!

1 quart strawberries, or 1
   pound frozen strawberries
2 cups sugar
1 cup water
1–2 teaspoons lemon juice

Wash and hull the strawberries. Or defrost frozen berries. Cut any very large berries in two.

In a saucepan, boil the sugar and water together to about 230° F., or the soft-ball stage, on a jelly (deep-fat-frying) thermometer.

Add the strawberries and simmer very gently for about 5 minutes, or until they are soft and almost translucent. Remove the berries and set them aside, reserving any juices.

Boil the syrup hard until well reduced and thickened to the point you like. Remember that it will thicken a little more as it cools. Return the berries and their juices to the pan. Stir in the lemon juice. Pour into hot sterilized jars and seal with paraffin or refrigerate.

Yield: 1½ to 2 pints

Apricot jam

Here is a delicious jam with an unusual flavor.

1 pound dried apricots,
   chopped
Sugar
Honey
1 tablespoon lemon juice
¼ teaspoon almond extract
Optional:
   ½ teaspoon grated lemon
   rind

Place the chopped apricots in a saucepan. Cover with water. Simmer until the apricots are soft and tender, about ½ hour. Add water if necessary to keep the apricots just covered.

With a slotted spoon, remove the fruit pulp from the pan and measure it. Return it to the pan. For every 1 cup of fruit, add ⅓ cup of sugar and ⅓ cup of honey. Add the lemon juice. Simmer until thickened, stirring occasionally, about ½ hour. Remember that the mixture will thicken a little more as it cools.

Stir in the almond extract, and lemon rind, if you like.

Pour into hot sterilized jars. Seal with paraffin, or refrigerate.

Yield: about 3 pints

Grape ketchup

This is an unusual condiment—particularly good with baked ham and with pork in general, and with many cold meats. It is a real favorite at my house. Try putting it in empty (sterilized) tomato ketchup bottles, and make your own label. While you are at it, why not put on your label one of the many Biblical references to the fruit of the vine? Here is a particularly beautiful one, from the Song of Songs: "The fig tree forms its early fruit and blossoming vines spread their fragrance" (2:13, NIV).

5 pounds grapes (red and
purple have the most
flavor)
Sugar
½ cup white vinegar, or
cider vinegar
1½ teaspoons ground ginger
1½ teaspoons ground cloves
1½ teaspoons cinnamon
1½ teaspoons ground
nutmeg
½ teaspoon salt
1 teaspoon pepper

Wash the grapes. Place them in a saucepan and crush well. Add 2 cups of water. Simmer the grapes until they are thoroughly soft: 10 to 15 minutes.

Force the grapes through a coarse sieve to remove the seeds and skins. Measure the pulp. Return it to the saucepan.

For every cup of grape pulp add ¾ cup of sugar. Add the vinegar. Boil the mixture for 20 minutes, then add the spices, and boil until the mixture is nicely thickened but still easily pourable. The ketchup will thicken a little more as it cools, so remove it from the heat while it is still slightly runny.

Yield: about 3 pints

Flavored vinegars and oils

These vinegars and oils are particularly easy to prepare, and they make handsome and delicious presents, with many uses: they are good not only in salad dressings, but also to give added flavor to mayonnaise, and to brush over fish or meat before or during broiling or grilling. Many stores sell pretty bottles (buy ones with corks or clamp-type tops), or you can save nicely shaped wine bottles, sterilize, and re-use them.

You should, of course, make labels for your homemade products. Here is a model that you might try adapting. (A Biblical concordance, which you can consult in any library or purchase for home use, will give you all the references in the Bible to any word you are interested in, with a line of context.)

Mint Vinegar
from the kitchen of
_____

Date
*Mint was a popular herb in
Biblical times, and was used
as well for the payment of tithes
(Matthew 23:23)*

Sprigs of fresh dill, basil,
tarragon, rosemary, sage,
thyme, or mint
White vinegar (wine or
distilled or cider vinegar)
or red wine vinegar
Optional:
A piece of lemon rind,
along with the tarragon,
rosemary, basil, or thyme
A clove or 2 with the
tarragon or rosemary
A little sugar with the
mint
A few celery seeds with
the sage
A few peppercorns with
rosemary or thyme in red
wine vinegar

HERBED VINEGARS

Cut sprigs of the fresh herb to fit the height of the bottle. Insert the herb into the bottle, using a wooden spoon if necessary.

Warm but do not boil the vinegar. Fill the bottle with vinegar. Distilled white vinegar is best with mint and sage. Try red wine vinegar with rosemary or thyme. Add optional ingredients. Cap tightly or insert a cork.

Let the bottle stand for about 10 days in a sunny spot, but not in direct sunlight, to blend the flavors.

SPICED VINEGAR

Here is an old Shaker specialty.

1 quart cider vinegar
4 tablespoons crushed black
  peppercorns
2 tablespoons ground ginger
2 tablespoons ground
  allspice
4 teaspoons salt
4 teaspoons sugar

Mix all ingredients and simmer briefly. Strain and bottle. Cap or cork.

LEMON OR LIME VINEGAR

2 or 3 unblemished lemons
  or limes
1 quart distilled or white-
  wine vinegar
Optional:
  1 bamboo skewer or thin,
    pointed wooden skewer

Cut the lemons or limes into quarters. If you wish, line them up on a skewer. Lay or insert them into a wide-mouthed bottle or jar. Cover with vinegar. Cap or cork.

Let sit for 10 days in a dark place to blend the flavors.

RASPBERRY VINEGAR

This gourmet treat is expensive to buy in the specialty shops but easy and fun to make at home. It adds a special taste to salad dressings and marinades, and has long been enjoyed as a drink, with club soda (or seltzer water) over ice:

1 quart raspberries, or
  frozen raspberries
  (without sugar) defrosted
1 quart white vinegar,
  white-wine, cider, or
  distilled
1¾ to 2 cups sugar

Put the raspberries into the vinegar in a large crock or pitcher, mashing them lightly. Let them stand overnight (or longer: up to a week), stirring occasionally.

Pour the mixture into a saucepan and add the sugar. Bring to a boil and simmer gently for 20 minutes. Strain and bottle.

Yield: 1½ quarts

Variations:

The same procedure can be followed for blackberries, strawberries, or peaches.

GARLIC OIL

Here is a garlic-flavored olive oil to add to salads.

10–15 cloves garlic, peeled
1 quart olive oil

Thread the garlic cloves onto a bamboo or other thin wooden skewer and insert it in the bottle. Fill the bottle with olive oil. Cap or cork.

Variation:

You can follow exactly the same procedure to make garlic-flavored vinegar. Use red-wine or white-wine or distilled vinegar.

Flavored mustards

There are many delicious ways of giving additional flavor to ready-made mustards, such as French Dijon mustard. Such mustards, presented in handsome jars with your label, make highly appreciated Christmas gifts. Here are two basic ideas.

½–⅔ cup finely chopped parsley, dill, tarragon, or chives—or a mixture
1 cup Dijon mustard

HERBED MUSTARD
Combine and blend until smooth. Store in the refrigerator.

1 cup Dijon mustard
4 teaspoons lemon or lime juice
Finely grated rind of 1 or 2 lemons or limes, to taste
Optional:
  ½ teaspoon sugar

LEMON OR LIME MUSTARD
Combine the ingredients thoroughly. Store in the refrigerator.

> When they had finished eating, Jesus said to Simon Peter, "Simon, son of John, do you truly love me more than these?"
> "Yes, Lord," he said, "you know that I love you."
> Jesus said, "Feed my lambs."
>
> John 21:15 (NIV)

Peach or strawberry spread for diabetics and dieters

While we're thinking of special treats for our loved ones at Christmas, let's give a thought to our diabetic friends and relatives, as well as to those who are on strict reducing diets. They must get awfully tired of the limited assortment of jams and preserves that are commercially available. So here are two delicious fruit spreads for them.

1½ teaspoons gelatin
¾ cup cold water
2 cups fresh chopped peaches or strawberries (or frozen fruit with no sugar)
2 teaspoons lemon juice
Grated rind of ½ lemon
Artificial sweetener to taste
⅛ teaspoon orange extract

Soak the gelatin in ¼ cup cold water.

Place the fruit in a saucepan with the lemon juice and rind. Add ½ cup water. Bring to a boil, reduce heat, and simmer for 8 to 10 minutes or until the fruit is soft. Stir frequently. Remove from the heat. Stir in the gelatin, artificial sweetener, and orange extract. Mix thoroughly.

Turn the fruit spread into small jars. (If you plan to keep the spread in the freezer, use freezer-proof containers.) Cover when cool. These spreads must be kept in the refrigerator or freezer.

Yield: about 1½ cups

Cheese balls

2 eight-ounce packages
  cream cheese, softened
4 ounces (about 1 cup) blue
  cheese, crumbled
1 tablespoon caraway seeds
4 tablespoons chives or
  green onions, chopped
1 tablespoon Worcestershire
  sauce, or brandy
1½ cups minced parsley
Chopped nuts, or finely
  minced parsley, or whole
  unblanched almonds

A cheese ball makes a handsome present. You can give it with a package of your favorite kind of crackers.

Blend all ingredients except the chopped nuts until completely mixed. Chill until the cheese mixture is easy to handle. Form it into a ball or a log. Or you can make several small balls or logs. Roll in chopped nuts. Or roll in minced parsley, or form into a pine-cone shape and stud with the almonds.)

Wrap well and refrigerate. Cheese balls will keep for 2 weeks in the refrigerator.

Chickadee pudding

One last item on our list! This Christmas pudding is for the chickadees and other seed-eating birds. Why a Christmas treat for the birds?

A beautiful legend has it that, on Christmas Eve night, the animals and birds can talk. Moreover, the swallows and chickadees can sing like nightingales.

Animals were honored by being the first witnesses, after Mary and Joseph, to the birth of Christ. Even before the shepherds appeared, and long before the Magi, the beasts came and beheld the Messiah. Legend relates that—on that dark but starry night so long ago—the rooster announced: "Christus natus est!" (Christ is born!—the animals all sound more like themselves in Latin!) The cow asked, "Ubi?" (Where?) The sheep answered "Bethlehem." "Eamus!" (Let's go!) said the donkey.

Because of these legends it has long been traditional, in many parts of the world, to provide extra food on this holy night for animals—in the barnyard, in the house, even in the fields nearby.

Ground suet
Flour
Sugar
Cornmeal
Old cake, bread, doughnuts
Wild bird seed
Peanut butter
Ground apples
Kitchen seeds: apples,
  squash, etc.
Nuts
Raisins
Bacon fat

So here is a delectable treat for the birds. (This recipe is taken from Forum Feasts *by Friends of the Forum School.) You might also think of special treats for your cat or dog or other favorite animal. Such treats for birds and beasts make nice presents to friends who have a special fondness for this part of God's creation.*

Mix all the ingredients, except the bacon fat, in whatever proportions you happen to have on hand. (Wouldn't it be restful if *all* recipes read like that?) Melt plenty of fat and, while it is hot, pour it over the mixture, stirring well. Pour the mixture into disposable aluminum pie plates. Freeze. Wrap up with a pretty ribbon.

CHRISTMAS EVE

No moment of the year has more beautiful or moving food customs than Christmas Eve. The "Eve" or "Vigil" of Christmas has for many centuries been the focus for a family meal of the very deepest solemnity but also of great joy.

This solemnity, this joy certainly have nothing to do with Santa Claus: he is a relative newcomer to the scene, and in many ways clearly a pagan interloper, with his roots deep in Nordic mythology. Rather, these emotions are deeply religious. Since Christmas Eve is still part of Advent—the very last moment of Advent—it involves, on the one hand, a final searching of the conscience and, in much of the Christian world, a final fasting and abstinence from meat before the feasting of Christmas and the Christmas season. On the other hand, Christmas Eve is already a celebration of the birth of Christ. So there is, on Christmas Eve, a sense of expectancy—a hush, as it were—and already a joy.

Thus, while the day of Christmas Eve was traditionally a day of abstinence from meat, the evening meal that was served was a feast as well—a feast within a fast, a jubilant abstinence, a joyful fast. In the countries of Eastern Europe, a great beautiful fish might be set out, preceded by several delicious, but meatless, soups. Along with the fish, in exquisite but often dairy-free sauces, came the handsomest of the vegetables, served in their most splendid form.

In many places the very number of courses was traditional, or even the number of elements included in a dish (see, for example, the Polish Twelve-Fruit Compote, page 139). But this ritual quality of the meal extended much further than that. It was, in many families throughout Christendom, one of the two or three most important meals of the year—one of those meals at which the family reaffirmed its bonds of love and solidarity—and every detail of the meal was full of meaning.

It is traditionally an evening meal, often preceded by a day of partial or total fasting, and at its close many a family through the centuries has attended a midnight liturgy together. In Russia, the meal began when the first star—symbolizing the star of Bethlehem—could be seen in the sky. In many places, it could not begin until all Christmas preparations had been completed, the house cleaned, in some places tools put away, and anything borrowed, returned. In Slavic countries, the floor and sometimes even the table are traditionally strewn with hay and straw in honor of the stable. A white tablecloth is placed over the straw on the table.

Special breads such as Stollen are shared in many German and

Austrian families. In Lithuania (and other Slavic countries) at the beginning of this meal, called the Vigilia, the father breaks thin wafers bearing religious motifs—the "bread of angels"—and distributes a piece to each member of the family, kissing each and wishing him or her a blessed Christmas. All these gestures symbolize the love and unity of the family in Christ.

An extra place is always set at the table in honor of those who are absent, and in case a lonely and weary traveler (perhaps Christ himself) might knock at the door seeking refreshment. Servants are included in the meal: all members of the household sit down together on this night. In many places, it is understood that no one should leave the table until the meal is over: another symbol of unity.

OYSTER STEW AND SCALLOPED OYSTERS

We will be looking, in the next few pages, at some Christmas Eve traditions drawn from several different cultures: Mexico, southern France, Italy, and Eastern Europe. But let's start with a couple of traditional dishes that in America are often served on Christmas Eve by families from different Christian denominations.

Each of these dishes is delicious served with French or Italian bread and a tossed salad. Why not try for dessert one of the marvelous dishes that follow: Buñuelos (Mexican Fried Cakes), perhaps, or Pompe à l'Huile (Provençal Christmas Eve Bread)?

Oyster stew

This is my mother's excellent recipe.

6 tablespoons butter
1½ pints oysters, drained
    (liquor reserved)
3 cups half-and-half
Salt
White pepper or paprika

Warm 4 bowls in the oven.

Melt 2 tablespoons of the butter in a double boiler. The water below should boil, but should not touch the bottom of the top pan. Add the oysters and cook them briefly—just until their edges start to curl.

Add the half-and-half and oyster liquor to the pan. Add salt to taste. Stirring constantly, bring the liquid *just* to the boiling point, but *do not boil.*

Place a tablespoon of butter in each bowl, and sprinkle in a little pepper or paprika. Divide the stew among the 4 bowls.

Yield: 4 servings

Scalloped oysters

1 stick butter
1¾ cups cracker crumbs
   (saltines, soda or oyster
   crackers, crushed)
1½ to 2 pints oysters
Salt
Freshly ground pepper
¼ to ½ teaspoon freshly
   grated nutmeg
4 tablespoons oyster liquor
1 cup cream or milk

Preheat oven to 425° F.

Butter a casserole or baking dish with 1 tablespoon of the butter. (Use an 8- or 9-inch square casserole, or any heatproof dish deep enough to hold three layers.) Place about a third of the cracker crumbs in the dish.

Lay half of the oysters on top of the crumbs. Sprinkle them with a little salt, pepper, and nutmeg. Pour on 2 tablespoons of oyster liquor and 2 to 3 tablespoons of cream. Dot with 2 tablespoons of butter.

Add another layer of crumbs—again about a third of the mixture. Add the other half of the oysters, more salt, pepper, and nutmeg, 2 tablespoons oyster liquor and 2 to 3 tablespoons of cream. Dot with 2 tablespoons of butter.

Cover with the remaining crumbs. Sprinkle with the rest of the cream, more salt, pepper, and nutmeg, and dot with the remaining butter.

Bake for 30 minutes.

Yield: 4 to 6 servings

MEXICAN CHRISTMAS EVE DINNER

Salad of the good night

ENSALADA DE NOCHEBUENA

2 beets, cooked and sliced
2 apples, cored and sliced
2 oranges, peeled and
   sectioned or sliced
2 bananas, sliced
Optional (Any or all of the
   following):
   1 jícama, sliced
   2 limes, sliced
   1 cup pineapple cubes
   2 carrots, sliced
   ½ cup radishes, sliced
1 tablespoon sugar
½ cup peanuts
Seeds from 1 pomegranate

This lovely fruit and vegetable salad is the traditional centerpiece of the Mexican Christmas Eve dinner; it is eaten only once a year. This is an abstinence dish, but it also certainly suggests the joyfulness of the meal.

Try serving this salad with Stuffed Red Snapper. Have Seviche as your first course, and Buñuelos for dessert.

Arrange the fruits and vegetables attractively on a platter or in a large glass bowl, sprinkling the sugar on them as you go. Sprinkle the peanuts and the pomegranate seeds on top.

Yield: 6 to 10 servings, depending on the "optionals"

Variation:

You can, if you like, make a mayonnaise dressing to spoon over the top of the salad. (Try flavoring it with a little Raspberry Vinegar, page 120.)

Marinated fish or shellfish

SEVICHE

1 pound mackerel (skinned
 fillets), pompano, porgy,
 or fillets of striped bass,
 or scallops
About 1½ cups lime or
 lemon juice
2 medium tomatoes,
 chopped
1 medium onion, sliced thin
1 fresh hot pepper, seeded
 and sliced thin, or canned
 serrano chilies, rinsed,
 chopped
Salt
Freshly ground pepper
Oregano
3 to 4 tablespoons vegetable
 oil
Optional:
 1 avocado, peeled, pitted,
 sliced
 1 lime, sliced thin

This specialty in many Latin American countries consists of raw fish "cooked" by being marinated for several hours in lemon or lime juice and spices. Seviche is a delicate and interesting dish.

Cut the fish into ½- to 1-inch squares, and put it into a glass or china bowl. Pour over it the lime or lemon juice to cover generously. Refrigerate for 3 hours, or until the fish is opaque. Turn the pieces occasionally.

Add the tomatoes, onions, hot pepper, salt, pepper, oregano, and vegetable oil to taste. Mix well.

Serve with slices of avocado and lime, if you wish.

Yield: 6 servings

Variation:

With the fish (not the shellfish), try adding, along with the hot peppers, 1 clove garlic, chopped.

Baked stuffed red snapper

1 red snapper, about 4
 pounds
Salt
Freshly ground pepper
½ pound fresh spinach or
 frozen spinach, defrosted
2–3 tablespoons sour cream
 or heavy cream
¼ cup finely chopped onion
¼ cup finely chopped
 walnuts or pine nuts
½ teaspoon freshly grated
 nutmeg
Lemon juice
Butter
White wine (optional)
Lemon wedges

The main dish at this dinner might well be a baked stuffed fish, such as a red snapper. There is, to my mind, hardly a more handsome sight to behold than a whole red snapper (complete with head and tail), stuffed, on a platter.

The stuffing can be bread crumbs (flavored with onion, garlic, parsley, salt, and pepper) or a mixture of cooked shrimp and crabmeat (with a little onion, lemon juice, and parsley). But here is my favorite stuffing for red snapper. It isn't authentically Mexican, but it is authentically good.

Rinse the fish and salt it inside and out. Sprinkle with pepper. Lay the fish in a large buttered baking dish.

Boil the spinach in a little salted water until it has just lost its raw taste—2 or 3 minutes. Drain thoroughly: put the spinach in a sieve and force the water out with the back of a spoon.

Put the spinach in a bowl. Stir in sour cream, onion, nuts, nutmeg, salt, pepper, and lemon juice to taste.

Stuff the fish with the mixture—don't pack it in too tight. Put any remaining stuffing in a small ramekin or casserole. Butter the top. Cover with aluminum foil. Close the fish with skewers or toothpicks. Butter the top.

Bake at 400° F. for about 45 minutes, or until the fish flakes easily. Baste occasionally with butter and white wine if you wish. Do not overcook! Bake the remaining stuffing for the last 20 minutes or so.

Serve with lemon wedges.

Yield: 4 servings

Mexican fried cakes

BUÑUELOS

These delicious crunchy fried cakes are very similar to those served on this night in many other countries. In Mexico, they are also served frequently on December 17, the feast of Oaxaca's patron, the Virgin of Solitude (what a beautiful title!).

4 cups flour
2 tablespoons sugar
1 teaspoon baking powder
1 teaspoon salt
2 eggs
¾ cup milk
1–2 tablespoons crushed anise seeds, or grated rind of 1 lemon or ½ orange (optional)
¼ cup melted butter
Vegetable oil for deep-fat frying
Confectioners' sugar and cinnamon; or granulated sugar, and cinnamon or anise seeds

Sift the flour with the sugar, baking powder, and salt. Beat together the eggs and milk, and stir them into the dry ingredients. Add the anise seeds, if desired. Stir in the melted butter.

Turn the dough out onto a floured surface and knead for 5 to 10 minutes, or until very smooth. Add more milk or more flour if necessary.

Divide the dough into about 20 pieces. Shape them into balls. Cover them with a cloth and let stand for 15 to 20 minutes.

On a lightly floured surface roll each ball out very thin into a large circle about the size of a tortilla.

Heat the oil to 370° F. Fry the Buñuelos one or two at a time in the hot oil, turning once or twice, until puffed and golden brown. Drain thoroughly on paper towels.

Serve hot, sprinkled with cinnamon and confectioners' sugar. Or pour over a spicy sugar syrup: boil ½ cup of sugar with ½ cup of water and a little cinnamon or a few anise seeds until the syrup is thick.

Yield: 1½ to 2 dozen Buñuelos

THE "BIG SUPPER" (GROS SOUPER) OF PROVENCE

In Provence, in the south of France, the Christmas Eve meal is called a "supper": that is, it is a simple repast, not very elegant (by French standards!). But it is full of charm and meaning. (A more elaborate meal—the *réveillon* dinner—is held after midnight mass.) No meat is served—again, in Catholic France this is an abstinence meal—and the central focus of the meal is a large, shared bowl of *aïoli,* the wonderful garlic mayonnaise that is a specialty of the region. The *aïoli* is served with snails or with fish, and with all kinds of vegetables.

For dessert, there are traditionally thirteen different sweets. (We tend to think of thirteen as an unlucky number; they do in France as well—generally. But on this night thirteen is *not* unlucky. There is an ancient legend that at Christmastime the forces of evil are powerless, because of Christ's power—even as an infant.) These thirteen desserts are not especially fancy: there are dried or glacé fruits, nuts, and some fresh fruits: apples, pears, perhaps a beautiful orange or tangerine. Perhaps there are some chocolates, maybe a few nougats, often a big tart. And at the very center of the platter is a large flat sweetbread often called *Pompe à l'Huile,* though it has many other names as well.

Garlic mayonnaise

AÏOLI

Serve this with any boiled or fried fish fillets, and with an assortment of vegetables, such as raw or boiled carrots, raw celery or fennel stalks, steamed artichokes, boiled new potatoes or fried potatoes, deep-fried zucchini strips, hard-cooked eggs.

4 garlic cloves, peeled
2 egg yolks
1½ cups or more olive oil or peanut oil
Lemon juice
Salt
Freshly ground pepper

Put the garlic cloves through a garlic press into a bowl. Beat in the egg yolks with a hand mixer or use the blender. Very gradually add the oil, beating well between additions, until the sauce has the consistency of mayonnaise.

Season to taste with lemon juice and salt and pepper.

Note: To make ordinary mayonnaise, just eliminate the garlic.

Provençal Christmas Eve bread

POMPE À L'HUILE

Incidentally, the French word pompe *here means "pomp"—as in "Pomp and Circumstance." This ceremonial bread, made with olive oil, has an unusual and delicious flavor.*

3 packages active dry yeast
½ cup lukewarm water (100–110° F.)
4¼ cups flour

In a bowl, sprinkle the yeast into the warm water. Stir in ½ cup flour. Cover lightly and let this mixture double in bulk and become spongy.

Grated rind of 1 lemon
Grated rind of 1 orange
1 teaspoon salt
⅔ cup brown sugar
1 cup olive oil
2 eggs
Optional:
  2 tablespoons orange-
  flower water (see Note)

In a large bowl, mix the remaining flour, the lemon and orange rinds, salt, and brown sugar. Stir in the olive oil and the eggs, mixing well after each addition. Add the yeast-flour mixture. Mix thoroughly; the dough should be rather soft. Knead for 8 to 10 minutes.

Place the dough in a greased bowl, turning the dough to grease the top. Cover the bowl and let the dough rise for 3 hours.

Punch down the dough and knead it briefly. Return it to the bowl, cover it, and let it rise again for 3 hours.

Make balls of dough about 3 inches in diameter. On a lightly greased baking sheet, lay the balls side by side, touching each other, in a circle. Let them rise once more for 30 minutes.

Bake at 350° F. for about 30 minutes, or until golden brown.

Optional: Brush, while still hot, with orange-flower water or diluted orange liqueur.

Yield: 1 circular bread

Note: I find the aroma of American orange-flower water unpleasantly "perfumey," and prefer using 1 teaspoon orange liqueur diluted in 1 tablespoon water.

ITALIAN CHRISTMAS EVE DINNERS

There are almost as many Italian Christmas Eve traditions as there are towns and villages in Italy. Here are just a few of the many interesting and delicious specialties. Throughout much of Italy, this traditional meal includes twelve courses, in honor of the Twelve Apostles. For an appropriate dessert, see the Cassata on page 27.

Pasta with anchovy sauce

You can use any kind of pasta you like. I am very partial to linguini and cappellini for this dish. Incidentally, there are some pasta shapes that would be appropriate here: little cross shapes called Maltese Crosses (Croci di Malta), little tubular ones called Hail Mary (Ave Maria)—they look like rosary beads—and others called Our Father (Paternoster) for reasons that aren't clear to me.

½ cup butter
¼ cup olive oil
4–6 cloves garlic, peeled
  and sliced paper thin
1 can anchovy fillets
Salt
Freshly ground pepper
Chopped parsley
Optional:
  1 teaspoon capers
  Crushed red pepper

Melt the butter in a frying pan or saucepan. Stir in the olive oil, garlic, anchovies and the oil they were packed in. Add salt and pepper to taste. Cook gently until the anchovies have dissolved.

Serve over hot, drained pasta with chopped parsley, and capers and crushed red pepper, if you wish.

Yield: ¾ to 1 cup sauce

Mixed fried fish, vegetables, and fruits

FRITTO MISTO, DI PESCE, DI LEGUMI, DI FRUTTI

One of the great specialties of many areas of Italy is the "mixed fry." The gran' fritto misto *typically includes all manner of deep-fried foods, including meat. On Christmas Eve, there will be no meat, but rather different kinds of fish, perhaps some vegetables as well—and maybe even some fresh fruit. This is a wonderful dish!*

You can use a combination of any of the following:

Seafood: Smelts, codfish, fresh tuna, whitefish, salmon, fillet of sole, halibut, small fish balls, baby eel, oysters, shrimp, scallops. Fish should be cleaned and cut into bite-sized pieces.

Vegetables: Zucchini, mushrooms, eggplant (sprinkle slices with salt and let sit for 20 minutes; wipe dry); partly cooked cauliflower or broccoli florets; artichoke hearts. Cut the raw or partly cooked vegetables into bite-sized pieces.

Fruits: Apple slices, pear slices, strawberries, cherries.

BATTER
1½ cups flour
½ teaspoon salt
3 tablespoons olive oil
2 eggs, separated
¼ cup dry white wine or water; if frying only fruit, you can use 2 to 4 tablespoons brandy
1 cup cold water
Vegetable oil for deep-fat frying
Optional:
A little freshly grated nutmeg. If frying only fish and vegetables, add up to 1 teaspoon each of crumbled basil and rosemary leaves to the batter; if only fruits, add 1 tablespoon sugar.

Mix the flour with the salt. Stir in the olive oil and the egg yolks, mixing well, then the wine and water. Let the mixture stand for 1–2 hours.

Just before you are going to prepare the Fritto Misto, beat the egg whites until stiff but not dry. Fold them gently into the batter. They do not need to be thoroughly incorporated.

Heat the oil to about 370° F. on a deep-frying thermometer.

Coat the foods completely with the batter and fry them a few at a time, turning once or twice, until they are golden on all sides. Do the fruits first, then the vegetables, then the seafood. Drain thoroughly on paper towels. Remove the cooked pieces to a hot dish while you cook the rest.

Arrange everything attractively on a large platter.

Serve hot with Salsa Verde (for fish and vegetables), or mayonnaise, or lemon quarters. Sprinkle the fruit with granulated sugar.

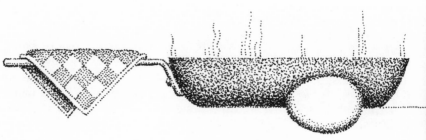

Salsa verde

1 one-inch slice Italian
  bread
Wine vinegar
2 anchovy fillets, drained
1 hard-boiled egg yolk
1 clove garlic, finely minced
1 bunch Italian parsley,
  stems removed, very
  finely chopped
1 tablespoon capers
About 1 cup olive oil
Salt
Freshly ground pepper

Soak bread slice in wine vinegar to cover for 15–20 minutes.

Chop the anchovies fine. Place them in a bowl and mash in the egg yolk. Mix in the garlic, parsley, and capers.

Squeeze the bread dry and add it to the mixture, pounding it to a paste. Very gradually add the olive oil—enough to make a fairly creamy texture. Beat well between additions. Season with salt and pepper to taste.

Yield: about 1¼ cups

O God, Who hast made this most sacred night to shine with the illumination of the true Light; grant, we beseech Thee, that as we have known the mystery of that Light upon earth, we may also perfectly enjoy It in heaven.

Collect for Midnight Mass

Christmas Eve eel

CAPITONE

Eel is a favorite in many parts of Italy on Christmas Eve. Here is a classic recipe.

6 eels
½ cup olive oil
1 medium onion, chopped
1 teaspoon chopped shallots
Salt
Freshly ground pepper
½ teaspoon chervil
½ teaspoon tarragon
1 cup tomato sauce
1 cup white wine
Chopped parsley

Skin the eels. (The best way is to get your fish merchant to do it. Barring that: put a noose around the eel's head and attach it to a nail high on the wall. Cut the skin around the neck, and gently but firmly—you may need pliers—pull the skin down and off.) Remove the intestines. Wash, and cut into 3-inch pieces.

Heat the olive oil in a frying pan. Sauté the eel with the onion and shallots. Season with salt and pepper to taste, and stir in the chervil and tarragon, tomato sauce and wine. Cover and simmer gently for 25 to 30 minutes, or until the eel is tender. Sprinkle with parsley.

Yield: 6 servings

Variation:

You can sauté ¼ pound chopped mushrooms along with the eel.

Pasta with gorgonzola sauce

PASTA AL GORGONZOLA

*1 pound spaghetti or green
 tagliatelle*
¼ cup (½ stick) sweet butter
*¼ pound Gorgonzola cheese,
 crumbled, approximately
 ¾ cup*
¼ cup heavy cream
*¼ pound ricotta cheese,
 approximately ½ cup*
*¼ cup chopped fresh
 parsley*
Juice of ½ to 1 lemon
Pinch of nutmeg
*Salt and freshly ground
 black pepper*
*½ cup freshly grated
 Parmesan cheese*

Cook the pasta in a large pot of boiling salted water until just tender.

Meanwhile, melt the butter in a large skillet. When it begins to foam, add the Gorgonzola and stir until melted. Add the cream and cook over medium heat, stirring constantly, for 3 or 4 minutes, until the sauce begins to thicken. Stir in the ricotta cheese, fresh parsley, and lemon juice. Add nutmeg, salt and pepper to taste.

Serve over pasta. Sprinkle with Parmesan cheese.

Yield: 4 servings

Variations:

You can add to the sauce ½ cup chopped onion and ½ cup chopped celery. Either sauté them in the butter or add raw at the end.

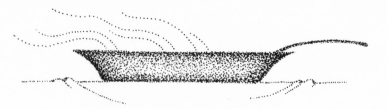

Orange salad

INSALATA DI ARANCE

A specialty of the Abruzzi, in the south of Italy. This unusual salad is served on Christmas Eve.

Oranges, peeled, sliced thin
Freshly ground black pepper
Olive oil

Arrange the orange slices on a handsome platter. Grind the pepper over them, and sprinkle them generously with olive oil.

Let the oranges marinate for ½ hour or more before serving.

Variation:
Serve with oil-cured (Greek) olives.

CHRISTMAS EVE IN EASTERN EUROPE

On Christmas Eve in many parts of Poland, the number of courses was set at fourteen: one for Christ himself, one for his Mother, and one for each of the Apostles. (In other areas of Poland and in other Slavic countries, the number of courses was always uneven: five, seven, nine, eleven; there is an ancient tradition, antedating Christianity, that uneven numbers are lucky.)

The first two courses were almost invariably a herring dish, followed by a soup. It might be a fish soup, but often it was a Borscht, perhaps with Mushroom Pockets.

Christmas Eve borscht with Polish mushroom pockets

"Vigil" (meatless) borscht is the classic Christmas Eve soup.

2 onions, chopped
2 celery stalks with leaves, chopped
2 carrots, chopped
8 medium beets, left whole, plus (optional) 1 extra
Optional:
  ¼ head Savoy cabbage, chopped, and/or ½ cup chopped parsley root
  1 turnip and/or 1 medium potato, peeled, chopped
  2 leeks, cleaned and chopped
  Dried or fresh mushrooms
2 quarts water
1 small bunch parsley, or parsley and dill, chopped
1 teaspoon salt
1 bay leaf
6 peppercorns
1 tablespoon softened butter (optional)
1 tablespoon flour (optional)
1 tablespoon lemon juice, or more to taste
Vinegar

Simmer all the vegetables (except the optional extra beet) in the water with the parsley, salt, bay leaf, and peppercorns for about 1 hour, or until tender. Remove the pan from the heat. Strain the broth.

At this point you have several choices: You may wish to peel the beets, cut them in thin julienne strips and return them to the broth. You may purée all the vegetables and return the purée to the broth. Or you can leave the broth clear. If you like the soup to be a more intense red, you can grate part or all of the extra raw beet into the soup, and simmer briefly.

Thicken the broth a little (if desired) by stirring in little balls of beurre manié (pea-sized balls of softened butter mixed with flour). Add the lemon juice and vinegar to taste, and taste for seasoning.

Borscht can be served with generous dollops of sour cream. Or horseradish can be added to it, or chopped hard-boiled eggs, or thick chunks of rye bread. But at this special meal, Mushroom Pockets (Uszka) are often set afloat in the Borscht (see page 134).

Note: To be completely authentic, Borscht must be made with *kvas*, fermented beet juice. To make kvas, pour 5 cups boiling water over 3 sliced cooked beets. Stir in ½ cup vinegar. Let it stand at room temperature for 3 to 4 days. One cup *kvas* can be substituted for part of the water, and *kvas* can be added, to taste, instead of or along with the lemon juice and vinegar.

continued

Christmas Eve borscht, continued

MUSHROOM POCKETS
Delicate little dumplings filled with chopped mushrooms, onions, and dill.

DOUGH:
2 cups flour
Pinch of salt
1 large egg
Water
Filling (see below)

FILLING:
2 tablespoons onions, finely chopped
2 cups mushrooms, finely chopped
2 tablespoons butter
Salt and freshly ground pepper to taste
Optional:
Chopped dill and/or parsley

In a bowl, combine the flour with the salt and the egg, and add enough water to make a firm dough. Turn the mixture out onto a floured surface and knead until the dough is smooth and elastic. Cover well and let the dough stand for 10 minutes.

Sauté onions and mushrooms in hot butter until golden brown. Add salt, pepper, and dill or parsley or both. Cool before using.

Divide the dough in thirds and roll it out paper thin. Cut into 2-inch squares, or even smaller.

Place ½ teaspoon filling a little to one side of each square. Moisten the edges with a little water, fold over, and press the edges gently but firmly together, to form a triangle.

Drop the pockets into a large pot of boiling salted water and cook until they rise to the top.

Yield: 6 to 8 servings

Sauerkraut, split peas, and mushrooms

In much of Poland and the Ukraine, this dish is invariably part of the Christmas Eve meal. The porportions may be varied.

½ cup dried split green or yellow peas (rinse, pick over to remove pebbles)
4 cups water
1 pint sauerkraut, rinsed, drained
1 onion, chopped
½ cup butter
½ cup chopped mushrooms
Salt
Freshly ground pepper
Optional:
1 can anchovy fillets, drained

Rinse and pick over the peas to remove any pebbles. Place in a saucepan with the 4 cups of water. Bring to a boil and cook for 2 minutes. Remove from the heat and cover. Let the peas sit for ½ hour. Return to the heat and boil until tender, about 30 to 40 minutes.

In a large saucepan, simmer the sauerkraut with water just to cover for about 20 minutes. Remove from the heat. Drain off all but a few tablespoons of the water.

In the meantime, sauté the onion in ¼ cup of the butter until it is soft and translucent. Remove it from the pan and reserve. In the remaining ¼ cup of butter, sauté the mushrooms over high heat until nicely browned.

Add the peas, onion, and mushrooms to the sauerkraut saucepan. Simmer the mixture, stirring, until thoroughly blended and heated through. Season to taste with salt and pepper.

Serve in a handsome bowl or on a platter, garnished with anchovy fillets, if you wish.

Yield: 4 to 6 servings

Variations:

Eastern Orthodox, for whom this is a day of strict abstinence (no dairy products being allowed), omit the sautéing in butter, and add the onion and mushrooms directly to the saucepan along with the sauerkraut.

The mushrooms are not invariably part of this dish and may be omitted.

Christmas Eve carp with black sauce

Carp is a large and handsome fish, with a long and distinguished culinary tradition. Monasteries in the Middle Ages often kept fish ponds stocked with carp. A strong-flavored fish, carp is best prepared with a sauce that is itself spicy or otherwise highly flavored. In Germany this extraordinary dish would be served with dumplings or noodles, and perhaps stewed cabbage; in Eastern Europe, with sauerkraut.

4–5 pound carp, scaled, cleaned, and filleted (see note)
Vinegar
Salt
3 cups diced parsnips, turnips, carrots, celery root (a mixture of all or several)
1 large onion, chopped
¼ cup butter (more if necessary)
⅔ cup gingerbread, grated
⅔ cup slightly stale rye bread crumbs
8 peppercorns
½ teaspoon ground allspice
1 bay leaf
¼ teaspoon thyme
½ teaspoon grated lemon rind
1½ cups red wine
3 tablespoons water
3 tablespoons black currant jam
⅔ cup blanched almonds, coarsely chopped
⅔ cup raisins
Juice of ½ lemon, or to taste

Cut the carp fillets into 2- to 3-inch pieces. Wash and rinse in vinegar. Season with salt and set aside.

In a large skillet, sauté the vegetables in the butter until nicely browned. Add the gingerbread and rye breadcrumbs and the seasonings. Stir in the wine and 3½ tablespoons vinegar. Simmer for 10 minutes.

Add the carp and simmer for about 15 minutes, or until the fish flakes easily. Add the water if the mixture seems too thick. Remove the fish to a hot dish.

Force the sauce through a sieve, and return it to the pan. (Discard the vegetables that remain in the sieve.) Add the currant jam, almonds, raisins, and lemon juice. Simmer for 10 minutes, then return the carp to the sauce.

The dish may be served immediately, but the flavor improves if it is kept overnight in the refrigerator and is then reheated before being served.

Yield: 6 servings

Note: Carp is full of many little bones. It can be sliced into steaks, but in that case you have to be very careful of all those little bones as you eat. So try to have your fish merchant fillet the fish for you, or do it yourself.

Herring in sour cream

6–8 pickled herring, drained
1 large onion, peeled,
 chopped
6 hard-boiled eggs, peeled,
 chopped
1 teaspoon lemon juice, or
 more to taste
1 cup sour cream
1 or 2 cloves garlic, finely
 chopped
Salt
Freshly ground pepper
Fresh dill and/or parsley,
 chopped

Cut the herring into small pieces. Mix them with the onion and eggs. Stir in lemon juice, sour cream, garlic, and salt and pepper to taste. Chill. Serve sprinkled with fresh dill or parsley.

Yield: 4 to 6 servings

Variation:
 Sometimes apple (peeled or unpeeled, cored, chopped) is included in this salad.

Noodles with poppy seeds

This is a traditional accompaniment to the Eastern European Christmas Eve dishes. The poppy seeds—both here, in rolls, and often in Kutia (next recipe)—are an important part of the meal, in Poland in particular.

8 ounces wide egg noodles
½ cup poppy seeds
3–4 tablespoons sugar
3 tablespoons butter, cut in
 small pieces
Salt

In a large saucepan of boiling salted water cook the egg noodles until tender. Drain well.
 Grind the poppy seeds with a grinder or a mortar and pestle. Combine with the sugar.
 Mix the poppy seeds and sugar thoroughly with the noodles. Toss with the butter and salt to taste.

Yield: 6 servings

Variations:
 Eastern Orthodox Christians eliminate the butter.
 This dish can also be flavored with the following: 1 teaspoon vanilla extract, 1 teaspoon lemon juice, the rind of ½ lemon, and ½ cup raisins. Mix the ingredients thoroughly with the drained noodles, poppy seeds, sugar, and melted butter. Serve hot.

It is written in Isaiah the prophet
"I will send my messenger ahead of you, who will prepare your way—
a voice of one calling in the desert,
'Prepare the way for the Lord, make straight paths for him.' "
Mark 1:2–3 (NIV)

Kutia

One of the traditional Christmas Eve dishes in many countries is whole or cracked wheat (sometimes rice), softened in water, cooked, sweetened with honey, and often flavored with spices, dried fruits, and/or nuts. Of all the traditional foods served at this meal Kutia is the most clearly ritual food. This ancient porridge must be served during the Christmas Eve meal in many cultures. In parts of the Ukraine, it traditionally begins the meal. First comes the Lord's Prayer and a blessing. Then the head of the family raises in the air a spoonful of Kutia, invoking God's grace, and greeting his family with the words "Christ is born!" to which they reply, "Let us glorify Him!" Then every member of the family partakes of the Kutia.

In the Middle East, almost the same dish is called Kahmieh; in Armenia it is Anoushabour. In Sweden there is a Christmas Eve porridge. And the various English and Western European Christmas puddings—originally called "frumenty" (from the Latin frumentum, *wheat)—are clearly in the same tradition.*

Many of these "abstinence" dishes are not only served on Christmas Eve but are often (with slight variations) ritual mourning dishes as well, served either at funerals or at commemorative liturgies. They are presumably the kinds of dishes that in pre-Christian times would have been eaten at, or left on, the graves of the dead. (See All Souls' Day, page 278.)

There are several different meanings to the ancient dish: It was eaten from a common dish, shared—thus symbolizing unity. It was made of grain, always a symbol of hope and immortality—of rebirth from a "dead" seed. It was eaten both on Christmas Eve and at funerals—symbolizing the spiritual unity of the clan, both living and dead members. Finally, Kutia is generally sweet and rich and flavored with poppy seeds, nuts, and fruits, suggestive of rest, happiness, and success.

1 cup whole or cracked wheat
Salt
⅔–1 cup honey or sugar
Optional (Any or all of the following):
Finely chopped or ground walnuts, almonds, and/or other nuts: about ½ cup
Ground poppy seeds, about ½ cup (to grind, see page 139)
Raisins or currants, or other chopped dried fruits, such as apricots (these are more characteristic of the Armenian Anoushabour)
Pomegranate seeds
½–1 teaspoon (to taste) cinnamon or vanilla or almond extract
Confectioners' sugar

Soak the wheat overnight in water to cover. Cook it in the same water until tender, adding more water as necessary and sprinkling in a little salt. Drain.

Mix the drained wheat with the honey or sugar to taste and any of the optional ingredients. Sprinkle with confectioners' sugar, if you wish.

Hungarian poppy-seed-and-walnut roll

MÁKOS ÉS DIÓS KALACS

In Hungary (and in several other Eastern European countries as well) this beautiful and delicious large rolled cake, filled with poppy seeds and walnuts, is the eagerly awaited dessert at the Christmas Eve dinner.

DOUGH:
1 package dry yeast
⅓ cup warm water
  (100–110° F.)
⅓ cup sugar
½ cup milk
6 tablespoons sweet butter
¾ teaspoon salt
Grated rind of 1 lemon
1 teaspoon vanilla extract,
  or 1–2 tablespoons dark
  rum
1 egg plus 2 egg yolks
About 3½ cups flour

FILLING:
¼ cup butter at room
  temperature
⅓ cup honey
⅓ pound ground poppy
  seeds (see Note)
2 tablespoons heavy cream
⅓ cup chopped raisins
⅓ cup chopped walnuts
Grated rind of 1 lemon or ½
  orange
½ teaspoon vanilla extract
½ teaspoon cinnamon
¼ teaspoon freshly grated
  nutmeg

EGG WASH OR ICING:
2 egg yolks beaten with 2
  tablespoons heavy cream
or confectioners' sugar
  mixed with a little milk
  or lemon juice

Sprinkle the yeast into the warm water and stir in 2 tablespoons sugar. Set aside until frothy.

Scald the milk with the butter, the remaining sugar, and the salt, stirring until the butter is melted. Cool until lukewarm and add the lemon rind and vanilla or rum. Pour the mixture into a large bowl.

Stir in the eggs and the yeast mixture. Gradually add enough flour to make a smooth dough that does not stick to your fingers. Turn the dough out onto a lightly floured surface. Knead for about 10 minutes, or until the dough is smooth and elastic, and the surface begins to blister.

Shape the dough into a ball and place it in a large buttered bowl, turning the dough to grease the top. Cover and let the dough rise until doubled in bulk—1 to 1½ hours.

Prepare the filling: Cream the butter with the honey. Stir in the ground poppy seeds, cream, chopped raisins and nuts, grated rind, vanilla, cinnamon, and nutmeg. Blend thoroughly.

Punch the dough down and knead briefly, 2 or 3 minutes.

On a lightly floured surface roll the dough into a rectangle a little less than ¼ inch thick, and about 15 by 22 inches. Spread the filling over the dough, leaving a 1- to 2-inch border free of filling. Roll up jelly-roll fashion, to make a long thin roll. Seal at the ends and along the seams.

Form the roll into a horseshoe shape, and place it on a buttered baking sheet. Cover it lightly and let it rise until almost doubled in bulk.

Brush the roll with an egg wash and bake it at 350° F. for about 50 minutes, or until golden brown. (If you wish to ice the roll, omit the egg wash.)

Optional: Ice when cool with confectioners' sugar mixed with a little milk or lemon juice.

Yield: 1 large rolled cake

Note: For poppy seeds to release their best flavor they need to be ground and steamed (or roasted) before use. They can be bought ground in some gourmet shops. Here is how to do it yourself: boil the seeds in water to cover for 30 minutes (or cover them with boiling water and let them soak overnight). Drain them and dry thoroughly. Then grind them in a poppy-seed grinder, or with a mortar and pestle, until they are very finely crushed.

Polish twelve-fruit compote

Among the Polish traditional dishes for Christmas Eve is a compote of twelve different fruits, in honor of the Apostles. This recipe is slightly adapted from the Polish Cookbook, *of the Culinary Arts Institute, which is full of interesting material and fine recipes.*

Use twelve of the fruits listed.

3 cups water
1 pound mixed dried fruits (pears, figs, apricots, and/or peaches)
1 cup pitted prunes
½ cup dark or golden raisins and/or currants
1 cup pitted sweet cherries, fresh, frozen, or canned
2 apples, peeled and sliced, or 6 ounces dried apple slices
½ cup cranberries
1 cup sugar
1 lemon, sliced
6 whole cloves
2 cinnamon sticks (3 inches each)
1 orange
½ cup grapes, pomegranate seeds, pitted plums, pitted peaches, and/or banana slices
½ cup fruit-flavored brandy or liqueur, such as kirsch, curaçao, or slivovitz

Combine water, mixed dried fruits, prunes, raisins and currants in a 6-quart saucepan. Bring them to boiling. Cover; simmer about 20 minutes, or until the fruits are plump and tender.

Add the cherries, apples, and cranberries. Stir in sugar, lemon, and spices. Cover; simmer 5 minutes.

Grate the peel of the orange; reserve. Peel and section the orange, and add to the fruits in the saucepan.

Stir in the grapes, pomegranate seeds, plums, peaches, and bananas. Add brandy or liqueur. Bring just to boiling. Remove from heat. Stir in the orange peel. Cover; let stand 15 minutes.

Yield: about 15 servings

Hazelnut torte

Another traditional dessert for the Christmas Eve dinner is a torte: a cake made primarily of ground nuts. Here is a marvelous, rich Austrian torte, made of hazelnuts (or walnuts).

6 eggs, separated, at room temperature
½ cup sugar
3 tablespoons dry breadcrumbs
Grated rind of 1 lemon
2 teaspoons fresh lemon juice
1 teaspoon vanilla extract
6 ounces hazelnuts, or walnuts, or a mixture of the two, finely ground
Buttercream icing (page 29), flavored with rum or vanilla and coffee, or whatever icing you prefer

Preheat the oven to 350° F. Butter and flour a 10-inch springform pan.

Beat the egg yolks until light and frothy. Add the sugar gradually, beating well after each addition.

In a small bowl, mix the breadcrumbs, lemon rind and juice, and vanilla extract. Add to the egg mixture. Stir in the ground nuts.

Beat the egg whites until stiff but not dry. Fold them gently but thoroughly into the batter. Pour the batter into the pan. Bake for 30 to 40 minutes, or until a straw inserted in the center comes out clean. Loosen the outer rim of the pan. Remove the torte from the pan when cool.

Slice the cake carefully into two layers. (If you prefer, you can leave it in one layer, and just sprinkle it with confectioners' sugar.)

Frost with buttercream icing, flavored with rum or vanilla, and coffee. (You can put jam or flavored whipped cream between the layers, if you like.)

Yield: 1 large torte

6

Christmas day and the Christmas season

Christmas is, next to Easter, the greatest holy day and feast in the Christian tradition. It commemorates the birth of Jesus Christ and the Incarnation.

No one knows, in fact, just when Jesus Christ was born. Though this seems hard for us to imagine, for the first several hundred years of the Christian era his Nativity was not celebrated. It was not until the fourth century, in Rome, that December 25 began to be celebrated as the feast in honor of his birth. Apparently, the date was chosen in conscious competition with a pagan feast in honor of the "Unconquered Sun God," the idea being to inspire people to turn from the worship of the material sun to that of the Lord.

By the mid-sixth century, the Twelve Days of Christmas, from Christmas Day to Epiphany, were considered a sacred and festive season. It is amusing to note the difference between the commercial and the traditional concepts of the Christmas season: the commercial one begins the day after Thanksgiving and extends until Christmas Eve. The *real*, traditional Christmas season *begins* at midnight on Christmas Eve, and extends through to Epiphany, on which we celebrate Christ's "Showing Forth" to the Magi, the first gentiles to acknowledge and worship him. This period has for many centuries been celebrated by music and caroling and the giving of Christmas plays, by feasting and holding open house, by charity to the poor as well as extra rations for animals.

Christmas Day has always been a feast day. St. Francis of Assisi practically snorted with indignation at the thought that Christmas, if it fell on a Friday, might ever be a day of abstinence. "The very walls," he said, "should have a right to eat meat today." There are a staggering assortment of food traditions associated with Christmas, both the day and the season. Some of them you will find in the recipes; others we do well just to evoke! Most of us would (for example) have difficulty laying our hands on a boar's head, a dish traditionally served up on a great platter on Christmas Day, in the medieval period.

142

Another traditional dish was the Christmas pie—the *enormous* Christmas pie—popular in England until well into the last century. Here is a traditional recipe (set in modern terms), and this is by no means the largest pie I've seen described:

Take a Pheasant, a Hare, a Capon, two Partridges, two Pigeons, and two Conies [rabbits]; chop them up, take out as many bones as you can, and add the livers and hearts, two kidneys of sheep, forcemeat made into balls with eggs, pickled mushrooms, salt, pepper, spice and vinegar. Boil the bones in a pot to make good broth; put the meat into a crust of good paste made craftily into the likeness of a bird's body; pour in the liquor, close it up, and bake it well; and so serve it forth, with the head of one of the birds at one end and a great tail at the other, and divers of his long feathers set cunningly all about him.

This English tendency to bake every creature under the sun into a pie became so marked in the southwest of Britain that the saying arose: "The devil dares not show himself in Cornwall, lest he should be baked in a pie."

In any event, throughout the Christian world, this season has long been celebrated as a time of good cheer, fellowship, and joy.

Many people today find, however, that there is a post-Christmas letdown. From Christmas Day on, it's just dried-up Christmas tree and turkey leftovers. (And we already had a turkey, a month before, for Thanksgiving!) The presents have all been opened (and some of the kids' toys already broken). How are we to keep our sense of joy of the Christmas season? Our sense not that something is *over*, but that something has begun. This is one of the good reasons for keeping the Advent season: it helps prepare us to rejoice.

Here are a few suggestions to help fight the post-Christmas secular letdown. First, don't just feed your family leftovers. (Even in small details, the body gets the message to the soul.) Day by day, let's break out some of the cookies or fruitcakes or other goodies we baked and squirreled away during Advent. If you didn't squirrel them away, then bake or buy them now. The point is to help our families and ourselves not merely to know but to *feel* that something wonderful has happened, and is continuing to happen, in our lives. So let's not just unload presents on our children on Christmas Day. When the last package is opened, they're depressed. Why wouldn't they be? Try doling out little presents throughout the whole twelve-day period—with perhaps one last, nice present for Epiphany.

This is the time to have parties and open houses, to see old friends and make new ones, to play Christmas records and go to concerts of Christmas music. If you have picture books or have received Christmas cards with beautiful paintings of the Nativity or the Adoration, look at them with your children. Focus as well on particular days of the season. Several of them bring in moving, somber notes: the feast of St. Stephen, on December 26, and that of the Holy Innocents, on the 28th—both being commemorations of martyrs.

Live the Christmas season—all twelve days of it—as richly, as joyfully (and sometimes sorrowfully), as *fully* as we possibly can.

Joy to the world! the Lord is come;
Let earth receive her King;
Let every heart prepare Him room,
And heaven and nature sing,
And heaven and nature sing,
And heaven, and heaven and nature sing:

Joy to the earth! the Saviour reigns;
Let men their songs employ;
While fields and floods, rocks, hills, and plains
Repeat the sounding joy,
Repeat the sounding joy,
Repeat, repeat the sounding joy!

Isaac Watts, "Joy to the World"

THE RÉVEILLON MEAL

In France and many other countries, it has long been traditional to sit down to a wonderful feast early on Christmas morning, after returning from a midnight church service. This meal might traditionally include oysters, wonderful sausages such as boudin (blood sausage), a roast turkey. In French Canada it would highlight a Tourtière, or meat pie. In France the dinner typically concludes with a Bûche de Noël, or Christmas Log.

French-Canadian meat pie
TOURTIÈRE

This French-Canadian dish dates back to the seventeenth century.

2 pounds ground pork
2 onions, finely chopped
1 clove garlic, finely minced
1 tablespoon finely chopped celery leaves
1 teaspoon savory
½ teaspoon sage
⅛ teaspoon ground cloves
2 bay leaves
1 teaspoon salt
Freshly ground pepper to taste
1 cup boiling water
3–4 tablespoons dry breadcrumbs
Pie dough for 2 nine-inch 2-crust pies
Optional:
2 tablespoons heavy cream

Mix the pork, onions, garlic, celery leaves, savory, sage, cloves, bay leaves, salt, and a few grindings of pepper in a large skillet. Add the boiling water. Simmer for about ½ hour, stirring frequently; the pork should be brown (not pink), and the mixture fairly dry. Drain off any excess fat. Taste for seasoning. Remove the bay leaves.

Sprinkle the bread crumbs in 2 uncooked pie shells. Spread the meat mixture on top. Cover each pie with a top crust. Seal and flute the edges, and make some incisions in the crust. (You might make a cross with the tines of a fork or some other symbolic shape or initial.) Optional: Brush crusts with cream.

Bake at 350° F. for 45 minutes, or until the top crust is golden.

Yield: 2 pies

Variations:
Use half pork, half ground beef or veal. You can also substitute for the savory and cloves 1 teaspoon cinnamon and ⅛ teaspoon nutmeg. This is another traditional version of the dish.

God rest you merry, gentlemen, Let nothing you dismay;
Remember Christ our Savior, Was born on Christmas Day.

Christmas carol

Christian log

BÛCHE DE NOËL

It has long been a tradition in Western Europe to burn a great log at Christmas time; this huge log was carried into the house and laid on the hearth with great ceremony. It was lit on Christmas night, and was to burn throughout the entire Christmas season. The log (sometimes the whole trunk of a tree) was generally chosen well in advance, and it was supposed to be lit with whatever wood remained from the yule log of the preceding year.

The eating of a pastry Bûche de Noël is a (delectable) culinary reflection of this tradition.

SPONGE CAKE

4 eggs, separated, at room temperature
1 cup sugar
¼ cup hot water
Grated rind of 1 lemon
1 teaspoon lemon juice
½ teaspoon vanilla
1 cup sifted flour
1 teaspoon baking powder
¼ teaspoon salt
A few tablespoons rum (optional)
Confectioners' sugar

Preheat the oven to 400° F. Grease a jelly-roll pan, 10 by 15 inches. Line the pan with waxed paper, and grease the paper.

Beat the egg yolks until light and lemon-colored. Gradually add the sugar, beating until very thick: about 5 to 7 minutes with an electric mixer. Beat in the hot water, lemon rind and juice, and vanilla.

Resift the flour with the baking powder and salt, and gradually beat into the egg mixture.

Whip the egg whites until stiff but not dry. Fold gently but thoroughly into the batter.

Pour it into the jelly-roll pan. Bake for 12 to 15 minutes, or until the cake is lightly browned.

As soon as the cake is done, sprinkle it with rum if you wish. Spread a clean, damp kitchen towel on the counter. Cover it with waxed paper. Sprinkle the paper with confectioners' sugar. Invert the cake onto the waxed paper. Peel the paper off the cake. Trim the edges if too crusty.

Roll up the cake along the long side with the towel and waxed paper. Let it cool at room temperature, for about 20 minutes.

MOCHA CREAM ICING

4 egg yolks
1¼ cups sugar
⅓ cup water
2 teaspoons vanilla extract
2 teaspoons powdered instant coffee
2 ounces unsweetened chocolate, melted, cooled
3 sticks (1½ cups) sweet butter, at room temperature

Beat the egg yolks until light-colored and thick.

Combine the sugar and water in a saucepan. Cook to the soft-ball stage: about 234° F. on a candy thermometer.

Beating constantly, add the eggs to the syrup. Continue beating until the mixture is cool. Stir in the vanilla extract, coffee, and chocolate. Gradually beat in the butter.

Cool the icing slightly in the refrigerator if it is too soft.

TO ASSEMBLE THE CAKE

Unroll the cake. Spread it with half of the icing. Without the paper and towel, roll the cake back up as tightly as possible without damaging it. Chill for several hours. Keep the icing refrigerated as well.

Trim the ends of the cake on the diagonal; reserve scraps. Frost the cake with most of the remaining icing. Cut the scraps to resemble knotholes. Set them on the Bûche and ice them. Using the tines of a fork, make marks on the surface of the cake to look like bark. Or using a spatula, you can give the surface a shaggy bark look.

You can decorate the surface, if you like, with tinted marzipan made to look like holly leaves and berries; almonds; mushrooms made of meringue; confectioners' sugar or colored sugar sprinkles.

Optional:
Marzipan, tinted with
food coloring
Almonds
Meringue "mushrooms"
Sugar sprinkles

Yield: 1 Christmas log

CHRISTMAS DINNER

Scandinavian pickled herring

4 fillets salt herring; remove
all fins and scales
1 carrot, sliced thin
2 red onions, sliced thin
2 bay leaves
¾ teaspoon whole allspice,
crushed
1–2 teaspoons mustard
seeds
1 half-inch piece fresh
ginger, peeled, sliced thin,
or 1 teaspoon ground
ginger
1 one-inch piece fresh
horseradish, peeled, sliced
thin, or 1 tablespoon
prepared horseradish
¾ cup cider vinegar
⅔ cup water
½ to ¾ cup sugar

Just as Herring Salad was a Christmas Eve specialty in Eastern Europe, we find it on the table for Christmas Day in much of Scandinavia.

Soak the herring in water at least 24 hours; change water once if convenient. Rinse, dry, and cut into 1-inch pieces. In a wide-mouth crock or glass jar, place layers of herring and vegetables, sprinkling them with the spices.

Combine the vinegar, water, and sugar. Bring the mixture to a boil, and stir until the sugar is dissolved. Pour over the herring.

Refrigerate. Let the herring marinate for at least 24 hours; longer is desirable.

Yield: 8 to 10 servings

Swedish Christmas spareribs

The main dish at a Swedish Christmas dinner is very apt to be pork: either ham or spareribs. If the choice is ham, see page 200. Here is a recipe for Swedish Spareribs, which provides a delicious variation from the traditions most familiar to Americans.

Try serving the spareribs with Pan-Fried Potatoes (page 44) and Spicy Applesauce (page 150).

5 pounds spareribs
1 tablespoon salt
1 teaspoon freshly ground
   black or white pepper
1 tablespoon ground ginger
   or dry mustard
A few tablespoons vegetable
   oil or bacon grease
2 cups water or stock

Rub the spareribs with the salt and spices. In a frying pan, brown the ribs in the oil. Place them on a rack in a roasting pan. Pour the water or stock into the pan. Bake at 350° F. for about 1½ hours.

Yield: 6 to 8 servings

Goose with fruit stuffing, German style

The Christmas goose: what could be more traditional? Goose is eaten in many countries for Christmas, and has been for centuries—though other birds and beasts have been popular as well. The bustard, now extinct, was long a favorite in England. The point always was, and still is, that you eat the handsomest, finest, tastiest creature you can lay your hands on and can afford, and prepare it in as delectable and handsome a way as possible. That is Christmas!

There are many good ways of preparing goose, but this is my absolute favorite. This recipe is slightly adapted from Marina Polvays' fine book All Along the Danube.

Try serving the goose with cabbage and mashed potatoes or Himmel und Erde (page 38).

1 goose, 10–12 pounds,
   fresh or frozen

STUFFING:
1 twelve-ounce package
   mixed dried fruit: about
   1½–2 cups
1 cup orange liqueur or
   brandy, or orange juice
1 cup orange juice
½ cup light or dark brown
   sugar
12 slices good white bread

If the goose is frozen, defrost it for 48 hours or more in the refrigerator, until completely defrosted. Remove the giblets and cut off as much fat as possible from the inside and all over the goose. Wash the goose, pat it dry with paper towels, and set it aside.

Chop the dried fruit and place it in a bowl. Mix orange liqueur and orange juice with brown sugar in a saucepan. Stir well. Bring the mixture to a boil, remove it from the heat immediately, and pour it over the fruit. Cover the bowl with foil, and let the fruit steep for 1 hour or more.

Cut off the crusts of the bread, and cut the bread into small cubes. Spread them on a cookie sheet and toast in a 400° F. oven, stirring the cubes occasionally until golden brown on all sides.

½ teaspoon ground ginger
1 teaspoon cinnamon
½ teaspoon nutmeg
¼ teaspoon ground allspice
⅛ teaspoon mace
2 eggs, well beaten
1 cup brandy or orange
   juice
Salt
Freshly ground pepper

Place the bread cubes in a large bowl. Add ginger, cinnamon, nutmeg, allspice, mace, and steeped fruit with its liquid. Toss lightly. Add the beaten eggs and ½ cup of the brandy. Toss until all the bread cubes are moistened.

Stuff the neck cavity with the mixture, fold over the skin and secure it with a skewer, or sew it up. Stuff the body cavity and cover the opening with a piece of foil, or close it with skewers, or sew it up.

Sprinkle the goose with salt and pepper all over. Place it on a rack in a shallow pan. Place in a preheated 400° F. oven, and roast for ½ hour.

Prick the skin all over with a fork (this will allow the grease to drip out). Reduce the heat to 350° F. Insert a meat thermometer into the thickest part of the breast without touching the breastbone. About every 20 minutes, pour fat out of the roasting pan, or spoon it out using a large kitchen spoon. Baste the goose frequently with the remaining ½ cup of brandy.

Roast for 2½ to 3 hours or until the thermometer reaches 185° F. Let the goose cool for 15 minutes, to let the juices settle; place on a heated platter and carve at the table.

CHRISTMAS STUFFINGS FOR TURKEY
If you are a real turkey lover, and just can't bear to eat any other creature for Christmas, do try a stuffing that is different from what you used for Thanksgiving. Here are two of the traditional festive Christmas stuffings: Chestnut and Oyster. And try serving your Christmas turkey with champagne!

3 cups peeled, cooked
   chestnuts (see Note)
½ cup sweet butter
1 small onion, chopped
½ cup celery, chopped
¾ cup dry breadcrumbs
2 tablespoons chopped
   parsley
½ pound pork sausage,
   thoroughly cooked,
   crumbled, drained, or 2
   cups oysters
½ teaspoon thyme
½ teaspoon marjoram, basil,
   or tarragon
Salt
Freshly ground black pepper
A little cognac, port, stock
   or milk

Chestnut stuffing for turkey

Chop the chestnuts coarse.

Melt the butter in a large skillet. Sauté the onion and celery until soft and golden brown. Add the chestnuts, breadcrumbs, parsley, sausage or oysters, thyme, marjoram, and salt and pepper to taste. Moisten lightly with liquid.

Stuff the turkey loosely. Do not pack the stuffing in.

   Yield: about 4½ cups (enough for an 8- to 10-pound turkey)

Note: About 5 cups unpeeled chestnuts will yield 3 cups cooked and peeled. To cook and peel chestnuts, place in a saucepan and cover with boiling water. Simmer for 15 to 25 minutes. Drain. As soon as you can handle them, remove the shells and inner skins (they are easiest to peel while hot). The chestnuts should at this point be tender enough to be chopped. If not, cover again with boiling water or stock and simmer until tender.

Oyster stuffing for turkey

½ cup chopped onions
1 stick (½ cup) butter
¼ cup chopped parsley
4 cups breadcrumbs (or diced slightly stale bread)
1½ cups drained whole or chopped oysters
½ cup chopped celery
1 teaspoon salt
½ teaspoon paprika
3 tablespoons capers

Sauté the onions in the butter until golden brown. Stir in the remaining ingredients, mixing thoroughly. Taste for seasoning.

Yield: about 5 cups, enough for an 8- to 10-pound turkey

Variations:

You can also add sautéed sliced mushrooms, and/or chopped cooked shrimp.

First parents of the human race, whose gourmandism is historical, you lost all for an apple, what would you not have done for a truffled turkey?

Brillat-Savarin, *The Philosopher in the Kitchen*

Spicy applesauce

Homemade applesauce is very easy to make: you just peel, core, and slice apples, and cook them in a saucepan with a little water, sugar, and whatever spices you like (cinnamon, nutmeg, cloves) until they are soft. But here is a somewhat unusual recipe for applesauce, adapted from an old Shaker recipe.

3 pounds apples (choose tart apples such as Granny Smiths)
About 1 cup brown sugar
Juice and grated rind of 2 lemons
1 teaspoon ground ginger, or ½ teaspoon each cinnamon and nutmeg
½ teaspoon salt

Peel, core, and chop the apples; there should be 6 cups. Place them in a saucepan and add the sugar (more or less depending on tartness of apples), lemon juice and rind, spice, and salt.

Add just enough water to keep the apples from burning: you won't need much. Cover and cook very, very slowly for 4 hours, adding water as necessary and stirring occasionally. Be careful not to let the apples scorch. Taste for seasoning.

Incidentally, such applesauce is yet another nice gift idea for Christmas.

Yield: 1½ to 2 pints

Red and green molded ice-cream dessert

There are many traditional desserts for the Christmas dinner, such as plum pudding and fruitcakes of all kinds. Many of them, however, are more to adult than to youthful tastes, and it is well to provide a dessert that the children will enjoy.

Here is a beautiful dessert, which can be made with almost any mold you have, from an elegant Bombe to an ordinary ring mold. It is exceedingly easy to make. You can, of course, use any combination of flavors that the children you are trying to please enjoy, but if possible pick up the green-and-red Christmas motif by using pistachio or mint, and strawberry or cherry.

Red and green have been Christmas colors since the Middle Ages when holly was used to decorate churches, though the tradition may go back to Roman Saturnalia customs. Holly was seen as symbolizing the burning bush that Moses saw and its prickly points and bright red berries like drops of blood were reminders that the Infant Jesus would one day wear a crown of thorns.

Ice cream: 2, 3, or 4 different flavors—about 1 pint of each. This will vary according to the number of flavors being used, the size of the mold you are using, and the number of children (and other ice creamers) you plan to serve this to

A mold of almost any shape; a simple ring mold does well

Soften the ice cream slightly. With a large spoon make a layer of one ice cream in the mold, pressing it down firmly. Continue with the other flavors. Choose the order in which you place the flavors so that contrasts in color will be as attractive as possible.

Place the mold in the freezer and freeze until the ice cream is hard again.

Just before serving, dip the base of the mold briefly (only briefly) in hot water, and unmold on a handsome platter.

The holly and the ivy,
When they are both full grown,
Of all the trees that are in the wood,
The holly bears the crown:

The rising of the sun
And the running of the deer,
The playing of the merry organ,
Sweet singing in the choir.

"The Holly and the Ivy"

Plum pudding with hard sauce

⅔ cup each:
currants
dark raisins
golden raisins
dates or prunes (the
  original "plums"), pitted,
  chopped
¾ cup chopped candied
  orange or lemon peel,
  citron or other candied
  fruit
½ cup good brandy, rum,
  Madeira, sherry, or cider
1 cup fine breadcrumbs
1 teaspoon cinnamon
½ teaspoon ground ginger
¼ teaspoon nutmeg
¼ teaspoon ground cloves
1 teaspoon salt
1½ cups dark or light
  brown sugar
1½ cups stout, ale, beer, or
  milk
4 eggs, well beaten
¼ pound (approximately ⅔
  cup) beef suet, finely
  chopped
¾ cup flour
1½ teaspoons baking
  powder
½ teaspoon baking soda
Freshly grated rind of 1
  lemon
Freshly grated rind of 1
  orange
½ cup finely chopped
  blanched almonds
⅔ cup peeled, cored,
  chopped apples

This famous pudding has long been served on Christmas Day, but its preparation is begun well before. Traditionally it is begun the Sunday before Advent, which is called in the Anglican (Episcopal) Church "Stir-up Sunday," from the collect which is always read on that day. It begins, "Stir up, we beseech Thee, O Lord, the wills of thy faithful people; that they plenteously bringing forth the fruit of good works, may by Thee be plenteously rewarded; through Jesus Christ our Lord. Amen."

According to tradition, the pudding is stirred before being cooked by each member of the family in turn. It was even prepared on board British ships at sea, where it was first stirred by the senior officer. The stirring is always from east to west, in honor of the journey of the Magi.

As we know it today (a pudding steamed in a pan or cloth) Christmas Pudding only dates from the eighteenth century. But it existed in Elizabethan times as "plum porridge," and in fact it goes back even further, to the medieval "frumenty" dishes. Plum Pudding is thus a distant cousin of the ritual Kutia (page 137).

Plum Pudding, like all old, traditional dishes, exists in many variations. (For example, it can be made with or without liquor; it can be done "Jamaican"-style, with the substitution of cherries and pecans for the raisins and almonds.) Here is a fine, classic recipe. If possible, prepare and steam the pudding early in Advent: it improves with age.

Combine the dried and candied fruits. Pour the brandy over them and let them sit for at least 1 hour.

Mix the crumbs with the spices, salt, and brown sugar. Pour the stout over them and let stand for a few minutes.

Blend the eggs with the suet.

Sift the flour with the baking powder and baking soda.

Combine all these mixtures and add the remaining ingredients: the rinds, the almonds, and the apples. Turn this mixture into a well-buttered and sugared 2-quart mold, or into two 1-quart molds. Cover well with aluminum foil.

Place the mold on a rack in a large pan. Pour in 2 to 3 inches of water. Cover the pot well. Steam for about 3 hours, or until the pudding is firm. (A knife will come out clean. You will need to unwrap the pudding to check. Rewrap and return if it's still too soft.) Store in the refrigerator; to reheat, steam for an hour or so.

Serve with Hard Sauce, or with vanilla ice cream.

Yield: 8 to 10 servings

1 stick (¼ pound) sweet
  butter, at room
  temperature
1–1¼ cups confectioners'
  sugar or brown sugar
1–4 tablespoons rum,
  brandy, or whiskey; or ½–
  1 teaspoon vanilla
  extract, coffee, or lemon
  juice
Optional:
  1–2 tablespoons heavy
  cream

HARD SAUCE

Cream the butter until soft and fluffy. Beat in the sugar gradually. Beat until well blended (an electric mixer does this quickly). Beat in the rum or other flavoring to taste. Beat in the cream, if desired.

When the sauce is completely smooth, chill.

Yield: about 1¼ cups

> England was merry England, when
> Old Christmas brought his sports again.
> 'Twas Christmas broach'd the mightiest ale;
> 'Twas Christmas told the merriest tale;
> A Christmas gambol oft could cheer
> The poor man's heart through half the year.
>
> Sir Walter Scott, "Lochinvar"

Mincemeat pie

The serving of Mincemeat Pie at Christmas goes back well into the Middle Ages in England. These pies were originally made in rectangular shapes, which came to be thought of as signifying the manger in which the Infant Jesus lay. Often the filling was set in with a hump in the middle, to suggest the shape of the swaddled child. Or sometimes a little figure of a baby was placed on top. Such pies were so clearly associated with Christmas that when the Puritans tried (unsuccessfully) to abolish the celebration of Christmas, they also forbade the eating of Mincemeat Pies.

Here, then, is a really old-fashioned way of making Mincemeat Pie: as a rectangular pie, suggesting in its lumpy shape the swaddled Babe.

Flaky Pastry, for one 7-by-
  11-inch rectangular pan
  (bottom and top crust)
  (page 250)
7 to 8 cups Old-Fashioned
  Mincemeat (page 116), or
  good store-bought filling

Preheat the oven to 400° F.

Roll out a crust to about 11 by 15 inches. Lay it in the pan. Fill with the mincemeat filling. Make a mound of filling toward the center. Cover with the top crust. Crimp the edges to seal and trim off excess crust.

You can also sketch out the outline of a baby, by pricking through the surface of the crust with the tines of a fork.

Bake for about 45 minutes, or until the crust is golden brown. Halfway through the baking, you may sprinkle the crust with sugar (it will give sparkle to the surface).

CAROL-SINGING PARTY

We get so little opportunity, it seems to me, to sing Christmas carols nowadays. Why not find a friend who can play the piano or a guitar, and organize an evening around this beautiful—and traditional—activity?

One of the traditional Christmastide dishes, in both Ireland and England, is a marvelous thing called "Spiced Beef." You could serve this dish for a carol-singing party some night during the Twelve Days. Singing these songs—some so old, some new—can be a deeply meaningful Christmas experience.

Christmas spiced beef

½ cup salt
1 four- to five-pound round or chuck roast
1 teaspoon cinnamon
1 teaspoon ground allspice
1 teaspoon ground cloves
A few grindings of black pepper
1 tablespoon brown sugar
3 cups hard cider
1 cup cider vinegar
1 bay leaf
4–6 onions, sliced
2–4 carrots, sliced
1–2 stalks celery, sliced
Optional:
1 cup Guinness stout

With the Spiced Beef try serving a fruit salad. Although the Mexican Salad of the Good Night (page 125) really belongs on Christmas Eve, if you didn't serve it then, serve it now. I think you will find the combination surprisingly good.

Rub the salt into the meat. Cover it in a bowl and let it sit refrigerated for 24 hours. Rinse it and pat it dry.

Rub the cinnamon, allspice, cloves, black pepper, and brown sugar into the meat. Place it in a bowl and add the cider, vinegar, bay leaf and 2 onions. Cover and refrigerate for 2 or 3 days—a week is even better. Turn the meat occasionally.

Place the meat in a large pan with the marinade and enough water barely to cover. Add the remaining onions, the carrots, and the celery. Cover the pot and simmer for about 3 hours, or until the meat is tender and fully cooked. If you like, add 1 cup of stout in the last hour of cooking. Serve hot or cold.

Yield: about 8 servings

Mulled cider

2 quarts cider
Peel of 1 orange or lemon
8–10 cloves
1 stick cinnamon
Sugar to taste
Optional:
Orange or lemon slices
Cloves

This is a fine drink for a carol-singing party. It is festive but nonalcoholic, so singers with parched throats can drink all they like and still keep their minds on the beautiful words they are singing.

Combine the cider, peel, cloves, and cinnamon in a saucepan. Add sugar to taste (most cider needs no extra sweetening). Bring to a boil, lower heat, and simmer for about 10 minutes, or until the flavors are well blended.

Optional: Stud the orange or lemon slices with cloves and float them on top of the cider in a punch bowl.

Yield: about 8 one-cup servings

ST. STEPHEN'S DAY
December 26

"Good King Wenceslas looked out, on the Feast of Stephen. . . ." This lovely old carol begins with a reference to the feast of the great—indeed the very *first*—martyr, St. Stephen, whose death is so movingly recounted in the book of Acts (Chapter 7). Precisely because he was the first person to die for the faith, he is honored by having his feast day right after Christmas.

Stephen has, since very early times, been considered the patron of horses. No one knows why—it may be because all domestic animals were treated especially well during the Christmas season, and horses were foremost among those servants of man. In many parts of Europe, horses were decorated on this day and brought to church to be blessed. They were then ridden three times (in honor of the Trinity, no doubt) around the church. Often the whole family would take a wagon or sleigh ride, called "St. Stephen's ride."

December 26 is called Boxing Day in England, because on the feast of St. Stephen the priest would empty the church alms box and distribute the money among the poor of the parish. Various workers also kept their own little boxes in which they saved "tips" throughout the year; on Boxing Day, they would open the boxes. (This is also, incidentally, the origin of our piggy banks: children in Germany and Holland stored their pennies in pig-shaped earthenware boxes, which they broke just after Christmas.)

St. Stephen's horseshoes
PODKOVY

> *On St. Stephen's Day in Poland and other Slavic countries, special breads were baked in the form of horseshoes. A trayful of these pastries makes a lovely Christmas present for a family.*

1 package dry yeast
½ cup warm milk (100–110° F.)
3 eggs
1 cup sour cream
2 teaspoons lemon juice
Grated rind of 2 lemons
5 cups flour
⅔ cup sugar
½ teaspoon salt
1 cup cold sweet butter, chopped in small pieces
½ cup shortening

FILLING:
½–¾ cup brown sugar
1 egg
½ teaspoon vanilla extract
Grated rind of 1 orange
Grated rind of 1 lemon
1½–2 cups finely chopped walnuts or other nuts

Melted butter
Optional:
   Heavy cream
   Glaze of confectioners' sugar and lemon juice, or confectioners' sugar

Sprinkle the yeast into the warm milk. Beat the eggs until light and fluffy. Stir in the sour cream, yeast mixture, lemon juice and rind.

Combine the flour, sugar, and salt. With two knives or your fingers, work the butter and shortening quickly into the flour mixture until thoroughly incorporated. Add the dry ingredients to the wet ingredients, beating well. If necessary, add a little more flour, just enough to make a fairly soft and nonsticky dough. Knead the dough briefly, until all the ingredients are well blended. Wrap the dough in waxed paper or plastic wrap. Chill for 1 hour.

Meanwhile, prepare the filling: Combine the brown sugar with the egg, vanilla extract, and rinds. Stir in the walnuts.

On a lightly floured surface, roll the dough out about ⅛ inch thick. Cut it into rectangles about 4 by 6 inches. (You can, in fact, make them any size you like.)

Brush the rectangles with melted butter and sprinkle lightly with the filling. Or use one of the variations. I find it nice to make two different fillings. Roll each rectangle up, starting on a long side. Form the roll into a horseshoe, and place on a lightly greased baking sheet. Optional: brush with cream.

Bake at 375° F. for about 15 minutes or until the horseshoes are nicely browned.

Optional: Coat with a confectioners'-sugar-and-lemon-juice glaze, or sprinkle with confectioners' sugar.

Yield: 2 to 3 dozen horseshoes

Variations:
Instead of using the filling, you can brush with preserves (try apricot, with a little fresh orange rind).

THE FEAST OF ST. JOHN
December 27

St. John was a complex and fascinating saint: a simple fisherman and a deep theologian; one of the Sons of Thunder, with his brother James, but always stressing the love of God.

John is often considered to have been Jesus' favorite among the Apostles: he is called "the disciple whom Jesus loved." He was present with the three Marys at the Crucifixion (most of Jesus' other followers and disciples had fled), and it is of him that Jesus said to his mother as he was dying on the cross, "Woman, behold thy son!" and to John that Jesus said, "Behold thy Mother!" From then on, Mary is said to have lived under John's care.

According to Christian legend, John traveled around Judea with Peter, and then went on to Asia Minor, where he founded the Seven Churches referred to in the Revelation. Legend also has it that the Emperor Domitian twice attempted to kill him: once by ordering him to drink a cup of poisoned wine. St. John took and blessed the cup—and the poison slithered away in the form of a snake. Because of this legend, there is in many countries a tradition on the day of his feast: a blessing of wine, in his name. Often, a special wine is prepared. At the dinner on that day, the father blesses the cup, then each member of the family takes a drink, saying to the others, "I drink to you in the love of St. John." Even children get a little sip.

John is said to have died at Ephesus as a very old man, having written his great Gospel, three Epistles, and the Book of Revelation.

St. John's wine

This recipe is from The Catholic Cookbook, *by William Kaufman.*

1 quart red wine
3 whole cloves
$\frac{1}{16}$ teaspoon ground
   cardamom
2 two-inch cinnamon sticks
½ teaspoon ground nutmeg
½ cup sugar

Pour the wine into a large saucepan. Add the remaining ingredients. Boil for 5 minutes (after 5 minutes the alcohol is virtually all evaporated). Serve hot.

Yield: 8–10 servings

THE FEAST OF THE HOLY INNOCENTS
December 28

The little children who were killed by King Herod in his attempt to do away with the Infant Messiah have been honored from very early times as martyrs. They were, after all, the very first to die for Christ. On their feast day, it has long been customary to serve some kind of "baby food" (often a hot cereal, with sugar and cinnamon added), especially to the youngest members of the family, or of the monastery or convent. Another tradition is the eating of some sort of light-colored pudding with a red sauce (such as raspberry or strawberry). The sauce is a reminder of the blood of these tiny martyrs. Is this too gory for you? Perhaps—but your children might surprise you!

ST. SYLVESTER'S DAY
December 31

St. Sylvester, whose feast day is December 31 in the West (January 2 in the Eastern Orthodox churches), was the first Pope after the Church emerged from the catacombs. He became Pope in 314, the year after Christianity began to be tolerated (under the Emperor Constantine), and no longer cruelly persecuted. Hardly anything is known about Sylvester. He established the Lateran basilica as the cathedral church of Rome, and built a number of other early important churches. (There were no real church buildings before his day, as the church had to meet "underground.")

In Vienna, Krapfen, or apricot-jam-filled doughnuts, are traditional on his day; eaten at midnight on New Year's Eve, they are said to bring good luck. Try them with an equally traditional Sylvester's Punch from Poland, or with champagne, or with coffee or tea.

Doughnuts filled with apricot jam

KRAPFEN

Sprinkle the yeast into the milk. Stir in 2 teaspoons sugar and ⅔ cup flour, and set the mixture aside until frothy.

Pour the butter into a large bowl. Stir in the remaining sugar, mixing thoroughly until creamy. Cool to lukewarm. Stir in the egg

2 packages active dry yeast
1 cup lukewarm milk, 100–110° F.
½ cup sugar
3½ cups flour, approximately
4 tablespoons sweet butter, melted
6 egg yolks
Grated rind of 1 lemon
1 teaspoon salt
1 tablespoon rum (optional)
1 cup apricot jam, approximately
Vegetable oil for deep-fat frying
Confectioners' sugar (optional)

yolks, mixing well after each addition, and add the lemon rind and salt. Add the rum, if you like. Stir in the sponge. Gradually, and beating constantly, sift in enough of the remaining flour to make a soft but not sticky dough. Continue beating the dough with a wooden spoon until it is smooth, about 3 to 5 minutes. Place the dough in a greased bowl, turning it to grease the top. Cover. Let it rise until double in bulk.

Punch the dough down, and knead for a minute or two. Let it rise for 15 to 20 minutes.

Divide the dough in two. On a lightly floured surface roll half of the dough out to a rectangle ¼ inch thick. With the floured rim of a glass (such as a wine glass) 2½ inches in diameter, mark out a series of circles *on* (but do not cut *through*) the surface of the dough. (Make your rows as neat as possible; this will simplify things later.)

At the center of each circle, place a generous teaspoon of jam.

Roll out the other half of the dough to a ¼-inch-thick rectangle identical to the first, and place it on top. You will see the lumps where the jam is.

Centering yourself on the lumps of jam, press down with the wine glass, through both thicknesses of dough, to cut out the doughnuts. (The object of this complicated-sounding procedure is simply to seal the edges without deforming the doughnuts.) Cover lightly and let them rise for 15 minutes.

Heat the vegetable oil to 370° F. Cook the doughnuts, a few at a time, 1 to 1½ minutes on each side, or until golden brown on both sides.

Drain thoroughly on paper towels.

Optional: Sprinkle with confectioners' sugar.

Yield: about 2½ dozen doughnuts

Sylvester's punch

PONCZ SYLWESTROWY

2 oranges, grated rind and juice
2 lemons, grated rind and juice
Sugar to taste (about 1 cup)
4 cups white wine
2 cups light rum

Here is a delicious (and potent) punch from Poland to serve on St. Sylvester's day.

Grate the orange and lemon rinds. Combine with the sugar, wine, and rum in a large pan. Add the strained juices of the orange and lemon. Heat (do not boil). Serve hot.

Yield: about 16 one-half-cup servings

Note: You can dilute this punch with hot water, if you wish.

NEW YEAR'S DAY

Coventry God-cakes

In Coventry, in England, it was long a custom to visit one's godchild on New Year's Day, and to offer him or her a blessing and a delicious little pastry called a "God-cake." Such little cakes were triangular, in honor of the Trinity, and they were filled with sweet things as a sign of this special bond: currants, fruit peel, and spices.

Let's be lavish and take along a God-cake for each member of the godchild's family!

RICH SHORT CRUST:
2 cups flour
1 teaspoon salt
1 tablespoon confectioners' sugar (optional)
8 tablespoons sweet butter, cold, cut into small pieces
1 egg, lightly beaten
1 tablespoon milk or water

FILLING:
¼ cup sweet butter, at room temperature
¼ cup sugar
¾ cup dried currants
¼ cup candied lemon peel, finely chopped
Grated rind of ½ lemon
¼ teaspoon nutmeg, preferably freshly grated
½ teaspoon ground allspice

Combine the flour and salt in a mixing bowl. If you wish, stir in the sugar. Using the tips of your fingers or 2 knives, work in the butter until the mixture resembles coarse meal. Make a well and add the egg and milk. Mix briefly with a fork. Form the dough into a ball. Wrap it in plastic wrap and chill it in the refrigerator for at least ½ hour.

Preheat the oven to 425° F. Butter 2 baking sheets.

To make the filling: Cream the butter with the sugar until fluffy. Stir in the remaining ingredients, blending thoroughly.

On a lightly floured surface, roll the dough out thin. Cut into 4-inch squares. Reroll the scraps. Place 1 heaping teaspoon of filling near one corner of each square, leaving ½ inch of dough uncovered. Lightly moisten the edges of the pastry. Fold from corner to corner to make triangles. Seal the edges with your fingers, then with the tines of a fork.

Place the cakes on the baking sheets and bake for 10 to 15 minutes, or until golden brown.

Yield: 12 to 15 God-cakes

Note: This crust can be used for all pies, tarts, and turnovers.

For a prebaked pie shell: Line a pie or tart pan with the crust. Cut a piece of foil or waxed paper a little larger than the pan. Press it in place over the crust, extending up the sides. Fill it with beans or rice to weight it down. Bake at 400° F. for 10 minutes. Remove the beans and foil and bake at 375° for another 5 to 10 minutes, or until golden brown. Try filling the prebaked crust with French Pastry Cream (page 251) or whipped cream (sweetened with confectioners' sugar and flavored with vanilla extract or a liqueur), and lay fruit over the surface in an attractive pattern.

Variation:

You can also use puff pastry. If you do, try to roll out the dough only *once:* puff pastry does not lend itself to being rerolled.

ST. BASIL THE GREAT
January 1

On January 1, Eastern Orthodox Christians celebrate the feast of St. Basil the Great; he died on that date in 379 (in the West, he is honored on January 2). He was born in 329 in Cappadocia (Turkey, today), to an extraordinary family: his grandmother, both his parents, two brothers, and a sister are also honored as saints. Basil preached eloquently against the Arian heresy, which denied the divinity of Christ, and he is one of the "Doctors" (or teachers) who helped to formulate the doctrine of the Trinity. He is thus one of those early Christians who first gave expression to what C. S. Lewis has called "Mere Christianity": that core of Christian doctrine which is our common heritage, shared by all denominations.

Basil was also a great bishop, showing extreme courage when threatened with torture and death by the Roman emperor, an Arian. And he was a monk; indeed he is considered the father of Eastern monasticism. Always a man of deep charity, he worked for peace and unity in the Church. He founded a large hospital for the poor, and is considered by the Orthodox the patron of charity and philanthropy.

St. Basil's bread

VASILOPITA

In Greece, on St. Basil's day, the Orthodox bake a wonderful aromatic bread called Vasilopita, *"Basil's Bread." The bread is blessed and distributed by the head of the household. The first slice is dedicated to Christ, the second to the Virgin Mary, and the third to St. Basil. Then the family is served, starting with the eldest. A silver coin has been baked into the bread, and the person who finds it has a special blessing from St. Basil for the coming year. Two sprigs of herbs—one over the other to form a cross—are also often baked in the bread.*

This slightly sweet bread has the most delightful fragrance, and it makes a large and handsome loaf.

continued

St. Basil's bread, continued

½ cup water
¾ teaspoon cinnamon
½ teaspoon aniseeds
¾ teaspoon freshly grated
  orange peel
2 bay leaves
½ cup milk
¾ cup sugar
½ teaspoon salt
¾ cup butter, softened
½ cup warm water (about
  100–110° F.)
2 tablespoons sugar
2 packages yeast
3 eggs, lightly beaten
6–6½ cups sifted flour
Melted butter
1 egg yolk, lightly beaten
Sesame seeds
For decoration:
  Whole blanched almonds,
  walnut halves, and/or
  maraschino cherries

Heat ½ cup water to boiling. Stir in the cinnamon, aniseeds, orange peel, and bay leaves. Remove from heat and allow the flavorings to steep until needed.

Scald the milk. Stir in ¾ cup sugar, the salt, and ¾ cup butter. Let cool.

Pour the warm water into a large bowl. Stir in 2 tablespoons sugar and the yeast. Let stand until frothy, about 10 minutes.

Pour the milk-butter mixture into the yeast mixture. Add the lightly beaten eggs, and mix well. Then stir in the spice liquid, first removing the bay leaves. Stir in 3 cups of the flour, a little at a time. Beat until smooth. Slowly add the remaining 3–3½ cups of flour. Add only as much as necessary to make a smooth and nonsticky dough.

Turn out the dough onto a floured surface and knead for about 20 minutes, until it is smooth and elastic. Place the dough in a greased bowl. Brush the top with melted butter. Cover lightly, and allow it to rise in a draft-free place until doubled in bulk, approximately 2 hours.

Punch the dough down, and knead again briefly, about 5 minutes. Remove from the dough a piece about the size of an orange. Reserve. Form the rest of the dough into 1 large round loaf (or 2 smaller loaves), and insert a coin. Place the loaf on a lightly greased baking sheet.

Divide the reserved dough in four parts and form them into the numbers of the new year. Set them on the bread, pressing them down gently.

Cover lightly and allow the dough to rise again for about 1½ hours, or until almost doubled in bulk.

When the loaf has risen, brush with beaten egg yolk and sprinkle with sesame seeds. Decorate with blanched almonds, walnuts, and/or cherries. Bake at 350° F. for 45 to 60 minutes (small loaves will be done sooner). The bread is done when it is a deep golden brown, and the bottom sounds hollow when tapped.

Yield: 1 large loaf (about 15 inches across), or 2 smaller loaves

Variations:
For a more pronounced anise flavor, add 1 tablespoon ouzo, when the spice liquid is mixed with the dough.

Albanian pie

LAKROR

*In Albania, the Orthodox have traditionally baked a special pie,
or* Lakror, *in honor of St. Basil—with a coin hidden in it. This pie is
commonly made with a phyllo pastry, and with one of several
delicious fillings. Here is a* Lakror *with a meat filling. One of its
charms is that both adults and children love it.*

3 tablespoons butter
1 large onion, finely
  chopped
1½ pounds ground meat,
  preferably a mixture of
  lamb and beef
2 cloves garlic
1 teaspoon salt
2 teaspoons oregano
Freshly ground pepper to
  taste
½ cup chopped fresh
  parsley
½ cup cooked rice
6 eggs
1 pound phyllo dough
¼ pound sweet butter (more
  if necessary)

In a large frying pan, melt 3 tablespoons of butter, and sauté the
onion gently until translucent. Add the meat, garlic, salt, oregano,
and pepper. Sauté until the meat is nicely browned. Drain off the
fat. Taste for seasoning.

Mix the chopped parsley, the rice, and the eggs, then add
them to the meat. Mix thoroughly.

Lay out the phyllo dough on a large surface. *Keep it covered
with a piece of plastic wrap (or a moist towel) when you are not
working with it; it dries out very easily.*

Butter a 9-by-12-by-2-inch pan. Melt the rest of the butter.

Take 1 sheet of phyllo dough and cut it to fit your pan. You
are going to need 20 identical pieces, so you may wish to cut
them all at once. (Remember to *re-cover* the ones you aren't ready
to use yet.) Lay the first sheet in the pan, and brush it well with
melted butter. Repeat this step 10 times.

After the tenth layer, place the meat filling over the dough,
spreading it out evenly. Then place 10 more layers of phyllo
pastry over the meat, buttering each sheet well. Butter the last
sheet especially well, and seal the edges by pressing down firmly
with your fingers.

With a sharp knife, and an up-and-down motion, score the
surface of the *Lakror,* making a pattern of squares or diamonds:
this will make it easier to serve later. You do not need to cut all
the way through to the pan, just cut through several of the top
layers.

Bake at 375° F. for about 45 minutes, or until golden brown.
This dish freezes and reheats very well.

Yield: 6 to 8 servings

EPIPHANY/TWELFTH NIGHT

The Feast of the Epiphany, also called the Feast of Kings, Twelfth Night, or the Last Day of Christmas, originated in Egypt during the course of the third century. Thus it is a more ancient feast than Christmas Day itself. Like Christmas, it was apparently established to compete with a pagan festival, in honor of the Egyptian sun god, celebrated at the winter solstice. The Christians began to observe a feast to honor the manifestation, or *epiphaneia*, of the true Savior; it celebrated not only Christ's birth but also the visit and adoration of the Magi, and soon it commemorated Christ's baptism in the River Jordan as a third important manifestation of Christ's divinity. This feast spread to the Western Church in the fourth century, at about the same time that Christmas—as the feast of Christ's nativity—was also becoming established.

It is still celebrated with the greatest solemnity in the Orthodox world. Specially blessed holy water is sprinkled in each room in the house, and after fasting, each person drinks some of the water. In many countries of the West as well, Epiphany has traditionally been a very important feast, with many lovely customs. Among the Spanish there are religious processions. In several Hispanic cultures toys for children are left in wooden shoes supposedly by Befana—an old lady whose name is a corruption of the word "Epiphany." (In Spain, Christmas is celebrated more quietly, and its observance is strictly religious.)

In England, Twelfth Night was traditionally celebrated with a delicious drink called Lamb's Wool, made of cider or ale, with roasted apples and sugar and spices. It was the custom to bless apple trees that night by pouring a libation of cider on them.

A common custom, in many cultures, is the baking of a cake containing a trinket or bean, the person who finds it in his piece becoming the king of the feast. Sometimes there are two trinkets, or one bean and one pea: one for a king and one for a queen. In the royal courts of the later Middle Ages, these customs were very popular; they derived from customs of the Roman Saturnalia, which fell at around the same time as Christmas. The Roman theme of the lordship of the feast was easily shifted to the Epiphany theme of kingship: that of Christ himself and of the Magi.

A very special Epiphany cake

This Epiphany cake, simple as it is to make, is unforgettable to children, and it brings home to them the meaning of Epiphany. In this cake, which looks studded with jewels like a crown, they can understand Epiphany as the recognition, by the Magi, of the Infant Jesus as Christ the King.

A couple of silver coins, or little trinkets, are baked into the cake. The children who get the coins are then king and queen for the next twenty-four hours. (If yours is a store-bought cake, you could make little slits in the icing before decorating the cake, and carefully insert coins.)

1 cake, homemade or store-bought

White icing, homemade or store-bought. You may wish to tint the icing yellow to suggest the gold of the crown. Use yellow (plus a drop or two of red) food coloring.

Lots of multicolored gumdrops, jelly beans, chocolate kisses, gold and silver balls—whatever your children like to use for decoration

Before baking the cake, drop two silver coins or beans, or two objects that won't melt, into the mixture in different parts of the baking pans.

After baking, and completely cooling, the cake, cover it with the icing. Then you can either decorate it yourself or you can let your children decorate it, trying to make the cake look like a crown. Letting *them* do it is of course more fun for them—and a lot more meaningful. (And what are a few gray hairs!) If there are enough children so that competition is a problem, or there are divergent ideas about what a crown should look like, you can always make cupcakes instead, and have each child decorate a small crown. In this case, just slip the coins into two of the muffin cups.

Parisian kings' cake

GALETTE DES ROIS

1 cup finely ground blanched almonds

2⅓ cups sifted flour

½ teaspoon salt

½ cup sugar

4 egg yolks

8 tablespoons butter, cut into little pieces

About 6 tablespoons cold water

1 egg yolk, lightly beaten with a little water

Mix the almonds thoroughly with the flour; mix in the salt and sugar. Add the egg yolks, the butter, and water as needed to make a firm dough. Work the paste gently with your fingertips. Form it into a ball, and let it rest in the refrigerator for about 1 hour.

Preheat the oven to 425° F. Lightly grease a baking sheet.

On a lightly floured surface, roll the paste out into a *galette* (a circle about ¾ inch thick). Insert a bean in the bottom surface of the *galette.* Cut the edges with a knife to make a perfect circle, with straight sides. With a sharp knife decorate the top with lozenge-shaped cuts or arabesques.

Place the *galette* on the baking sheet. Brush with egg yolk, lightly beaten with a little water.

Bake for 25 to 30 minutes, or until the *galette* is golden brown.

Spanish kings' bread

ROSCÓN DE REYES

This recipe is reprinted from Penelope Casas' The Foods and Wines of Spain.

1 package dry yeast
¾ cup warm water (100–110° F.)
1 tablespoon orange-flower water or strong tea
½ teaspoon grated lemon rind
6 cloves
¼ pound butter
1 tablespoon lard or vegetable shortening
½ cup sugar
½ teaspoon salt
2 eggs
1 tablespoon brandy (preferably Spanish) or cognac
½ cup milk, scalded and cooled
5 cups unbleached flour
Candied fruit slices
1 egg, lightly beaten
1½ tablespoons sugar, preferably coarse

Dissolve the yeast in ¼ cup of the warm water. Simmer the remaining ½ cup of warm water with the orange-flower water or tea, lemon rind, and cloves for 10 minutes, covered. Cool. Discard the cloves.

Cream together the butter, lard, sugar, and salt. Beat in the 2 eggs, then add the brandy, milk, the water-and-lemon mixture, and the softened yeast. Gradually mix in the flour with a wooden spoon until a soft and slightly sticky dough is obtained. Knead on a floured working surface, adding more flour as needed, about 4 minutes, until smooth and elastic. Place the dough in a large oiled bowl, turn to coat with the oil, cover with a towel, and place in a warm spot, such as an unlit oven, to double in size, about 2 hours.

Punch down the dough and knead about 5 minutes. Insert a good-luck coin—perhaps a silver dollar or half dollar—or some other appropriate object, such as a miniature ceramic animal.

Shape the dough into a large ring, pinching the ends to seal. Place on a lightly greased cookie sheet. Decorate with the fruit slices, pushing them slightly into the dough. Let the ring rise in a warm spot about 1 hour, or until doubled in size. Brush with the egg, which has been mixed with a teaspoon of water, sprinkle with sugar, and bake in a 350° F. oven for 35 to 40 minutes, or until a deep golden brown.

Yield: 1 large bread ring

Variations:

A very similar bread is made in various parts of southern France, such as Bordeaux. It is often called a "crown" for this Feast of Kings. It is decorated with candied citron, rather than with the fruit slices.

Lamb's wool

This Old English and Irish punch, which dates from the Middle Ages, probably gets its name from the whiteness of the flesh of the roasted apples as they float in the cider.

6 baking apples, cored
2 tablespoons to ½ cup
  brown sugar
2 quarts sweet cider, or
  hard cider, or ale—or a
  mixture of cider and ale
⅛ teaspoon nutmeg
¼ teaspoon cinnamon
¼ teaspoon ground ginger

Roast the apples in a baking pan at 450° F. for about an hour, or until they are very soft and begin to burst. (An alternative—and quicker—procedure is to peel and boil the apples until they are very soft and flaky.) You may leave the apples whole, or break them up.

In a large saucepan, dissolve the sugar a few tablespoons at a time in the cider or ale, tasting for sweetness. Add the spices. Bring to a boil and simmer for 10 to 15 minutes. Pour the liquid over the apples in a large punch bowl, or serve in large heat-resistant mugs.

Yield: About 8 one-cup servings

Nuts make a nice accompaniment to Lamb's Wool (they were originally roasted in with the apples).

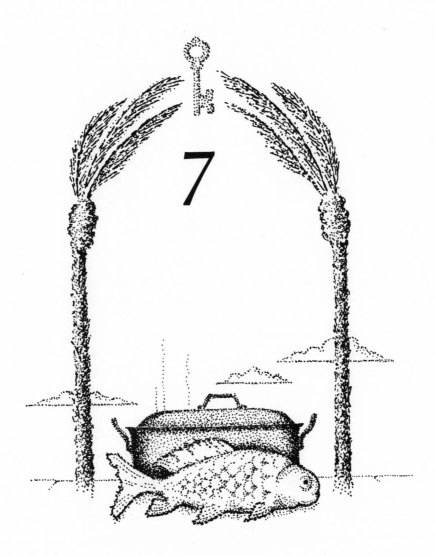

7

Lent

The very early Christians commemorated the hours Christ suffered on the cross and the days he lay in the tomb: from Good Friday morning until Easter morning every year they prayed and fasted—a total fast. This was called the Passion Fast.

Little by little this period started earlier and the severity of the fast mitigated. At first it went through Holy Week, then eventually by the third century it lasted for forty days—a commemoration of Christ's forty days of fasting and temptation in the desert. (Moses had also spent forty days in fasting and prayer on Mount Horeb.)

The character of this season also evolved somewhat in emphasis. Originally, it had focused exclusively on the Passion and on Christians' reliving of this sorrow. (This is still the essential focus of Holy Week.) But, as the duration of the period was extended, a theme of sorrow for sin, of repentance, developed. Lent became what is called a penitential season.

Fasting has been, since the beginning, an intrinsic part of Lenten penance, though not of course the only important element. The wearing of "sackcloth and ashes," as in the Jewish tradition, the turning away from all pleasures, culinary and otherwise: this is what Lent means.

Fasting is a voluntary abstinence from food, with a moral or religious end in view.

Although fasting is contrary to one of our natural inclinations, or rather one of our most habitual needs, it is nevertheless a custom of the greatest antiquity.

Brillat-Savarin, *The Philosopher in the Kitchen*

Lenten fasting has involved two things historically: a reduction in the amount of food eaten (meals often being taken later in the day as well) and a change in diet. In the West, from at least the seventh century on, Roman Catholics were to eat no meat, no dairy products, no eggs in Lent. (Only the prohibition against meat is today officially binding, and only on Ash Wednesday and Good Friday.) Among the Eastern Orthodox groups, fasting practices have always been, and still are, markedly more austere: not only no meat or dairy products but also no fish (except shellfish), no wine or olive oil during most of the days in Lent. Among the Orthodox, Lent is called "the Great Fast." (Christians in the Protestant traditions generally moved away quite soon after the Reformation from all Lenten fasting.)

The particular foods given up were—obviously—not forgone because they were considered evil: after all, Christians ate them happily, indeed voraciously, the rest of the year. The giving up of flesh and of foods that come from flesh (dairy products, eggs) is a symbolic renunciation of the world, and a giving up of one whole set of particularly vivid culinary pleasures during this period of prayer and turning to God.

Lenten practices and restrictions have given rise over the centuries to many dishes, necessity being the mother of invention. Almond milk replaced cow's milk. Thick soups and hearty vegetables replaced meat. Fish was of course a favorite, though those who could not afford fresh fish got awfully tired of salted herring: the herring was one of the symbols or emblems of Lent. And when, as Easter approached, Lent was hung or burned in effigy, it was often in the form of a huge herring.

There is a good deal of old Lenten culinary humor. In Italy they make an elaborate dish composed of many kinds of fish called a *cappon magro*: a fast-day (or scrawny) capon. There are jokes about chickens and rabbits being dipped in water and "rebaptized" as fish. But, although people grumbled and moaned, especially toward the end of Lent, and dreamed of eggs and meat, since everyone else was fasting too, and since the forbidden foodstuffs were hardly even made available during Lent, for centuries people did it: they kept Lenten abstinence from Ash Wednesday through Holy Saturday. Though in recent years there has been a marked reduction in Lenten observance, many Christians still find it essential to their spiritual lives to abstain from certain foods, to fast, often to practice other forms of self-denial as well in Lent.

A LENTEN SAMPLER

Italian bean and vegetable soup

MINESTRONE DI MAGRO

Practically every town and many a family in Italy has its own minestrone; the variations on this basic soup are endless. During Lent, minestrone is made di magro—*meatless—that is, without the bacon or ham or tiny meatballs that would otherwise be added. But these soups don't need meat to be rich and interesting: the variety of beans and vegetables, and often pasta, makes them a wonderful first course or even main dish, when served with good crusty Italian bread and cheese.*

2 cups dried beans (white, red kidney, or pinto)
2 quarts water
1 tablespoon olive oil
1 clove garlic
½ cup olive oil
1 onion, chopped
2 cloves garlic, minced
2 stalks of celery, chopped
2 carrots, sliced
2 potatoes, diced
5 large tomatoes, peeled and chopped, or 5 canned Italian plum tomatoes, drained, chopped, or 5 teaspoons tomato paste
1 tablespoon fresh parsley, chopped
1 teaspoon basil, rosemary, or borage
1 clove
¼–½ head green or Savoy cabbage, finely shredded
1–2 cups fresh spinach, chopped
Salt and freshly ground pepper to taste
Optional:
½ cup pasta, any variety
Large croûtes (recipe below) and/or grated Parmesan cheese

Wash and pick over the beans; remove any pebbles. Cover with warm water and soak overnight.

Rinse the presoaked beans. Cook them in 2 quarts of water, to which you have added 1 tablespoon olive oil and 1 clove garlic, for 1 to 2 hours, or until tender. Optional: purée half or more of the beans (in a blender or with a potato masher). Set aside.

In a large soup pot, heat ½ cup olive oil. Sauté the onion, minced garlic, celery, and carrots, until they are translucent and begin to brown. Add the beans and their cooking liquid, the potatoes, tomatoes (or tomato paste), parsley, basil, clove, cabbage, and spinach. Add salt and pepper to taste. If the soup seems too thick, add more water.

Cover and simmer for 15 minutes. Add the pasta, if you wish, and cook for another 15 minutes. If using long pieces of pasta, break into shorter lengths before adding to water.

This soup is often served with large croûtes (especially if no pasta has been added) and/or sprinkled with Parmesan cheese.

Yield: 6 to 8 servings

Variations:

They are practically infinite, and all delicious, but here are a few basic ideas. Decide whether you want an extremely varied soup—in terms of textures, colors, tastes—or a simpler, more homogeneous soup. If today you wish a rich, varied, exciting soup, full of contrasts, you might like to:

Combine two (or more) kinds or colors of beans. (Cook each kind separately, however, as different varieties of beans cook at different rates.)

Add a wider variety of extra vegetables: 2 or 3 zucchini, chopped; ½ head red cabbage, finely shredded; 1 or 2 leeks, carefully washed and chopped; a cup or two of Swiss chard, chopped; some fresh (or frozen) peas. (If you add this many vegetables, you will need to increase the amount of water, and you will be increasing the number of servings produced.)

Increase the spices: for example, add more basil, or add a little marjoram. Add more garlic.

If you prefer a simpler, "quieter" and, as it were, more meditative soup:

Stick with white beans, and aside from the tomatoes or tomato paste, use just a few vegetables: potatoes, cabbage . . .

Purée part of the beans.

You might also like to substitute rice (a classic variation) for the pasta.

One last variation:

In Genoa, they make one of my very favorite soups, a minestrone based on white beans, to which they add, just before serving, 5 to 6 teaspoons of Pesto. Pesto—made of fresh basil leaves, nuts, olive oil, and Parmesan cheese—adds a wonderful bite to the soup; I recommend it highly, and provide a recipe on page 266.

CROÛTES

1 loaf Italian bread, preferably slightly stale
Olive oil

Preheat the oven to 400° F.

Slice the bread into ½-inch slices. Cut off the crusts. Brush with olive oil.

Place the slices on a baking sheet and bake for approximately 5 to 8 minutes on each side, or until golden brown.

Variations:

Use butter instead of olive oil, though this is of course more French than Italian. Rub the croûtes with a peeled clove of garlic, for a little added flavor. For smaller croûtes—croutons—just cube the slices of bread, and proceed with the recipe.

When you fast, do not look somber as the hypocrites do, for they disfigure their faces to show men they are fasting. I tell you the truth, they have received their reward in full. But when you fast, put oil on your head and wash your face, so that it will not be obvious to men that you are fasting, but only to your Father, who is unseen; and your Father, who sees what is done in secret, will reward you.

Matthew 6:16–18 (NIV)

French onion soup for Lent
SOUPE À L'OIGNON GRATINÉ, AU MAIGRE

Traditionally, French family cookbooks—such as the Livre de Cuisine de Tante Marie (Aunt Mary's Cookbook)—*provided not only recipes but also menus, for each of the months of the year. Each of these sets of menus was divided into two groups:* maigre *and* gras. Maigre, *which literally means "skinny," having no fat, also refers to dishes that contain no meat or meat stock; these were the abstinence dishes, served on Fridays and during Lent. (*Gras *means fat, meaty.)*

This hearty soup is typical of French maigre *fare (at other times it is often made with beef or chicken stock). With crusty French bread or thick* croûtes, *a salad, and some fruit, it makes a whole meal.*

4 tablespoons butter
1 tablespoon olive oil
6 cups thinly sliced yellow onions
Salt
1 teaspoon sugar
3 tablespoons flour
2 quarts water
1 cup red wine
1 bay leaf
Freshly ground pepper to taste
1 loaf of French bread
Olive oil or melted butter
¼ cup grated Parmesan cheese
About 6 very thin *slices of Swiss cheese*

Melt 3 tablespoons of butter and 1 tablespoon oil in a large, heavy saucepan. Add the sliced onions and coat them well with the fat. Cover the pan, and cook the onions over fairly low heat for about 20 minutes, stirring occasionally, until they are soft and translucent. Uncover the pan and raise the heat to moderately high. Stir in 1 teaspoon salt and the sugar (to help brown the onions). Cook for 20 to 25 minutes, stirring frequently, until the onions are golden brown.

Lower the heat. Stir in the flour and 1 more tablespoon butter. Cook slowly, stirring, for 2 to 3 minutes to brown the flour. Remove from the heat. Add the water and the wine, a little at a time, blending them with the onion mixture. Add the bay leaf. Simmer partly covered for about 30 minutes. Season to taste with additional salt and pepper.

Prepare large *croûtes* from the French bread and some of the oil or butter (see page 173).

Pour the soup into a large casserole or into 4 to 6 individual bowls. (They must be ovenproof.) Sprinkle a little of the grated cheese over the soup. Place a layer of *croûtes* over the surface of the casserole (or bowls). Then lay the thin slices of Swiss cheese over the surface. Spread the rest of the Parmesan on top. Sprinkle with a little oil or melted butter. Set the casserole (or bowls) in the oven, at 350° F., for about 20 minutes, or until the cheese has melted.

Run the casserole (or bowls) briefly under the broiler to lightly brown the top.

Yield: 4 to 6 servings

Rumanian Lenten eggplant

What is Lenten about this dish is that it is neither stuffed with meat nor cooked in butter—two common preparations for eggplant in Rumanian cuisine. Elimination of butter from the Lenten diet is characteristic of Eastern European Christians, especially Orthodox but also some Roman Catholics as well. Eastern Orthodox cooks would also replace the olive oil in this recipe with some other oil.

Lenten though it may be, this is a delicious dish—a cousin to the Italian caponata. *Served hot or cold, it makes a fine side dish. It can also be served hot as a main dish, with cornbread (which in Rumanian is called* mamaliga*), or with a crusty wheat bread and cheese and a salad. After all, one of the ideas of Lent is not just to avoid meat, but to eat less, and more simply.*

2 large eggplants
Salt
½ cup olive oil or vegetable oil
2 large onions, chopped
2 leeks or 8–10 scallions, finely chopped
2 large tomatoes, coarsely chopped (or 2½ cups canned plum tomatoes, drained, chopped)
2 tablespoons dill weed
Freshly ground pepper
1 tablespoon flour
½ cup parsley, finely chopped
8–12 black olives, preferably oil-cured

Cut the eggplants into ½-inch cubes. Set the cubes in a large colander and sprinkle them generously with salt. Allow them to drain in the sink or over paper towels for 20 to 30 minutes. Pat the cubes dry and set aside.

In a large frying pan heat a few tablespoons of oil. Stir in the onions and leeks (or scallions) and sauté them gently for about 8 minutes, until they are soft, transparent, and lightly browned. Remove them from the pan and reserve.

Heat the rest of the oil in the skillet and sauté the eggplant cubes over high heat, turning them frequently, until they are nicely browned. Return the onions and leeks to the skillet, add the tomatoes, dill weed, salt and pepper to taste. Cover and simmer for 8 to 10 minutes.

Sprinkle the flour over the mixture, and stir in the parsley and olives. If the pan seems too dry, add a little water. Simmer gently, uncovered, for 3 to 5 minutes.

Taste for seasoning.

Yield: 4 to 6 servings as a main dish; 8 or more as a side dish

Variations:

Not so Rumanian, but delicious: add 1 to 2 tablespoons capers; 2–4 anchovy fillets; 1–2 tablespoons pine nuts.

---

*. . . dust you are
and to dust you will return.*

Genesis 3:19 (NIV)

Polish Lenten mushroom "cutlets"

KOTLETY Z GRYZBÓW

This is one of a number of amusing Lenten dishes in which a non-meat item—in this case, mushrooms—is made to resemble meat, to console Lenten fasters. And they are properly consoled: this "cutlet," served with buttered noodles and a salad, makes an excellent main dish.

1 pound fresh mushrooms
1 cup chopped onions
3 tablespoons butter
2 or 3 hard rolls, cubed
  (about 2 cups)
½ cup milk
3 eggs, lightly beaten
2 tablespoons chopped
  parsley
½ teaspoon salt
Freshly ground pepper to
  taste
½ cup breadcrumbs, more if
  needed
Butter as needed for
  sautéing the cutlets

Chop the mushrooms. In a large frying pan, sauté them with the onions in 3 tablespoons of butter.

Soak the cubed hard rolls in milk for about 10 minutes. Add to the mushroom-onion mixture. Blend in the eggs, parsley, salt, and pepper.

Form the mixture into cutlet-shaped patties; each patty should take 3 to 4 tablespoons of the mixture. Press the patties onto the breadcrumbs.

Fry in butter until crisp and brown on both sides.

Yield: about 14 "cutlets"

Variation:

You can substitute dried mushrooms for part or all of the fresh mushrooms. They are a favorite among the Polish for their rich and interesting flavor. Just a few ounces of dried mushrooms, simmered in hot water until tender, add an interesting flavor to this popular dish.

Armenian stuffed trout

The association between Lent and fish goes far back in Armenia— at the very least to the thirteenth century, when the extraordinary Marco Polo, who traveled from Italy to China, relates:

There is a monastery here (in Armenia) called St. Leonard's, notable for the following miraculous occurrence. You must know that there is a great lake formed of water that issues from a mountain just beside the church of St. Leonard. And in this water no fish is found, big or little, at any season of the year, except that they begin to appear on the first day of Lent and continue every day throughout Lent till Holy Saturday, that is, the eve of Easter. During all this period there are fish in plenty; but at every other season there is not one to be found.

This is one of the traditional Armenian Lenten dishes, served for special company.

5 tablespoons olive oil
1 cup finely chopped onions
¼ cup pine nuts
1 cup cooked rice
½ cup chopped parsley
¼ cup minced dill or 2
   teaspoons dried dill weed
Salt and freshly ground
   pepper to taste
Grated rind of 1 lemon
5 good-sized brook trout,
   cleaned, dressed (heads
   left on)
Juice of 1 lemon

Heat the olive oil in a large skillet. Sauté the onions gently for about 5 minutes, or until soft and translucent. Add the pine nuts and sauté until they are golden, turning often.

Blend in the cooked rice, parsley, dill, salt, pepper, and lemon rind. Stuff the fish with the mixture. Close the fish with skewers, or sew them shut.

Lay the fish in a large oiled pan. Sprinkle them with salt and squeeze over them the lemon juice. Bake at 350° F. for about 20 minutes, or until the fish flakes easily. Garnish them with lemon wedges.

Yield: 5 servings

Variations:

My friend Alice Antreassian, in her marvelous *Armenian Cooking Today*, provides a somewhat similar recipe, but she uses 1 large fish (such as a 4-pound snapper or striped bass) rather than the trout. Rather than rice she uses 1 cup packaged bread stuffing. And she adds to the stuffing ¼ teaspoon allspice and ¼ cup currants. There is lots of room for "play" here; for example, the currants could be an addition to the rice stuffing. And her stuffing could as easily be used in trout, mine in larger fish.

Dough for a 9-inch pie-
   crust
1¼ pound salmon, cod, or
   haddock (or a mixture)
2 tablespoons lemon juice
2 tablespoons butter
2 pears, peeled, cored, and
   thinly sliced
2 apples, peeled, cored, and
   thinly sliced
1 cup good white wine
2 tablespoons lemon juice
2 tablespoons brown sugar
5 cubebs, finely crushed (see
   Note)
⅛ teaspoon ground cloves
⅛ teaspoon nutmeg
¼ teaspoon cinnamon
½ cup raisins
10 prunes, pitted and
   minced
6 dates, minced
6 dried figs, minced
3 tablespoons damson or
   red currant jelly

A medieval Lenten tart

TART DE BRYMLENT

One of the earliest collections of recipes that we have from England is entitled Forme of Cury *(that is, Manner of Cookery). It was written around 1390, for King Richard II.*

Here, then, is a medieval English Lenten dish from this old cookbook. (It has been nicely adapted for modern cooks by Lorna J. Sass, in To the King's Taste.)

This dish is typically medieval in its strong use of spices and in its surprising combination of fish with fruit. Although it may sound peculiar, it is really, believe me, very good. And the combination of colors is very attractive.

Preheat the oven to 425° F. and bake the pie crust for 10 minutes. Let cool.

Cut the fish into 1½-inch chunks, salt lightly, and sprinkle with 2 tablespoons lemon juice. Set aside.

Melt the butter in a large, heavy skillet and toss the pear and apple slices in it until they are lightly coated.

Combine the wine, lemon juice, brown sugar, spices, and dried fruits, and add to the mixture in the skillet. Cover and simmer about 15 minutes, or until the fresh fruit is soft but still firm. Check the flavoring, and drain off excess liquid.

Paint jelly on the pie crust. Combine fish chunks with fruits and place the mixture in the crust. Bake at 375° F. for 15 to 25 minutes, or until the fish flakes easily.

Yield: 6 to 8 servings

Note: The cubeb, an aromatic pepper commonly used in medieval times, can still be bought in many spice stores.

FILLING:
6½- or 7-ounce can tuna, preferably packed in olive oil
2–3 tablespoons peeled green chilies, chopped
2 tablespoons wine vinegar

TOPPING (any or all of these):
Chopped cucumber
Wedges of avocado
Chopped tomato
Shredded lettuce
Mexican Tomato Sauce (see below), or use store-bought taco sauce

Lenten tacos or tostadas

TACOS, TOSTADAS DI VIGILIA

Both tacos and tostadas are prepared for Lent in the ways described below. (They might also be eaten on Fridays: the term vigilia *in Spanish refers to meatless days—days of "vigil"—in general.)*

Flake the tuna into a bowl, mixing in the olive oil as well. (If your tuna is packed in water, drain it carefully, and when you flake the tuna into the bowl, add 1 tablespoon olive oil.)

Add the chilies and vinegar.

Serve on tostadas, or in tacos, with various toppings.

Yield: 6 tacos or tostadas

1 medium tomato, unpeeled, chopped
½ medium onion, chopped
2 canned serrano chilies, or other fresh hot chilies, chopped
Salt to taste (about ½ teaspoon)
Pinch of sugar
1–2 tablespoons chopped fresh green coriander (cilantro)
Optional:
Few tablespoons cold water

MEXICAN TOMATO SAUCE

SALSA CRUDA

Mix all the ingredients in a blender until well mixed, but not too smooth. Serve as soon as possible: this sauce is best when very fresh.

Yield: about 1¼ cups sauce

Maltese almond cakes

KWARESIMAL FOR LENT

This is a traditional and quintessentially Lenten treat, particularly in Malta, and Italy as well. (In Italy, they are called Quaresimali; both names derive from the Latin Quadragesima, *"Lent.") The idea was to make a delicious sweetmeat that contained neither butter nor eggs, both of which were given up for Lent. The result is a nutty, citrus-flavored sort of cookie (or sliced loaf) with an unforgettable flavor and an attractive chewy texture. This recipe is adapted from* Recipes from Malta *(by Anne and Helen C. Galizia).*

10 ounces (1⅛ cups) slivered blanched almonds
3½ cups flour, sifted
1½ to 1¾ cups sugar
1 teaspoon cinnamon
2 teaspoons orange extract
Grated rind of 2 lemons
Grated rind of 2 tangerines or 2 oranges
Approximately 1½ cups water
Optional:
Honey and toasted slivered almonds

Toast the almonds on a baking sheet for about 5 minutes at 400° F. Reset the oven for 350°. Grind one-third of the almonds.

Mix the ground almonds with the flour, sugar, and cinnamon. Add the orange extract and the rinds. Mix well. Blend in the slivered almonds. Gradually, add enough water to make a stiff dough (the dough will be sticky). Form the dough into cakes about 7 inches long, 2 inches wide, and 1 inch thick.

Bake for 35 minutes.

Optional: While they are still hot, brush the Kwaresimal with honey, and sprinkle with slivered toasted almonds.

Let the cakes cool for about 20 minutes, then with a serrated knife cut them into slices about ⅜ inch thick.

Yield: about 60 slices

Variations:
Here are a few of the classic variations:
Hazelnuts can be substituted for the almonds.
You can if you prefer grind all of the nuts, or fewer of them. You can also insert some whole blanched almonds. Remember that the more nuts you grind to powder, the more liquid you will need to make the dough; and the fewer nuts you grind, the less liquid.

In Malta these cakes would often be made with orange-flower water, which is hard to obtain here. Orange extract or liqueur (or other liqueur, or rum) can be used as part of the liquid.

Fasting is one of the wings of prayer.

St. Augustine

Pretzels

The pretzel is a very ancient bakery item, which traditionally was eaten only during Lent. It appeared each year on Ash Wednesday and disappeared on Good Friday. It goes back at least to the fifth century: there is a Roman manuscript in the Vatican Library dating from that period which shows a Lenten pretzel. As to the shape: it is made in the form of two arms crossed in prayer. The word bracellae, *"little arms," became in German* Bretzel, *then* Pretzel. *These early Christians ate no dairy products in Lent, so the pretzel was made only of flour, salt, and water: it was as simple as it could be.*

1 tablespoon honey or sugar
1½ cups lukewarm water (100–110° F.)
1 envelope active dry yeast
1 teaspoon salt
4 cups flour
Coarse or kosher salt
1 egg, beaten

Add the honey to the water; sprinkle in the yeast and stir until dissolved. Add 1 teaspoon salt. Blend in the flour, and knead the dough until smooth.

Cut the dough into pieces. Roll them into ropes and twist into pretzel shapes. You can make small pretzels with thin ropes, or large ones with fat ropes, but remember that to cook at the same rate, your pretzels need to be all the same size.

Place the pretzels on lightly greased cookie sheets. Brush them with beaten egg. Sprinkle with coarse salt.

Bake at 425° F. for 12 to 15 minutes, until the pretzels are golden brown.

A BIBLICAL DINNER

No recipes have come down to us from the time of Christ. But we do know what raw materials were available to the Jews of Palestine in that period, and we know what cooking methods were used. And of course there are many references to food and to various dishes in the Bible itself. So here are a menu and some recipes that are, I think, quite authentic versions of the food that Jesus and his followers would have eaten. This is a sort of Lenten culinary pilgrimage to the Holy Land at the time of Christ.

MENU
Broiled Fish, Biblical Style
Lentils with Cumin and Coriander
Cucumbers with Cumin and Yogurt
Wheat and Barley Loaves, Flavored with Mint and Olive Oil
Biblical "Fruitcakes"

Broiled fish, biblical style

St. John's Gospel closes with the wonderful story of how the Apostles are out fishing on the Sea of Tiberias—and catching nothing. All of a sudden Jesus—the Risen Jesus—is standing on the beach, but his disciples don't recognize him. He calls out, "Friends, haven't you any fish?" When they answer no, he says, "Throw your net on the right side of the boat and you will find some." (John 21:5, 6, NIV.) They do, and pull in an incredible load of fish. At this point John recognizes Jesus, then Peter, who jumps into the sea and swims toward Him.

Jesus had some bread, and had prepared a charcoal fire. He said to his disciples as they came ashore, "Come and have breakfast," and he cooked them a breakfast of fresh fish on the beach.

2 pounds fresh or defrosted fish: any small fish, fish fillets, fish steaks, or larger fish, split
Salt
4 cloves garlic, chopped
Olive oil
Red wine vinegar or lemon juice (see Note)
Lettuce
Greek olives or other strongly flavored olives
Optional:
½ cup chopped fresh mint leaves

Clean, rinse, and salt the fish. Rub with garlic, and brush with oil.

Preheat the broiler. Place the fish in an oiled pan. Broil small fish about 3 inches from the flame, larger fish about 5 inches away. Broil split fish skin side down. During the cooking, baste generously with olive oil and a little vinegar or lemon juice.

Serve the fish on a bed of lettuce, surrounded by Greek olives. Sprinkle with mint leaves, if you wish.

Yield: 4 to 6 servings

Note: The lemon juice is less authentic than the vinegar. Lemons were rare and expensive at the time of Christ, and verjuice (the juice of sour grapes or other sour fruit) or vinegar provided tartness where this was desired. So do whichever you prefer—but I do find the vinegar very tasty on this broiled fish.

Cucumbers with cumin and yogurt

Cucumbers were always a favorite (the Hebrews had missed them and onions terribly while they were in the wilderness: Numbers 11:5). Our yogurt is presumably a first cousin to the forms of curdled milk they used.

2 cucumbers, peeled and grated
1 medium onion, finely chopped
1 teaspoon cumin seed, heated briefly in a dry skillet, or 1 teaspoon ground cumin
3 cups plain yogurt, lightly whipped
Salt to taste
Freshly ground pepper to taste

Combine all ingredients and chill for 1 hour or more.

Yield: 6 to 8 servings

Lentils with cumin and coriander

It was for a dish probably quite like this one that Esau sold his birthright (Genesis 25). Lentils, especially strongly spiced, were a popular dish at the time of Christ.

1 cup dried lentils
5 cups water
2 medium onions, chopped
2 cloves garlic, chopped
¼ cup olive oil
1 teaspoon ground cumin
1 teaspoon ground coriander
½ teaspoon salt
Freshly ground pepper

Rinse the lentils and carefully pick over to remove any pebbles.

Bring 5 cups of water to a boil in a large saucepan. Add lentils, and boil for 2 minutes, then remove them from the heat and set aside for 1 hour.

In the meantime, sauté onions and garlic in olive oil. When the lentils have soaked for 1 hour, add the onions, garlic, cumin, and coriander to the pan with the lentils.

Cook, partly covered, for 1 hour or more, stirring occasionally, until the lentils are quite soft and the water is mostly absorbed. Add more water if necessary to keep the dish from drying out too much, but the mixture should be very thick.

Add salt and freshly ground pepper; taste for seasoning.

Yield: 4 to 6 servings

Variations:

Leftover meat, especially lamb, cut into small pieces, can be added to this dish. Even the ancient Hebrews had leftovers!

Wheat and barley loaves

Barley was, at the time of Christ—and indeed always has been—the grain of the poor. The loaves that Christ multiplied, along with the fishes, were barley loaves. So here is a bread recipe that calls for part barley flour. If the bread were made entirely of barley flour, it would hardly rise at all: barley is essentially unleavenable, hence its lack of popularity. But I think you will find that the taste in bread is very pleasant and interesting. The Jews at the time of Christ flavored their bread with spices such as mint (used here), or cinnamon, or coriander.

1 teaspoon honey
2 cups warm water
   (100–110° F.)
1 envelope dry yeast
1 cup barley flour
2 teaspoons salt
About 5 cups flour
¼ cup olive oil
2–3 teaspoons crushed dried
   mint leaves

Mix the honey with the water in a large bowl. Sprinkle in the yeast and let sit until foamy.

Stir in the barley flour and the salt. Gradually add the all-purpose flour, mixing well between additions. Add the olive oil and the mint. Mix thoroughly.

Place the dough on a lightly floured work surface. Knead it for about 15 minutes, or until it is shiny and elastic. Add more flour, while you are kneading, if the dough is too sticky.

Form the dough into a ball, and place it in a greased bowl. Cover with oiled wax paper and a towel, and let the dough rise until approximately doubled in volume—1½ to 2 hours. When a finger inserted into the dough leaves a hole that remains, the dough is ready.

Punch the dough down with your fist. Put the dough on your work surface and cut it in half with a knife. Knead each half into a ball. Cover the balls, and allow them to rise for 15 minutes.

Form each ball into a large flattish loaf and place on an oiled pan. Make several slashes—or a cross—with a very sharp knife on the top of each loaf.

Bake for 45 minutes at 350° F. The loaves are done if they sound hollow when tapped on the bottom. (These loaves won't brown as much as regular bread.)

Yield: 2 eight-inch flattish loaves

Variations:

For a more pronounced barley flavor, increase the proportion of barley to flour. Just remember that the bread won't rise as much. Substitute cinnamon or coriander for the mint.

Biblical "fruitcakes"

We know that the Jews of Biblical times ate "cakes" of pressed fruits. For example, in I Samuel 25:18 Abigail brings to David, among other things, "two hundred cakes of pressed figs" (NIV). Here are some delicious cakes made of dates and figs, with walnuts and cinnamon and honey. Cinnamon was a rare and expensive spice at the time of Christ, and would have been used for special occasions.

1 cup coarsely chopped
  dried figs
1 cup coarsely chopped
  pitted dates
¼ cup honey
½ teaspoon cinnamon
2 cups chopped walnuts

Mix the fruits, the honey, and the cinnamon. Form the fruit mixture into small cakes (about 2 inches across) or into little balls.

Roll the balls or press the cakes onto the chopped nuts, coating them well.

Yield: about 12 cakes, or 20 balls

Variations:

Use chopped toasted almonds instead of the walnuts; substitute dried apricots for one of the other fruits.

MID-LENT SUNDAY:
MOTHERING SUNDAY

The fourth Sunday in Lent, or Mid-Lent, has many different names. Its liturgical name is "Laetare" or "Rejoice" Sunday, from the first words of the liturgy for that day: "Rejoice, O Jerusalem." Many Christians over the centuries rejoiced, among other things, because Lent was now half over!

The English name for this day is "Mothering Sunday." This term arose from a custom connected with the ancient idea of the Church—"Jerusalem"—as our Mother. On this day, Christians have traditionally gone to the church in which they had been baptized and confirmed, to their Mother Church. And on this day it has also been a custom for people to visit their own mothers. Servants, apprentices, and children in boarding school were even given a special holiday to do this. You took your mother flowers and a cake, and asked for her maternal blessing. The cake was called a "Simnel," from the fine-quality white flour (Latin *simila*) with which it was made. The great seventeenth-century poet Robert Herrick put it nicely:

I'll to thee a Simnel bring
'Gainst thou go'st a-Mothering
So that, when she blesseth thee,
Half that blessing thou'lt give me.

This day was thus the original—the Christian—Mother's Day.

Simnel cake

There are many recipes for Simnel Cakes. Here is a description of how one kind, from Shrewsbury, was made.

They are raised cakes, the crust of which is made of fine flour and water, with sufficient saffron to give it a deep yellow color, and the interior is filled with the material of a very rich plum cake, with plenty of candied lemon peel and other good things. They are made up very stiff, and boiled for several hours, after which they are brushed over with egg, and then baked. When ready for sale, the crust is as hard as if made of wood.

I'm not quite sure I'm ready for that cake but here is a traditional recipe that, with its almond paste layer and topping, makes a delicious and unusual light fruitcake. I hope that you—and your mother—will agree.

1½ sticks (¾ cup) sweet
  butter, at room
  temperature
1 cup sugar
4 eggs
2 cups all-purpose flour
1 teaspoon baking powder
½ teaspoon salt
1½ cups currants, lightly
  tossed with flour
½ cup mixed candied fruit
  peel, lightly tossed with
  flour
About 2 cups almond paste,
  homemade (see below) or
  store-bought
Flavoring for almond paste
  (optional, see below)
Glacéed cherries (optional)

Preheat oven to 350° F. In a large bowl, cream the butter with the sugar until fluffy, then beat in the eggs one at a time, blending thoroughly after each addition.

Sift the flour with the baking powder and salt. Blend the flour gradually into the butter-sugar mixture. Stir in the currants and candied fruit peel and mix lightly but thoroughly.

Grease an 8-to-10-inch round cake pan and line with greased parchment or waxed paper. Pour in half of the batter.

Roll out half of the almond paste to the same diameter as the cake pan and lay it on top of the batter. Then pour on the remaining batter. Smooth out the surface of the cake.

Bake at 350° F. for about 1 hour and a quarter, or until the cake pulls away slightly from the sides of the pan.

Roll out the remaining almond paste to the same diameter as the pan and lay it on top of the cake. If you like, make patterns on it with the tines of a fork. Return the cake to the oven for 5 to 10 minutes, or until the almond paste melts a little into the cake.

Let the cake cool in the pan for 10 to 15 minutes, then remove it carefully to a rack.

If you wish, you can decorate the top of the cake, while it is still somewhat warm, with glacéed cherries.

ALMOND PASTE:
1 cup finely ground
  blanched almonds
1 cup superfine sugar
1 egg, separated; beat the
  yolk and the white lightly
Optional flavorings:
  1–3 teaspoons brandy or
    rum
  a few drops almond
    extract
  1 tablespoon fresh lemon
    juice

Combine the almonds and sugar, blending well with a fork. Mix in the egg yolk. Add just enough of the flavorings and egg white to form a thick paste. Knead briefly until smooth. If the mixture is too wet, add a little more sugar.

Variations:

You can vary, increase, decrease, or eliminate the fruits, according to taste—and what you have on hand. If you eliminate the fruits entirely you might wish to flavor the batter with a little cinnamon or allspice (¼ to ½ teaspoon) or vanilla extract (about 1 teaspoon).

HOLY WEEK

Holy Week is the final and most sorrowful part of Lent. Christians attempt to relive the Crucifixion on Good Friday and the events leading up to and surrounding it. The week begins with Palm Sunday (also called Passion Sunday), on which Christ entered triumphantly into Jerusalem, and ends with Holy Saturday, still a fast day but one on which cooks are busily preparing the Easter feast. In a number of countries such as Poland families take their food—their Easter ham, their hard-boiled eggs, their special breads—to church to be blessed by the priest.

PALM SUNDAY

Greek Palm Sunday baked fish

PSARI PLAKI

Fish is plentiful in the Aegean waters that surround Greece, and the Greeks have many marvelous ways of preparing the numerous varieties available to them.

But during Lent, Greek Orthodox Christians give up their wonderful fish (as well as meat and other things). Only on Sundays do the Greeks eat fish. Palm Sunday is a joyful day, and the Greeks put aside their Lenten austerity to eat delicious Psari Plaki: fish baked in white wine with tomatoes, onion, and garlic, and spiced with oregano.

2 pounds fish fillets (such as halibut, haddock, cod, bluefish, red snapper), or 3 pounds whole fish (such as striped bass, sea bass, bluefish, red snapper)
½ cup olive oil
5 scallions, chopped
2 cloves garlic, minced
2 cups chopped tomatoes (peeled and seeded)
1 cup parsley
1 teaspoon oregano
1 teaspoon salt
Freshly ground pepper to taste
1 cup white wine
2 onions, sliced into rings

Place the fish in an oiled baking pan.

Heat the olive oil in a large frying pan, add the scallions and garlic, and sauté gently for 3 to 5 minutes, or until the scallions are translucent and lightly browned. Add the tomatoes, parsley, oregano, salt, pepper, and white wine. Cover and simmer for 10 minutes.

Pour the sauce over the fish. Decorate with onion rings. Bake at 375° F. until the fish flakes easily. This will take approximately 45 minutes for a whole fish, 20 minutes for fillets.

Yield: 4 to 6 servings

Variations:

The scallions, garlic, tomatoes, and so on can just be sprinkled over the fish before baking, and the wine poured over and around the fish. In Salonika, instead of white wine they use ½ cup sweet red wine such as mavrodaphne or port, and they add to the sauce just a pinch of cinnamon.

HOLY THURSDAY

Thursday of Holy Week is the evening on which the Last Supper occurred. This day bears various names in different languages, and many beautiful traditions are associated with it. In English, it is called Maundy Thursday, from Christ's *mandatum,* or command (and example) that Christians in authority must be first in willingness to serve. Since the seventh century it has been traditional in much of Europe for religious superiors and secular rulers to wash the feet of their subordinates, or of the poor, just as Christ washed the feet of his Apostles.

In Central Europe this day is called "Green Thursday." "Green" may well derive from the ancient Germanic word *grunen,* to mourn. (This is, after all, the day before Christ's Passion.) Another possibility is that this "green"—which often involves the eating of bitter greens, such as tansy and dandelion—is a reminiscence of the "bitter herbs" of the Jewish Passover meal.

In any case, in many countries of Europe, something—or in some places, *everything!*—eaten this day must be green. Here is a menu, with some recipes.

MENU
Seven-Herb Vichyssoise
Fish with Herb Butter
Spinach
Mixed Green salad
Lime Sherbet, or Pistachio Ice Cream, or Vanilla Ice Cream with
Crème de Menthe

Seven-herb vichyssoise

This is a classic Vichyssoise—cold leek (or onion) and potato soup—but with a refreshing greenness and a symbolic touch added. There is an old French tradition of preparing on Holy Thursday a soup made with seven greens. Vendors in the Old French Market of New Orleans would call out to the housewives: "Buy your seven greens for good luck!"

2 cups potatoes, peeled and sliced
2 cups leeks (carefully washed) or onions, sliced
2 quarts water or chicken broth
Salt
1 to 2 cups mixed chopped greens (see Note)
½ cup heavy cream
White pepper
Juice of 1 lemon
Watercress leaves to garnish

Place the potatoes, leeks, and water in a large saucepan. Add 1 teaspoon salt. Bring to a boil and simmer, partly covered, for about 20 minutes, or until the potatoes and onions are tender. Add the greens and simmer for 5 to 10 minutes longer, or until the greens are tender.

Purée the mixture in a blender, adding the heavy cream as you blend.

Pour the soup into a serving bowl or tureen. Add the white pepper to taste and the lemon juice. Taste for seasoning. If you plan to serve the soup cold, oversalt it slightly. Check for consistency: if the soup seems too thick, you can add a little milk or chicken broth or water; if it is too watery, add a little more cream. Chill for several hours. (This soup is also good hot. When reheating it, do not bring it to a boil.)

Garnish with the reserved watercress leaves.

Yield: 6 servings

Note: Ideally, a combination of seven of the following greens should be used to make this soup: watercress, spinach, chicory, green onions, collards, mustard and turnip greens; beet, carrot, and radish tops; or dandelion greens.

Herb butter

1 stick (½ cup) softened
  butter
2 tablespoons (or more) of
  one or a mixture of the
  following chopped herbs:
  chervil, tarragon,
  rosemary, chives, parsley

This makes a delicious sauce for any sautéed, broiled, or poached fish.

Mix the ingredients well with a fork.

Rosemary buns

PANINI DI RAMERINO

In Italy, it is an old tradition to visit seven churches on Holy Thursday and, in Florence, to eat Rosemary Buns marked with a cross. These are a delicious continental cousin to the English Hot Cross Bun.

1 package dry yeast
1¼ cups warm water
  (100–110° F.)
2 teaspoons sugar
1 teaspoon salt
¾ cup olive oil
4–4½ cups sifted flour
¾ cup golden raisins
3 tablespoons rosemary
  leaves
Optional:
  1–2 tablespoons sugar

Sprinkle the yeast into the warm water in a mixing bowl. Stir in the sugar and let sit until frothy. Add the salt and ¼ cup of the oil. Gradually mix in 3½ cups of the flour. Toss the raisins with ½ cup of flour, and add them to the dough.

On a lightly floured surface knead the dough until smooth and elastic, about 10 minutes. Add more flour as necessary to make a fairly stiff dough (the oil will soften it). Place the dough in a greased bowl, turning to grease the top. Cover with a towel and let the dough rise in a draft-free spot until doubled in bulk, about 1½ hours.

While the dough is rising, sauté the rosemary leaves in the remaining olive oil until golden brown.

Return the risen dough to the lightly floured surface. Make a hole and pour into it the rosemary and oil. Knead for about 5 minutes to work them thoroughly into the dough.

Cut the dough into 2 dozen buns and place them about 1½ inches apart on greased baking sheets. With a sharp knife, cut a cross into the top of each bun. Cover lightly and let rise until almost doubled in bulk.

If you wish, sprinkle with sugar. Bake at 425° F. for 10 minutes, then reduce the heat to 375° and continue baking until the buns are golden brown.

Yield: 2 dozen buns

GOOD FRIDAY

Good Friday, the day on which Jesus suffered and died on the Cross, is the most sorrowful day of the Christian year. Traditionally, this was a day of mourning. No work was done. No games were played; there was to be no laughing or joking. Many cities were strangely silent, for from the evening before, Maundy Thursday, until Easter morning, no churchbells would ring (little children in Catholic countries were told that the bells had flown to Rome to be blessed by the Pope, or by St. Peter himself).

Christians have traditionally spent this day in prayer—often in church, perhaps in three-hour services commemorating Christ's three hours on the Cross. Many followed processions of various kinds: funeral processions, in some countries; elsewhere, there were Stations of the Cross. (This is a devotion in which one meditates on each of fourteen moments of Christ's Passion, from his condemnation to death to his entombment.) There were (and in some places still are) passion plays. In many Protestant churches beautiful music is played, such as Bach's *St. John's Passion.*

Christians have, since the very earliest times, fasted on this day, and many Christians who do not otherwise observe Lent as a time of fasting do keep this ancient tradition. Many Irish Christians keep what is called the Black Fast: nothing but plain tea. But what people *do* eat on this day often has strong symbolic meaning.

There are many pious superstitions about Good Friday—such as that it is a lucky day for sowing (since Christ blessed the ground, the soil, by his burial), but that it is bad luck to use a hammer or nails (a hammer and nails had fixed Jesus to the cross). In England it was considered good luck to bake on Good Friday, and to plant parsley—but bad luck to wash clothes.

On the 9th of April (1773), being Good Friday, I breakfasted with him on tea and cross-buns.

On April 18 (1783), being Good-Friday, I found him at breakfast, in his usual manner upon that day, drinking tea without milk, and eating a cross bun to prevent faintness; we went to St. Clement's church, as formerly.

Boswell, *Life of Johnson*

Greek lentil soup

In Greece and a number of other countries it is customary to eat something on Good Friday to which vinegar is added, in memory of the vinegar that Christ was offered on the cross. To this good soup the vinegar adds a symbolic touch.

1 pound lentils
10 cups water
4 medium onions, chopped
2 cloves garlic, chopped
2 stalks celery, chopped
2 carrots, chopped
½ cup vegetable oil
6 sprigs parsley, chopped
1 bay leaf
1 tablespoon tomato paste
Salt and freshly ground
  pepper to taste
2 tablespoons wine vinegar
  or cider vinegar

Rinse and pick over the lentils, removing any pebbles. Bring the water to a boil in a large pan. Add the lentils, and boil for 2 minutes. Remove from the heat and let the lentils stand for 1 hour.

In the meantime, sauté the onions, garlic, celery, and carrots in the oil.

When the lentils have sat for an hour, add to them the vegetables, along with the parsley, bay leaf, and tomato paste. Simmer, partly covered, until the lentils are tender. In the last few minutes of cooking, add the salt and pepper.

Just before serving, add the vinegar. You might wish to do this at the table—and to explain why you are adding it.

Yield: 8–10 servings

Good Friday buns from England

The Hot Cross Bun is the most famous, and probably the oldest, of the many English buns. Unlike today, when it is to be found throughout Lent, the Hot Cross Bun was originally eaten only on Good Friday. According to tradition, Father Rocliff, a monk and the cook of St. Alban's Abbey, in Hertfordshire, on Good Friday in 1361 gave to each poor person who came to the abbey one of these spiced buns marked with the sign of the cross, along with the usual bowl of soup. The custom was continued and soon spread throughout the country—though no other buns could compare, it was said, with Father Rocliff's.

Hot Cross Buns became enormously popular in England in the eighteenth and nineteenth centuries. Street cries were commonly heard on Good Friday:

Hot Cross Buns, Hot Cross Buns,
One a penny, two a penny,
Hot Cross Buns!
If your daughters won't eat them,
Give them to your sons;
But if you have none of those little elves,
Then you must eat them all yourselves!

Hot Cross Buns had the reputation of never becoming moldy. As Poor Robin's Almanac for 1733 declared:

Good Friday comes this month, the old woman runs
With one or two a penny hot cross buns,
Whose virtue is, if you believe what's said,
They'll not grow mouldy like the common bread.

Hot Cross Buns, and other forms of Good Friday bread, were considered blessed, and were believed to provide powerful protection against disease and danger.

1 package dry yeast
¼ cup warm water (about 100–110° F.)
1 teaspoon white or light brown sugar
1 cup milk
½ cup sweet butter
⅓ cup brown or raw sugar
1 teaspoon salt
2 eggs, beaten
4 to 4½ cups sifted flour
1 teaspoon cinnamon
½ teaspoon ground cloves
½ teaspoon nutmeg
½ teaspoon ground ginger
⅔ cup dried currants
Optional:
   ⅓ cup finely diced or julienned citron

FROSTING:
2 tablespoons milk
4 tablespoons confectioners' sugar (more, if needed)
Grated rind of 1 lemon

Sprinkle the yeast into the lukewarm water. Stir in 1 teaspoon sugar. Let sit until frothy.

Scald the milk. Add the butter, sugar, and salt. Stir until blended. Cool to lukewarm. Beat the eggs until light, and combine with the milk mixture. Add the yeast.

Sift 3½ cups of the flour with the spices into a mixing bowl. Make a well, and pour in the yeast mixture. Beat for 5 minutes.

Toss the currants, and citron, if you like, with the remaining ½ cup of flour. Mix into the dough.

Place the dough on a lightly floured surface and knead until the dough is smooth and elastic, adding more flour if necessary. The dough should be fairly firm: otherwise it will not take the cuts for the cross.

Place the dough in a greased bowl, turning to grease the top. Cover the dough with a towel and put it to rise in a draft-free spot until doubled in volume; this will take about 2 hours.

Punch the dough down. Shape it into 2 dozen buns. Place them 1½ to 2 inches apart on well-greased cookie sheets or in muffin pans. With a sharp knife cut a cross on the top of each bun. Allow them to rise until doubled in bulk, 30 to 45 minutes.

Bake at 400° F. for about 20 minutes.

For the frosting: Mix the milk with enough sugar so that the icing is not runny. Add the rind. Brush a cross on the top of each bun.

Yield: about 24 buns

Variations:
Try varying the spice ratios: for example, eliminate the cinnamon, and use only the other spices (increasing their quantities proportionately). You can also substitute allspice for the ginger.

Eliminate the icing: the icing on Hot Cross Buns is considered by some purists to be new-fangled.

Cornish saffron buns

Cornwall has been famous for its use of saffron since the Middle Ages. Saffron was cultivated in Cornwall, and in other parts of England as well, from around the fourteenth century until the latter part of the eighteenth century. On Good Friday, the custom in Cornwall is to eat saffron buns and clotted cream.

To make Cornish Saffron Buns, follow the recipe for Hot Cross Buns, but make these adjustments: (1) For the spices in the Hot Cross Bun recipe, substitute 2 teaspoons ground nutmeg. (2) When you add the yeast to the flour, also add ¼ teaspoon saffron that has been steeped in 1½ teaspoons of warm water for 10 minutes. (3) Use ½ cup mixed candied fruit peel, shredded, instead of the optional citron. (4) Make a softer, less firm dough than for the Hot Cross Buns (these do not have to take the knife cuts). That is, use a little less flour in the dough.

8

Easter

Easter is the single most important and the most ancient of Christian festal days. Not that Christmas is unimportant, but Easter is the day on which Christianity began. Each Sunday is a little Easter. This religion of the worship of Christ as the Son of God dates from the discovery that the tomb was empty, that Christ had risen from the dead.

Easter is a moment of rejoicing. To some degree, in some places, this rejoicing bears a mark of deep solemnity. This has been especially true of Eastern Europe. But the theme of Easter joy is clear in many humorous old customs and superstitions. It was long traditional that preachers should at some point in their sermons on that day make their listeners laugh: this was "Pascal laughter." In the highlands of Scotland they used to say (maybe some still do) that on Easter morning the sun dances for joy.

With Easter rejoicing goes Easter feasting. There are dozens of beautiful traditional dishes from all over the world for this great feast.

The meat most commonly served has always been lamb, often a whole baby lamb or at least a large joint. The eating of this animal carried on a continuity with the Jewish Passover, at which a lamb was sacrificed and eaten. It has also, for Christians, carried the important meaning of Jesus as the Lamb of God, who by his death atoned for the sins of the world. This importance of lamb at Easter feasts can also be seen in the Greek soup Mageritsa (page 196), traditionally made of all parts of the lamb. In the Campania region of Italy, around Naples, there is a lovely Easter soup called *Benedetta* (Blessed), whose principal ingredients are lamb, eggs, Romano cheese, and "Easter Water," the holy water blessed on Holy Saturday. In many countries, lamb cakes or lambs formed out of sugar or chocolate have been prepared especially for Easter.

Ham is also eaten at Easter, often along with lamb. Pork is an ancient Indo-European favorite and is commonly served at feasts. We have blessings for Easter hams that go back far into the Middle Ages. Whereas lamb stresses continuity with the Judaic tradition,

194

the eating of pork points up the discontinuity: pork was (and is) considered "unclean" in Jewish dietary law, but in Christianity all foods are "clean."

Perhaps the most famous Easter food is the Easter egg, which has universally been associated with the Resurrection. Even in pre-Christian times a symbol for rebirth, it was taken over by Christians as the perfect symbol of Easter: new life emerges from the "tomb" of the shell. So for many hundreds of years people in many lands have broken their Lenten fasts by eating Easter eggs. In England, an important part of the meal was Easter eggs with green (herb) sauce; in many places, eggs have been baked into beautiful Easter breads.

Everywhere there has been an attempt to serve forth on the table (often set in white) foods worthy of the occasion. This does not mean that expensive delicacies have had to be imported from afar. People who have been fasting for many long weeks don't need Beluga caviar and French truffles to be grateful to God at their Easter feast. They are happy just to be eating again all the things they had forgone for Lent. Many of the most famous Easter foods are clearly "Lent is over!" dishes. For example, the delicious cold Pascha (page 205) of so many Eastern European countries is made of farmer cheese and cream, butter, eggs, and sugar: just about everything (except meat) that had been given up for Lent.

It is, then, the most basic foodstuffs, lovingly, painstakingly, and often gloriously prepared and beautifully decorated with religious symbols, that people ate, and eat, joyfully, once again each year at Easter.

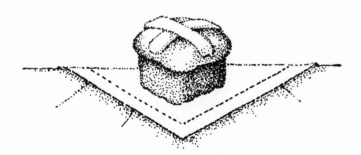

Greek lamb soup

MAGERITSA

It is with this soup—served with bread, cheese, and eggs—that Greek Orthodox Christians have traditionally broken their Lenten fast, after the midnight service, early on Easter morning. This meal is eaten by the light of the Resurrection candles that are distributed in church to each member, and brought home carefully, still burning. A traditional greeting is given: the triumphant words "Christ is risen!" meet the jubilant answer "He is risen indeed!"

In Greece this soup is made of the entrails of the lamb that has been slaughtered and will be spit-roasted for the Easter feast. (Every part of the lamb—symbolic of Christ—is precious.) Since lamb innards are hard to find in this country, this version of the soup is made with small pieces of lamb meat.

2 pounds boned lamb leg or shoulder, very finely chopped
1 onion, chopped
2 stalks celery, chopped
2–4 tablespoons olive oil
8 cups (2 quarts) water or stock
1½ teaspoons salt
2 teaspoons parsley, chopped
2 teaspoons dry mint, or 4 teaspoons chopped fresh mint
1½ tablespoons dill weed, or 3 tablespoons chopped fresh dill
½ cup raw rice
4 eggs
Juice of 2 lemons

In a large pot, sauté the meat a little at a time until nicely browned. (You will probably not need any oil, but can use the fat that the meat renders. Discard excess fat as it accumulates.) Remove the meat and drain on paper towels. Pour out the remaining fat from the pot.

Sauté the onion and celery in the olive oil until golden brown. Return the meat to the pot and add the water, salt, parsley, mint, dill weed, and rice. Bring to a boil. Cover, reduce heat, and let simmer for about 20 minutes, or until the rice is fully cooked.

Just before serving, prepare an egg-lemon mixture: Beat the eggs well. Gradually beat in the juice of 2 lemons. Add 2 cups of the hot soup slowly to the egg mixture, beating constantly. Stir this mixture gradually back into the soup, stirring constantly. Return the soup to the heat and stir vigorously until it is thickened. *Do not boil.* Serve immediately.

Yield: 8 to 10 servings

Variation:

If you are able to procure lamb innards, such as tripe, lungs, heart, and liver, you can use them to make this soup. Wash them thoroughly in cold running water. Scald the tripe. Chop the organs coarse. Cook in salted water to which the juice of 1 lemon has been added. You can add the organs progressively to the water: the tripe will take about 40 minutes to cook, the lungs and heart about 30 minutes, the liver about 15 minutes. Simmer until all are tender. Drain. Strain and reserve the broth to use in the soup. Chop the meat fine. Sauté the meat with the onion and celery, and proceed as above.

Easter pie

TORTA PASQUALINA

This extraordinary torta *is a Genovese Easter specialty. When made completely from scratch, it is a difficult and time-consuming dish because it requires many layers of thin dough. I have simplified it here by the use of phyllo pastry, which can be bought in many groceries (and in shops specializing in Greek or Balkan foods). By using this very thin pastry, we can keep one of the old traditions associated with this dish: the use of thirty-three layers of dough, one for each year of Christ's life. The eggs pick up the Easter theme—one egg for each of the Apostles? The greens, presumably, evoke the renewal of life in the spring.*

2 pounds beet greens or spinach, or around 10 canned artichoke hearts (see Note)
½ onion, finely chopped
4 tablespoons olive oil
2 tablespoons chopped parsley
1 teaspoon marjoram
1 cup freshly grated Parmesan cheese
1¼ pounds ricotta cheese
¾ cup heavy cream
Salt
1 one-pound package phyllo pastry (see Note)
1 cup olive oil (more if needed)
12 medium eggs
Freshly ground pepper
4 tablespoons melted butter

You will need a 12-inch springform pan (or a large, deep pie or baking pan of similar or slightly larger dimensions); it should be 2 to 3 inches deep.

If using beet greens or spinach, wash them carefully in several changes of water. Chop fine, and cook until just soft in as little water as possible; press out the moisture. If using canned artichoke hearts, drain and chop coarse.

In the olive oil sauté the onion until it is soft and translucent, but not brown. Add the well-drained greens or artichokes, and mix them well with the onion. Sauté gently together for a minute or two. Remove from the heat. Add 1 tablespoon of the chopped parsley, ½ teaspoon of the marjoram and ½ cup Parmesan. Mix well. Let cool.

Mix the ricotta with the cream. Add ½ teaspoon salt.

Remove the phyllo pastry from its package, but keep it covered carefully with plastic wrap or a moist towel as much of the time as possible: it dries out *very* easily.

Brush the baking dish with oil. Lay in place the first layer of pastry, extending the edges up the sides of the pan; brush lightly with oil; trim off dangling edges. Continue the same procedure for 15 more pieces of pastry: 16 in all. If you are using a 12-inch pan, your pastry may well be a little too narrow for the pan. Just lay each layer of pastry at a slightly different angle from the preceding one, so that you are moving around the pan.

Spread the 16th layer with the cooked vegetable mixture. On top of this spoon the ricotta and cream. In this filling make 12 wells. Into each well break an egg: try to keep the eggs (especially the yolks) confined to their own wells as much as possible. Sprinkle the eggs with salt, pepper, and the rest of the parsley, marjoram, and Parmesan. Pour the melted butter over the top.

continued

Over this filling place the remaining 17 layers of the phyllo pastry, following the same procedure as before. Brush the top layer generously with oil. Press down the edges firmly, and trim off excess pastry.

Bake at 375° F. for about 1 hour, or until the pie is golden brown. Serve hot, lukewarm, or cold.

Yield: 12 servings

Note: Beet greens are the most completely traditional, but the others are common substitutes.

One pound should be enough phyllo, but you may be 1 or 2 sheets short. If you want to be certain to have enough, buy an extra package.

Easter pâté (from the Berry region of France)

PÂTÉ DE PÂQUES, DU BERRY

This elegant pâté is a variation on the basic culinary themes of Easter: the reintroduction of meat into the diet after Lenten fasting, and the use of hard-boiled eggs. It makes a beautiful first course. Served with a crisp green salad—and perhaps a nice wine, or a bottle of Champagne—it can be a meal unto itself on any day during the Easter season.

FLAKY PASTRY:
2¾ cups flour
12 tablespoons (1½ sticks)
  unsalted butter
1 teaspoon salt
½ cup ice water

Prepare the pastry: Sift the flour onto a work surface or pastry board. Make a well in the center. Add the butter and the salt. Using a pastry blender, or two knives, or your fingers, mix the butter into the flour until it has the consistency of cornmeal.

Make another well in the center of the dough. Add the water, mixing it in lightly with your fingers or a fork. (Do not work the dough any more than absolutely necessary.) Form the dough into a ball, wrap in a plastic bag or damp towel, and let it rest in the refrigerator for 2 hours.

Prepare the filling: Hard-boil the eggs, peel them, and trim off ½ inch from the end of each, so that they will fit together perfectly, end to end, in the pâté.

In a frying pan, cook the sausage meat for about 8 to 10 minutes over low heat, so that it will render some of its fat. Drain off the fat and pat the sausage well with paper towels. Mix the sausage with the ham, veal or chicken, onion, parsley, breadcrumbs and egg. Add the salt, pepper, and *quatre-épices*, and taste the mixture for seasoning.

FILLING:

4 eggs
½ pound sausage meat
¼ pound boiled ham, chopped very fine or ground
¼ pound raw boneless veal or chicken breast, chopped very fine or ground
1 onion, very finely chopped
3 tablespoons fresh parsley, very finely chopped
3 tablespoons breadcrumbs
1 egg
Salt and freshly ground pepper to taste
⅛ to ¼ teaspoon Quatre-épices or allspice
1 egg yolk, lightly beaten, mixed with a little water

When the dough is properly chilled, roll it out on a lightly floured surface to a thickness of ¼ inch (or even a little thinner). Cut the dough into 2 rectangular pieces, one of which should be 1 inch longer and wider than the other. The dimensions of the larger piece should be about 8 or 9 inches by 14 or 15 inches.

Place the larger piece of dough on a buttered baking pan. Place half of the filling mixture onto the dough, spreading it out but leaving 2 inches free along the edges of the dough. On top of the filling, place the hard-boiled eggs, fitting them end to end, and pressing them down slightly into the filling. Spoon the rest of the filling mixture over the eggs. Moisten the edges of both pieces of the dough slightly.

Cover the filling with the remaining (the smaller) rectangle of dough. Fold the edges of the bottom piece over, to cover the edges of the top piece. Seal the edges with the tines of a fork. Make several slits in the lid, to form a design and to let the steam escape. Mix the egg yolk with a little water, and brush this lightly on the surface of the pâté.

Bake at 400° F. for 10 minutes. Reduce the heat to 350° and continue baking for 50 minutes, or until the surface of the pâté is nicely browned.

Yield: about 6 servings

Note: Quatre-épices is a blend of spices much used in French cooking, and available at many gourmet and spice shops in this country.

A strict observance of Lent made possible a pleasure which is unknown to us now, that of "un-Lenting" at breakfast on Easter Day.

If we look into the matter closely, we find that the basic elements of our pleasures are difficulty, privation, and the desire for enjoyment. All these came together in the act of breaking abstinence, and I have seen two of my great-uncles, both serious, sober men, half swoon with joy when they saw the first slice cut from a ham, or a pâté disembowelled, on Easter day. Now, degenerate race that we are, we could never stand up to such powerful sensations!

Brillat-Savarin, *The Philosopher in the Kitchen*

Easter lamb with beans

This is one of the classic ways of preparing leg of lamb. (Lamb is the most traditional meat to serve at Easter: it maintains the Passover tradition, and refers to the ancient Christian theme of Christ as the Lamb of God.)

One little note on the rosemary flavoring: There is a charming legend that on the flight to Egypt the Holy Family stopped to rest and the Virgin laid her blue cloak over a rosemary bush: that is how rosemary got its beautiful fragrance and rosemary flowers their blue color. Oregano is also delicious with lamb, and typical of both Italian and Greek preparations.

1 leg of lamb, 7–8 pounds
Salt
Freshly ground pepper
Rosemary or oregano
Juice of ½ lemon
4 cloves garlic, peeled and cut into slivers

THE BEANS:
1 pound cannellini beans, cooked, or 4 to 5 cans cannellini beans, drained
2 cloves garlic, peeled and crushed
Rosemary
Salt
Pepper

Remove the tough fell, and trim off some of the remaining fat. Let the meat sit at room temperature for ½ hour or so before cooking. Rub the roast with salt, pepper, and rosemary or oregano, and sprinkle it with lemon juice. Cut small gashes in the meat and insert slivers of garlic.

Roast in a large roasting pan at 350° F. for approximately 2 hours for meat that is rare to medium. For well-done meat, increase the cooking time by approximately ½ hour. (The reading on a meat thermometer will be 175° F. for a well-done roast; 120° for rare.)

During the last half hour of cooking, put the beans in the pan next to the roast; sprinkle with crushed garlic, rosemary, salt, and pepper, and spoon the pan juices over the beans.

Yield: 8 servings

April 11 [1773], being Easter-Sunday. . . . I repaired to Dr. Johnson's. . . . We had a very good soup, a boiled leg of lamb and spinach, a veal pye, and a rice pudding.

Boswell, *Life of Johnson*

Baked glazed Easter ham

Second only to lamb as the traditional meat for Easter is pork. In many countries, Suckling Pig is served. (There is a marvelous Roast Suckling Pig recipe on page 34.) Ham is also a favorite, and here is one of the most delicious and festive-looking ways of preparing it; here too are a few suggested garnishes.

Ham is nice served with Baked Sweet Potatoes or Potato Puffs (pages 203 and 45) and a green vegetable or a salad.

1 cooked ham (see Note)

GLAZE:
½ cup brown sugar
½ teaspoon dry mustard
1 tablespoon grated orange
  rind
½ teaspoon allspice
¼ cup (or more if necessary)
  any of the following:
  sweet pickle juice
  cider
  fruit juice or syrup (see
    below)
  white wine, red wine, or
    beer
Whole cloves

Strip off the rind and cut off the excess fat from the ham. Score the remaining fat layer in diamond shapes. (Cut diagonal lines going in one direction across the ham; then cut a second set to intersect the first.) At the corners of the diamond pattern, stud the ham with the whole cloves. Place the ham in a large baking or roasting pan.

Mix the sugar, mustard, orange rind, and allspice. Add enough liquid to moisten it slightly. Apply this mixture to the surface of the ham.

Bake the ham at 350° F. for 1½ hours or more, depending on size (the ham needs to heat through). Baste frequently with the cooking juices and with the remaining liquid.

Garnishes and Variations:

Fruits make a delicious and traditional garnish for glazed ham. Particularly nice are:

Slices of pineapple arranged on the top surface of the ham about halfway through the baking time, and brushed with honey and the pineapple and cooking juices.

Canned peach halves. Drain the peaches; use the juice to baste the ham. Place the peach halves on a baking pan. Dot each with a little brown sugar and butter. Moisten lightly with syrup or bourbon. When the ham is done, place the peaches under the broiler for a minute or two to heat and brown lightly. Surround the ham with the peaches.

Note: The cooked ham may be smoked or unsmoked, boned or unboned. For an unboned ham, calculate about ½ pound per person; if the bone is still in, figure ¾ to 1 pound per person. For the glaze, you may need to increase or decrease the amount of ingredients, depending on the size of your ham. This quantity will be adequate for a 5-pound ham. Traditionally, a Swedish Christmas ham is decorated with softened butter or a butter-cream icing, applied with a decorator tube. Apply the butter or icing to a cold ham, or just before serving if the ham is served hot. Use any motifs you like: strictly decorative or more specifically Christian.

Pesse pie

In Scotland Pesse Pie is an old tradition for Easter. The word Pesse comes from the Hebrew Pesakh, from which are derived many other Easter terms, such as Pascua and Paschal. This is a chicken pot pie—glorified by the addition of bacon, baby onions, mushrooms, and cream—and appeals to grownups and children alike. It makes a pleasing centerpiece for an Eastertime brunch.

1 chicken, about 3½ pounds (whole or cut up)
2 teaspoons salt
1 bay leaf
4 peppercorns
2 stalks celery, coarsely chopped
½ onion, chopped
1 carrot, coarsely chopped
¼-pound chunk of lean bacon, or ¼ pound thick-sliced bacon
10–12 tablespoons butter
12 small white onions
12 mushrooms, coarsely chopped
4 tablespoons flour
1½ cups milk
½ teaspoon thyme
1 tablespoon parsley, chopped
1 egg yolk
2 tablespoons heavy cream
Salt and freshly ground pepper to taste
White wine or milk
Crust for a 9- or 10-inch pie pan
1 egg, lightly beaten

Put the chicken in a large saucepan, cover it with water, add salt, and surround it with the bay leaf, peppercorns, celery, onion, and carrot. Bring the water to a boil, cover the pot, and turn the heat down: the chicken should simmer gently (not boil) until the flesh is tender; this will take about 1 to 1½ hours. Remove the chicken from the pan; when it has cooled enough to handle, take out the bones, and cut the meat into bite-sized pieces. (You may discard the cooking water—or keep it for making soup, broth, etc.)

Remove the rind from the bacon and cut it into sticks about 1 inch by ¼ by ¼ inch. Place them in water to cover and simmer for 8 to 10 minutes. Drain. Sauté them in 1 to 2 tablespoons butter.

Peel the baby onions. At each root end, cut a small X shape. Brown them in 2 to 3 tablespoons of butter. Pour in water to cover them halfway, cover the pan, and let them simmer for 10 minutes. Drain off the liquid; reserve the onions.

Sauté the mushrooms in 2 to 3 tablespoons more butter until brown. Reserve.

Melt 4 tablespoons of butter in a heavy saucepan and add the 4 tablespoons of flour. Stirring constantly, cook for 2 to 3 minutes over medium heat. Add the milk, reduce the heat slightly, and stir constantly until the mixture is smooth and thick. Remove from the heat. Stir in the chicken, bacon, onions, and mushrooms. Add the thyme and parsley.

Beat the egg yolk into the cream, and add to the mixture. Taste for seasoning. If the mixture seems too thick, you can thin it with a little white wine or more milk.

Pour the mixture into a deep-dish pie pan: a 9-inch pan should be large enough unless your chicken was especially big, in which case you may need a 10-inch pie pan.

Cover with the crust. Make several vents in the surface to allow the steam to escape. Brush the surface with beaten egg, and bake at 425° F. for 10 minutes. Then reduce the heat to 350° and bake for another 20 to 30 minutes or until the crust is nicely browned.

Yield: 6 servings

Baked Sweet Potatoes

Delicious and foolproof.

6 medium sweet potatoes
  (yams or yellow Jersey
  sweet potatoes)
½ stick (¼ cup) sweet butter
¾ cup dark-brown sugar
½ teaspoon salt
Grated rind of ½ lemon
¼ teaspoon ginger, or 2
  tablespoons lemon juice
Optional:
  2 to 4 tablespoons cognac
  or dark rum
  3 tablespoons chopped
  pecans or slivered
  almonds

Cook the sweet potatoes in boiling water to cover until just tender, about 15 minutes.

Preheat oven to 350° F. Butter a shallow baking dish or casserole.

Peel the sweet potatoes and slice them lengthwise. Lay them in the baking dish. Melt the butter in a saucepan. Stir in the brown sugar, salt, lemon rind, ginger or lemon juice, and, if you like, the cognac or rum. Stir until well blended. Pour the mixture over the sweet potatoes. Sprinkle the top with the nuts.

Bake uncovered for 30 minutes, basting once or twice.

Yield: 6 servings

Variations:

You can sprinkle about ¼ cup raisins in with the sweet potatoes, or add a little orange marmalade to the sauce.

Fresh asparagus

By Easter, many of us in the different parts of the country can lay our hands on fresh asparagus, one of the real treats of the season. (If you can't get it yet, postpone this dish till Pentecost.) You can serve asparagus hot with Hollandaise Sauce (page 41), or Herbed Breadcrumbs (page 39), or cold with a Vinaigrette Sauce (page 39)

2 pounds asparagus (choose
  spears as identical in size
  as possible)

Wash the asparagus carefully, getting all grit out of the tips.

Cut or snap off the bottom part of the spears, making the stalks all about the same length and removing all the white. If you wish, you can peel the bottom few inches of the stalks with a knife or vegetable peeler.

Bring 2 inches of lightly salted water to a boil in a large skillet. Lay the asparagus in the skillet and boil until the stalks are just tender when pierced with a fork: no longer!

You may find it easiest to remove the asparagus from the pan with a slotted spoon. Drain thoroughly on paper towels.

If serving cold with vinaigrette, allow the asparagus to marinate in the sauce for at least ½ hour before serving.

Yield: 4 to 6 servings

Russian Easter bread

KULICH

This is the great, traditional Russian Easter bread. Tall, like a crown—or a Russian onion-domed church—and with the initials XB, "Christ is risen," on the top, this bread is always brought to the priest on Holy Saturday to be blessed and sprinkled with holy water. It is served on Easter Day with the cold Pascha.

The decorated top of the loaf is not eaten: rather it is placed back on the loaf as lower slices are removed.

1 package dry yeast
¼ cup warm water (about 100–110° F.)
¾ cup lukewarm milk
4 tablespoons melted butter
¼ cup sugar
½ teaspoon salt
2 teaspoons grated lemon rind
1 teaspoon vanilla extract
2 teaspoons brandy or rum
2 eggs
3 cups flour
¼ cup blanched almonds, chopped
¼–½ cup golden raisins, plumped in hot water, drained
Optional:
  ¼ cup mixed candied orange and lemon peel and/or other candied fruits

ICING:
1 cup confectioners' sugar
1 tablespoon milk
½ teaspoon vanilla

You can bake the bread in a two-pound coffee can, or make 2 loaves, using 2 one-pound cans.

Sprinkle the yeast in the warm water, stirring to dissolve.

In a large bowl, combine the milk and the melted butter. Stir in the sugar, salt, lemon rind, vanilla extract and brandy. Stir in the yeast. Beat in the eggs, one at a time. Mix in the flour, a little at a time, adding only enough to make a soft dough.

Turn the dough out onto a floured surface and knead for 10 to 15 minutes, or until it is smooth and elastic. Place it in a greased bowl, turning to grease the top. Cover and place in a warm, draft-free spot for 1 to 1½ hours, or until doubled in bulk.

Punch the dough down and turn it out onto the floured surface again. Press the dough flat and work into it the almonds and raisins and candied peels and fruits, if used.

Break off a piece of the dough a little larger than a golf ball; set it aside for making the initials for the top of the cake. Form the rest of the dough into a large ball and press it, seam down, into the greased coffee can(s). (It should only fill *half* of the can.) Roll out the small piece of dough into a rope about 30 inches long. Cut it into 4 pieces. Cross two strands to form the X and from the other two form the B. Place the letters gently but firmly on top of the dough.

Cover the can lightly with wax paper and let the dough rise for about 30 to 45 minutes, or till it *just* reaches the top of the can: no higher!

Bake the bread at 375° F. for 40 to 45 minutes, or until golden brown, and until a toothpick stuck into the center of the top comes out clean.

Frost with a confectioners' sugar icing. (It is this icing that makes the Kulich so look like the onion-domed Russian churches.) Mix the confectioners' sugar with the milk and vanilla. Let the icing drip down the sides of the cake.

Yield: 1 large loaf or 2 smaller loaves

Pascha

This is an absolutely beautiful and delicious dish; versions are prepared in Poland, Russia, the Ukraine, and Latvia. It is made in a tall mold (or flower pot), then turned out onto a large platter and decorated. Cool and rich, it tastes like a cross between ice cream and cheesecake. It goes wonderfully with the sweet Easter breads, such as Kulich (opposite), or with the various Easter cakes.

1 whole egg
4 egg yolks
2⅓ cups sugar
1 cup heavy cream
2 pounds farmer cheese
½ pound sweet butter, at
    room temperature
1 tablespoon vanilla extract
1½ cups fruit: raisins and/
    or dried currants, mixed
    candied fruit peel
1 cup blanched almonds,
    chopped
2 tablespoons freshly grated
    orange or lemon rind
For decorating:
    Candied fruit peel,
    maraschino cherries, or
    nuts
    Fresh strawberries to
    place around the base
    and on top

Beat the egg and the yolks until thick and lemon-colored. Gradually add the sugar, and beat until the mixture is thick and creamy. Pour into a saucepan and add ½ cup of the cream.

Heat over medium-low heat, beating constantly, until the mixture begins to thicken. *Do not boil.* Remove the pan from the heat and continue beating until the mixture has cooled to lukewarm.

In a mixing bowl, combine the cheese, butter, the other ½ cup of cream and the vanilla. Cream until the mixture is smooth. Add the egg mixture, then the fruits, almonds, and orange or lemon rind. Blend thoroughly.

Line a flower pot or Pascha mold (see Note) with 2 thicknesses of cheesecloth. Place the pot over a bowl (to catch liquid), and pour the Pascha mixture into the pot. Put a layer or two of cheesecloth over the top, set a plate on it and something heavy on the plate. (The purpose is to press the extra liquid out of the Pascha and into the bowl below.) Chill overnight or for a day or two.

Remove the top cheesecloth. Unmold the Pascha onto a large platter, and remove the rest of the cheesecloth.

Decorate the Pascha with the candied fruit peel or maraschino cherries or nuts to form the letters XB or CR (Christ is risen) on one side, and on the other side a cross. You may use the Western cross form or the Orthodox cross, or any other cross design that you prefer (see Note). In Russia, Pascha is often decorated with an angel and a lily, as well as the cross.

Around the base and on top of the Pascha, place fresh strawberries. Serve chilled.

Yield: 14 to 16 servings

Note: Molds can be purchased at some Eastern European specialty and liturgical stores, such as the Synod Bookshop, 75 East 93rd Street, New York, N.Y. 10028.

See "The Exaltation of the Holy Cross" (page 267) for various cross motifs.

Ukrainian pretzel cookies

KRENDLI

During Lent a simple pretzel was traditional fare; for Easter the pretzel is sweet and full of butter and eggs and wonderful flavor. Such pretzels are, in the Ukraine, favorite delicacies for Christmas as well.

2 sticks (1 cup) sweet
  butter, at room
  temperature
1¼ cups sugar
2 egg yolks
Grated rind of 1 lemon
1 tablespoon lemon juice
¼ teaspoon salt
2½ cups flour
½ cup coarsely ground
  blanched almonds

Cream the butter with 1 cup of the sugar until fluffy. Stir in the egg yolks one at a time, stirring well after each addition. Add the lemon rind, lemon juice, and salt. Gradually add the flour, mixing thoroughly.

Chill the dough for about 1 hour, then place it on a lightly floured surface. Break off small handfuls of dough and, using your fingers and a rolling pin, pinch and roll the dough out to ropes about ¼ inch thick and 8 inches long. If you prefer smaller pretzels, make ropes 6 inches long. Form the ropes into pretzels (it isn't easy: this is cookie not bread dough, and is very fragile; the ropes have to be cajoled into pretzel shapes). Once you have formed a pretzel, you can then improve on its shape by molding the dough. If your pretzel looks fat, pinch the ropes to make them thinner: they should be ¼ inch or a little less. Flatten the pretzels slightly on top.

Transfer the pretzels as you prepare them to a buttered baking sheet, placing them 1½ to 2 inches apart. Sprinkle them with the remaining sugar and with the almonds. If almond pieces fall to either side, you can just press them into the sides of the cookies.

Bake at 375° F. for about 12 minutes, or until golden brown. Wait for a minute or two before removing the pretzels from the baking sheet. Let cool on a rack.

Yield: about 3 dozen pretzel-shaped cookies

Variations:

You can also flavor this dough with vanilla extract or with rum or brandy. Use about 1 teaspoon of whichever you prefer.

Swiss Easter tart

OSTERFLADEN

This delectable tart is an old specialty of the German-speaking parts of Switzerland. Easter just wouldn't seem like Easter without it! Some versions contain groats or rice, and appear to be cousins of the Italian Easter specialty pastiera. All contain cream (or milk) and eggs—and are thus typical "Lent is over" Easter dishes.

Here is a particularly light and lovely version, slightly adapted from The Swiss Cookbook, *by Nika Hazelton.*

⅔ cup blanched almonds, ground
⅔ cup sugar
1¾ cups light cream
⅔ cup milk
1 tablespoon cornstarch or rice flour
4 eggs, separated
½ cup raisins, soaked in water to plump
Grated rind of ½ lemon
1 tablespoon kirsch (optional)
2 nine-inch pie shells, unbaked

Preheat the oven to 325° F.

With a fork, mix the almonds with the sugar. Add the cream, and beat until smooth. Combine the milk and cornstarch to make a smooth paste. Beat it into the almond mixture.

Add the egg yolks, one at a time, beating well after each addition. Stir in the raisins, lemon rind, and Kirsch, if you wish. Just before baking, beat the egg whites until stiff but not dry, and fold them into the mixture.

Pour into the unbaked pie shells, making sure that the raisins are evenly distributed between the shells. Bake for about 1 hour, or until the tops are nicely browned and a knife inserted into the center of one comes out clean.

Serve cooled but not chilled.

Yield: 2 nine-inch tarts

Bread of Easter brightness

LAMBROPSOMO

This large, round loaf of sweet, spicy bread is traditional in Greece at Easter. It is a spectacular sight, with its five scarlet eggs, set like great jewels in the form of the cross.

2 packages dry yeast
¼ cup warm water (100–110° F.)
½ cup sweet butter, melted
¾ cup scalded milk
3 eggs
⅓ cup sugar
½ teaspoon salt
1 teaspoon cinnamon
½ teaspoon nutmeg
4½–5 cups flour
5 hard-boiled eggs, dyed red
1 egg, lightly beaten
Sesame seeds

Sprinkle the yeast into the warm water; stir to dissolve.

In a large bowl, stir the butter into the milk. Add the eggs, one at a time, the sugar, salt, and spices. Beat until smooth.

Stir in the yeast and 2 cups of the flour, and mix well. Gradually add enough of the remaining flour to make a smooth dough. (If the dough is too sticky, add more flour.)

Turn the dough out onto a floured surface and knead for 10 to 15 minutes or until it is smooth and elastic. Place in a greased bowl, turn to grease the surface, cover, and let rise in a warm, draft-free spot for about 1½ to 2 hours, or until doubled in bulk.

Punch the dough down, turn it out again onto a floured surface, and knead for 3 to 5 minutes. Form it into one large, flat, round loaf and place it on a lightly greased baking pan. With your thumb, make 5 deep depressions in the loaf: 1 in the center, and 4 around the edges, to form a cross. In each depression set an egg firmly but carefully.

Cover lightly and let the dough rise for about 1½ hours, or until again doubled in bulk. Brush the top of the loaf with beaten egg and sprinkle with sesame seeds.

Bake at 350° F. for 45 to 55 minutes, or until the loaf is golden brown and sounds hollow when rapped.

Yield: 1 loaf about 12 inches in diameter

Lamb cake

In a number of countries—Italy and Poland among them—a Lamb Cake is made for Easter, in a special mold. (These molds are easy to find in department and bakery-supply stores in this country.) Here the cake is iced with a thick white frosting, applied with a decorating tube, to give a woolly effect.

Vegetable oil or shortening
2 cups sifted flour
3 teaspoons baking powder
¼ teaspoon salt
½ cup butter
1 cup sugar
1 teaspoon vanilla
¾ cup milk
3 egg whites

FROSTING:
2 egg whites
¼ teaspoon cream of tartar
6 tablespoons cold water
1½ cups sugar
1 teaspoon vanilla
Jelly beans or currants for the lamb's eyes and mouth

Preheat the oven to 375° F. Grease the mold well with shortening or oil, brushing the oil into all crevices. Dust lightly with flour.

Resift the flour with the baking powder and salt; resift once more.

Cream the butter, and blend in the sugar gradually, creaming well after each addition. Add the vanilla to the milk.

Add the flour mixture to the butter-sugar mixture, alternating with the milk-vanilla. Stir just until the batter is smooth.

Whip the egg whites until stiff but not dry. Fold them into the batter.

Pour the batter into the front half of the mold. Fill the ears carefully. Cover with the second half of the mold; close tightly.

Place, front side down, on a baking sheet, and bake for 25 minutes. Gently turn the mold over and bake for another 25 minutes. Remove the pan from the oven, and let the mold cool on a wire rack for 10 minutes. Remove the back first, and let cool 5 minutes longer. Turn the cake out on a rack to cool completely.

When it is cold, frost.

For the frosting: Place the egg whites, cream of tartar, water, and sugar in the top of a double boiler, over medium heat. Cook, beating, until the icing is stiff enough to stand in peaks: about 8 to 10 minutes. Remove from the heat. Add the vanilla. Beat for a few minutes to cool. Apply with a decorating tube, using a star head, in short, wavy strokes.

For the eyes and mouth, use currants or jelly beans, or tint a small amount of icing the desired hues.

Yield: 1 lamb cake

Variations:

You can mix some coconut in with this or any other white icing. Apply the icing to the cake. Then coat the lamb generously with more coconut.

You may also wish to surround the lamb with "grass": coconut tinted with green food coloring. Other optional details include a pretty ribbon or little bell tied around the lamb's neck.

9

Pentecost

Pentecost is traditionally one of the greatest of Christian holy days, the other two being Easter and Christmas. It is the birthday of the Church, as a teaching, preaching, baptizing body.

Pentecost, or the Feast of Weeks, was originally a Jewish festival, falling fifty days (seven weeks) after Passover. The first fruits of the corn harvest were offered to the Lord, as commanded in Deuteronomy 16:10. The giving of the Law to Moses was also celebrated.

It was at this great Jewish festival, when many people were gathered in Jerusalem, that the Holy Spirit descended on the Apostles, Mary, and other disciples of Jesus.

When the day of Pentecost came, they were all together in one place. Suddenly a sound like the blowing of a violent wind came from heaven and filled the whole house where they were sitting. They saw what seemed to be tongues of fire that separated and came to rest on each of them. All of them were filled with the Holy Spirit and began to speak in other tongues as the Spirit enabled them (Acts 2:1–4, NIV).

A dramatic event. An important one as well. From that moment the Apostles led by Peter began to preach the Gospel. Many in the crowd, hearing the Good News, repented and were baptized.

Throughout the Middle Ages, and beyond, in both Catholic and Protestant countries, Pentecost and the week following it were holy days and holidays.

Pentecost's popularity as a festival has not been due exclusively to its Christian meaning. As in Jewish culture it was primarily a nature festival, so in the early centuries of our era it became a Christian focus for the ancient Indo-European nature cults, with their yearly games and maypoles, songs and dances. In Poland, the name for Pentecost is "Green Holy Day"; in the Ukraine it is the "Flower Feast." Thus, Pentecost, the feast of the birth of the Church, is also the festival of new buds, new birth in nature.

210

A shoot will come up from the stump of Jesse; from his roots a Branch will bear fruit.
The Spirit of the Lord will rest on him—the Spirit of wisdom and of understanding, the Spirit of counsel and of power, the Spirit of knowledge and of the fear of the Lord—and he will delight in the fear of the Lord.

Isaiah 11:1–2 (NIV)

Pentecost has been considered a very holy day, one when the Holy Spirit was especially near at hand. Sometimes people would go to the top of a mountain to pray. It has been a favorite moment for baptisms, and the English name for this feast, Whitsunday, refers to the white robes of the newly baptized.

The Middle Ages had a strange and delightful way of celebrating the religious meaning of Pentecost. In the ceiling of the church there would be a large aperture called "the Holy Ghost Hole." And on Pentecost, to the sound of trumpets or some other windy noise, down through the hole would be lowered a great disk, often painted blue with golden rays, and with a white dove, symbol of the Holy Spirit, painted on it. In some places pigeons or doves would be released into the church through this hole. Elsewhere roses were dropped. A few churches tried dropping burning straw. Alas, unlike the flames described in Acts, this fire did not hover *over* the faithful but fell right *on* them; the practice was discontinued.

Throughout much of Europe Pentecost is a traditional time of communal feasting and family picnicking. It has been curiously neglected in this country. Let's try to remedy that!

The culinary traditions connected with this feast focus on the dove as symbol of the Holy Spirit. People have traditionally eaten dove or some other small bird (as on the feast of the Ascension, because Jesus "flew" to heaven). The Rock Cornish hen makes a nice approximation of the dove. Along with some other dishes pleasing as picnic fare, you will find below a Dove Bread and a Pentecost Cake.

BROILED AND ROAST ROCK CORNISH HENS

Here are two superlative recipes for this dovelike creature. Both feature mint, which can be bought fresh (or grown in your garden) at this season, and which has a wonderfully refreshing aroma and taste. Try serving with either dish a Yogurt Sauce, also flavored with mint.

Broiled rock cornish hens

2 Rock Cornish hens, fresh
   or defrosted
Salt
Freshly ground pepper
¼ cup sweet butter, melted
4 tablespoons lemon juice
Grated rind of ½ lemon
1½ tablespoons very finely
   chopped fresh mint

Remove the giblets. Cut the hens in two lengthwise, removing the backbones. Wash the hens and pat dry. Season lightly with salt and pepper. Place on a broiler pan, skin side down.

Combine the melted butter, lemon juice and rind, and mint. Brush over the hens.

Broil 6 inches from the heat for about 8 minutes, or until the hens are beginning to brown. Turn skin side up, and baste again. Broil for approximately 12 more minutes, or until the hens are nicely browned, and the juices run clear when the hens are pricked with a knife at the joints.

Yield: 4 servings

Variation:

Try broiling hens over coals, basting often; cooking time should be about 30 minutes.

Roast rock cornish hens

2 Rock Cornish hens, fresh
   or defrosted
Salt and pepper
⅓ cup breadcrumbs
3 tablespoons coarsely
   chopped fresh mint
Grated rind of ½ orange
2–3 tablespoons chopped
   walnuts or pine nuts
Dry white vermouth, stock,
   or water
3 tablespoons butter, melted
2 tablespoons orange juice
Grated rind of ½ orange

Preheat oven to 350° F.

Remove the giblets. Wash inside and out. Pat dry. Season inside and out lightly with salt and pepper. Truss.

Mix the breadcrumbs with the mint, orange rind, and nuts. Moisten lightly with liquid. Add salt and pepper to taste.

Fill the hens lightly with the stuffing.

Place on a baking pan. Roast for 60 to 70 minutes, or until the hens are golden brown, the joints move easily, and the juices run clear when pricked with the point of a knife. Baste frequently with the butter mixed with the orange juice and grated rind.

Serve hot or at room temperature. Try them with mint-flavored Yogurt Sauce.

Yield: 2 roast hens, serving 2 generously or 4 lightly

Note: You can make more stuffing if you like and put it in the oven, in a covered ovenproof dish, for the last 15 to 20 minutes that the hens are cooking.

YOGURT SAUCE

1 cup plain yogurt
1 tablespoon fresh lemon
   juice
Grated rind of ½ lemon
4 tablespoons fresh mint,
   coarsely chopped

Combine the ingredients. Pour over hens, or serve separately in a bowl.

Peas with prosciutto

2 tablespoons butter
1 small onion, chopped
2 cups shelled fresh grean
  peas
Chicken stock
Pinch of sugar (optional)
⅓ cup prosciutto, chopped
  or cut into strips
1 tablespoon chopped
  parsley

Melt the butter in a saucepan and sauté the onion until it is translucent. Add the peas and chicken stock just to cover. If you like, add a little sugar. Cook over medium heat until the peas are just tender.

Two or three minutes before the peas are done, drain any excess liquid and stir in the prosciutto and the parsley.

Yield: 4 servings

Twelve-fruit salad

It has long been traditional to list twelve fruits or graces of the Holy Spirit in the lives of believers, Galatians 5 having provided the essential idea. The twelve are charity, joy, peace, patience, benignity, goodness, long-suffering, mildness, faith, modesty, continency, and chastity.

This is a wonderful season for fresh fruit. What could be more fitting or appetizing for this feast than a mixed fruit salad?

12 kinds of fresh fruit. Here
  are some possibilities:
  grapes (combine different
  varieties), strawberries,
  blackberries, raspberries,
  peaches, nectarines,
  plums, apricots,
  pineapple, apples,
  bananas, melon (combine
  different varieties),
  oranges, grapefruit, kiwi,
  mangoes
Sugar (optional)
Lemon juice

Wash, hull, peel, slice the fruit as necessary. If you are using melons, cut into bite-sized chunks or melon balls.

You can either mix all the fruits together in a large bowl, or lay them in an attractive pattern (perhaps with twelve as an organizing motif) on a bed of greens.

Sprinkle with a little sugar if you wish, and with a little lemon juice.

If you like, you can serve this salad with Curry Mayonnaise.

CURRY MAYONNAISE
Combine the ingredients.

1 cup mayonnaise
¼ teaspoon ground ginger
½ teaspoon curry powder
1 teaspoon honey
2 tablespoons lime juice

Yield: about 1¼ cups sauce

Italian dove bread

COLOMBA DI PASQUA

It must be said that this is an Easter rather than a Pentecost bread. But I think we will steal it—rob Peter to pay Paul, as it were—and claim it for Pentecost, for which it is symbolically so appropriate.

1½ teaspoons active dry yeast
2 tablespoons warm water, about 110° F.
6 tablespoons sweet butter
⅓ cup sugar
2 teaspoons grated lemon rind
1 teaspoon vanilla extract
½ teaspoon almond extract
3 egg yolks
2 eggs
¼ teaspoon salt
⅓ cup warm milk
3–4 cups flour

ALMOND PASTE
TOPPING:
½ cup almond paste
1 egg white, lightly beaten
3 tablespoons sugar
16–20 whole blanched almonds (optional)
1 egg white
Sugar

Sprinkle the yeast into the warm water.

In a large bowl, cream the butter with the sugar. Add the grated lemon rind, and the vanilla and almond extracts.

Beat the egg yolks and eggs until thick and lemon-colored. Stir them into the butter mixture.

Dissolve the salt in the milk. Stir the milk and the yeast into the butter-egg mixture. Mix thoroughly. Stir in the flour, a little at a time, to make a soft dough. Turn the dough out onto a floured board and knead for about 10 minutes, or until it is firm and elastic. Place the dough in a greased bowl, turning to grease the top of the dough. Cover with a towel. Let the dough rise in a draft-free place until doubled in bulk—about 1 to 1½ hours.

Punch down the dough. Knead it again briefly on a floured board.

Divide the dough into two pieces. I find that the bird's proportions come out better if one of the pieces is a little bigger than the other. With the smaller piece make an oval shape about 5 by 8 inches, for the wings. Place the wings across the width of a baking sheet. With the other, larger piece, roll out a triangular shape about 12 inches high with a 5-inch base and a 1-inch top. Lay the triangle over, perpendicular to the oval. Twist the narrow end of the triangle one way to form the head of the dove. Pinch the dough to form a beak. Flatten the head down well on the pan: otherwise it will bounce up. Twist the wide end of the triangle in the opposite direction to form the tail. Spread it out and flatten it down well. Cut slashes in the tail and wings to resemble feathers.

Make the almond-paste topping, mixing all the ingredients together until smooth. Spread the paste over the wings and tail. Press the almonds into the wings, if you wish. Cover the dove loosely with a towel, and allow it to rise for 20 minutes, or until slightly puffy. Brush the entire dove with beaten egg white. Sprinkle the wings and tail generously with sugar.

Bake at 325° F. for about 45 to 50 minutes, or until the bread sounds slightly hollow when tapped. If the dove browns too fast, cover it with foil.

Cool on a wire rack.

Yield: 1 large dove, about 9 by 13 inches

Pentecost cake

At Pentecost a few years ago the usefulness of food for teaching religious ideas really became apparent to me. I was trying to explain to my children what Pentecost was, and their eyes were getting that glassy look that mothers know so well. I was losing them fast. Then (providential inspiration?) I declared, "We are going to bake a cake to eat on the great feast of Pentecost. How shall we decorate it?" Now, as it happens, my children love to decorate cakes and cookies. Their eyes brightened and their ears pricked up. We made a pretty wild-looking bakery item, with flames and doves and rays of light, but we all had a wonderful time, and they certainly knew what Pentecost was by the time we were through.

Any cake, iced with white icing (or colored icing, if you prefer)

For decorating: Tubes of decorator icing and/or sprinkles in various colors; and/or strawberries, cherries, or other small fruits. Before deciding, read Concepts.

Concepts, taken from the ancient traditions of Christian art:

Red flames—that hovered over the Apostles

White dove—in honor of the Holy Spirit; if the cake has white icing, you can outline the dove in red or another color

Rays of yellow (gold)—perhaps surrounding the dove, to suggest divinity

7 of some shape (small doves? rays of light?)—to suggest the sevenfold gifts of the Holy Spirit (a list derived essentially from Isaiah 11:2): wisdom, understanding, counsel, fortitude, knowledge, piety, and fear of the Lord

12 strawberries or other fruits—to suggest the fruits of the Holy Spirit (page 213)

Arthur, the good King of Britain, whose prowess teaches us that we, too, should be brave and courteous, held a rich and royal court upon that precious feast-day which is always known by the name of Pentecost.

Chrétien de Troyes, *Yvain*, trans. by W. W. Comfort

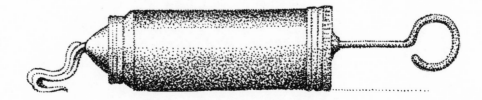

10

Thanksgiving

Thanksgiving—that is, the feast of thanksgiving celebrated on the fourth Thursday in November—is, of course, an American holiday. It was established in this country and is celebrated only by Americans.

The Pilgrim Fathers of Massachusetts decided sometime in late October or early November of 1621 to celebrate three days of rejoicing for their survival through the first hard winter and for the fruits of their first harvest, and for peace with their Indian neighbors. Their Indian friends Squanto and Chief Massasoit showed up with ninety or so braves to join in the feast. As to the menu: Governor Bradford had sent out hunters and they returned with various fowl. The Indians brought with them five deer. And there were apparently lobsters and oysters; frumenty; cranberries cooked in honey; homemade cakes and ale.

This first Thanksgiving, these three days of rejoicing, were clearly modeled on the old European tradition of the harvest-home festival, with eating and drinking, the singing of harvest songs, the playing of athletic and other games.

From this beginning, Thanksgiving soon became something of a tradition, though it was not celebrated every year, nor always at the same time of year, nor was it originally or reliably even called "Thanksgiving." But in 1863, close to 250 years after this feast was first celebrated, President Lincoln proclaimed Thanksgiving a national holiday. And it is altogether appropriate that Americans should set aside this day to give thanks to God: our cup runneth over.

The idea of a feast of thanksgiving has universal and venerable precedent. Gratitude to God (or to the gods: the powers that be) for the fruitfulness of the earth is deeply rooted in the religious heart of man.

The Jews had, and have today, three celebrations that are at least in part agricultural festivals: Passover, Pentecost, and Tabernacles or Succoth. Sacrifices were traditionally offered at the temple in thanksgiving for the harvest and festive meals held.

Christianity brought a new perspective to the ancient tradition. "Eucharist" itself means "thanksgiving," and God is thanked, sacrifice offered every time the Eucharist is celebrated. This is why the eucharistic feast became the fundamental Christian meal, imparting beauty and symbolism to all other feasts.

By the end of the first century Christians had ceased to observe the ancient Jewish agricultural festivals. Their new celebrations would thenceforth commemorate events in the life of Christ and of His Church, and by the third century, of His Mother and of the saints, many of them martyred for their faith. But Pentecost and (as we will see in Part Three) a few saints' days, such as St. Michael's and St. Martin's, did come in time to be celebrated in part as harvest or thanksgiving festivals.

The thanksgiving banquet is, in all its many forms, a beautiful tradition. Here are recipes for an old-fashioned, family-style American Thanksgiving, with an interesting twist or two.

Our harvest being gotten in, our governor sent four men on fowling, that we might after a special manner rejoice together after we had gathered the fruit of our labors. The four in one day killed as much fowl as, with a little help beside, served the company almost a week. At which time, amongst other recreations, we exercised our arms, many of the Indians coming amongst us, and among the rest their greatest king Massasoit, with some ninety men, whom for three days we entertained and feasted, and they went out and killed five deer, which they brought to the plantation and bestowed on our governor, and upon the captain and others. And although it be not always so plentiful as it was at this time with us, yet by the goodness of God, we are so far from want that we often wish you partakers of our plenty.

From a letter by Pilgrim Edward Winslow to a friend in England
shortly after the colonists' celebration of their
first successful harvest

Roast turkey

Wild turkeys were unquestionably among the fowl brought back by Governor Bradford's hunters, though they had certainly gone looking for the more traditional ducks and geese. This recipe, which produces an absolutely superlative turkey, calls for a high oven temperature. That is what roasting really means: cooking with a hot fire, on a spit or grill. Frequent basting is essential: a turkey is a very dry bird.

Wild rice—an authentic American treat—goes well with turkey. (Several wild-and-white-rice blends are also available, at a lower price.)

Along with the turkey and Cranberry Sauce, you might serve a green vegetable such as broccoli or Brussels sprouts, and a green salad. Cornbread is a pleasant and authentic addition—corn having been essential to the Pilgrims' survival during those first few years in the new land. Perhaps two desserts: why not?—it's Thanksgiving!

1 10–12-pound turkey
½ lemon
Salt
Freshly ground pepper
Bread stuffing with apples
   and prunes (opposite)
Melted butter, or a softened
   stick of butter

Preheat oven to 450° F.

Rinse the turkey; pat dry; rub the cavities with half a lemon; sprinkle with salt and pepper. Stuff. Sew up the opening, or close with skewers. Tie the wings to the body with string. Place the bird on a rack in a large roasting pan. Baste with plenty of melted butter, or rub with a stick of softened butter.

Start roasting the bird with its breast down, for 20 minutes. Turn it and roast for 20 minutes on each side, basting the turkey each time after you turn it. Then set the turkey breast up, and roast until it gets nice and brown all over. Baste frequently—every 15 minutes—with butter. After an hour or so, you may wish to turn the oven down to 375° if the turkey seems to be getting too brown too fast. But 2 hours of roasting should be plenty for a 10- to 12-pound bird. Don't overcook. A turkey is done when its legs move easily, and when the flesh feels soft and the skin is brown and crisp-looking.

For easier carving, let the turkey sit for a few minutes after removal from the oven.

I think that no gravy can compare with the natural sauce composed of the butter and cooking juices left in the pan. They are delicious by themselves. Scrape into them all those little bits of brown left in the pan.

Bread stuffing with apples and prunes

One of the traditional stuffings for goose is a mixture of apples and prunes, but they are delicious as well as part of a bread stuffing for turkey.

3 cups diced slightly stale
    bread (see Note)
½ cup melted butter
1 cup peeled, cored,
    chopped tart apples
1 cup pitted, chopped
    prunes
½ to ¾ cup chopped
    walnuts or pecans
1 teaspoon salt
¾ teaspoon paprika
2 tablespoons lemon juice

Combine the ingredients. Stuff the turkey lightly.

Yield: about 5 cups, enough for a 10-pound turkey

Variations:

You can use mixed dried fruits instead of prunes; use blanched almonds for the nuts.

This stuffing also makes a delicious and unusual filling for acorn-squash halves. Pour a little cream or stock over the top.

Note: Use good-quality bread. Try combining white or oatmeal with some rye bread or whole- or cracked-wheat bread. I don't remove the crusts: they just add character to the stuffing.

Cornbread

Try, along with your turkey, a cornbread made with good old-fashioned coarse-ground cornmeal. It has true grit and great flavor.

1 cup flour
1 teaspoon salt
4 teaspoons baking powder
1 cup stone-ground (coarse)
    cornmeal
1 cup milk
2 eggs
4 tablespoons sweet butter,
    melted
2 to 4 tablespoons brown
    sugar or molasses

Preheat the oven to 375° F. Butter a 9- or 10-inch square baking pan.

In a large bowl, sift together the flour, salt, and baking powder. Stir in the cornmeal.

In a bowl, mix the milk with the eggs and butter. Stir in the molasses or brown sugar. Blend the wet into the dry ingredients. Stir only until the mixture is just moistened.

Pour into the baking pan. Bake for about 20 minutes, or until the cornbread is golden brown and a knife inserted in the center comes out clean.

America! America! God shed his grace on thee
And crown thy good with brotherhood From sea to shining sea!
Katharine Lee Bates, ''America the Beautiful''

Cranberry-orange sauce

The Pilgrims ate a lot of cranberries, which grew wild in the bogs of New England. Following the example of the Indians, they generally boiled cranberries with maple syrup or honey. I have to admit that the Pilgrims didn't have any oranges, so this recipe isn't authentic; it's just good. These two fruits make a nice combination. And what would Thanksgiving turkey be without cranberry sauce?

½ cup water
1½ cups sugar
4 cups cranberries
1 orange, peeled, seeded, chopped
2 tablespoons freshly grated orange rind

Place water and sugar in a saucepan. Stir until the sugar is dissolved. Bring to a boil, and add the cranberries. Boil, stirring, just long enough for the berries to pop, but not to cook them very much. Cool. Add chopped oranges and grated rind. Taste for sweetness; add more sugar if desired. Chill thoroughly.

Yield: about 5 cups

Pumpkin pie

There was apparently no pumpkin pie at the very first Thanksgiving, but it has long been associated with this feast. This recipe makes a marvelously spicy pie.

3 eggs, lightly beaten
¾ cup brown sugar
½ teaspoon salt
¾ teaspoon ground ginger
½ teaspoon cinnamon
½ teaspoon nutmeg
½ teaspoon ground cloves
1 tablespoon molasses
1 teaspoon vanilla
1¾ cups canned pumpkin (or mashed cooked pumpkin)
1 cup heavy cream
1 nine-inch unbaked pie shell, with a high fluted rim

Preheat the oven to 450° F.

Beat the eggs with sugar, salt, and spices. Add molasses and vanilla, pumpkin and cream; mix well. Adjust seasonings. Pour the mixture into the crust and bake for 10 minutes. Lower the oven temperature to 400° F. and bake until a knife inserted into the center of the pie comes out clean: this will take 35 to 45 minutes.

Yield: 6 to 8 servings

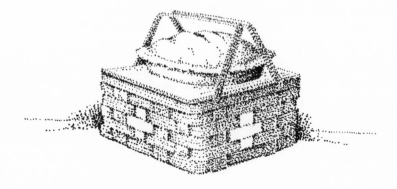

Steamed cranberry pudding

I am one of those people who think you can hardly ever eat enough cranberries, and this recipe is just maybe my very favorite of all. I still remember the first time I ate Cranberry Pudding, with its unctuous sauce; I couldn't believe how good it was!

1½ cups flour
2 teaspoons baking soda
⅛ teaspoon salt
¼ teaspoon ground ginger
⅛ teaspoon ground cloves
⅔ cup water
3 tablespoons sweet butter
⅓ cup molasses
¼ cup brown sugar
2¼ cups cranberries (chop, if desired)

Butter generously a pudding steamer. Dust with flour.

Sift the flour with the baking soda, salt, ginger, and cloves.

In a saucepan heat the water with the butter, stirring until the butter is melted. Stir in the molasses and brown sugar. Cook, stirring, until the mixture is well blended. Add gradually to the flour mixture, stirring until the mixture is smooth. Add the cranberries and mix well.

Pour the mixture into the pudding steamer. Cover it tightly.

Place the pudding steamer on a wire rack or vegetable steamer in a large pot with a tightly fitting lid. Pour an inch or so of water into the pot. Bring it to a boil, cover the pot tightly and reduce heat. Steam the pudding for about 2 hours, or until the pudding is firm and a knife inserted into the center comes out clean. Check occasionally to be sure that the water has not boiled away.

Serve warm with hot sauce poured over each slice.

SAUCE FOR THE PUDDING

1 cup sugar
1 cup heavy cream
⅓ cup butter
1 teaspoon vanilla

Combine the sugar, cream, and butter in the top of a double boiler. Heat thoroughly, stirring frequently, until the butter is melted. Add the vanilla and serve hot.

Yield: 6 to 8 servings

Celebrate the Feast of Tabernacles for seven days after you have gathered the produce of your threshing floor and your winepress. Be joyful at your Feast—you, your sons and daughters, your menservants and maidservants, and the Levites, the aliens, the fatherless and the widows who live in your towns. For seven days celebrate the Feast to the Lord your God at the place the Lord will choose. For the Lord your God will bless you in all your harvest and in all the work of your hands, and your joy will be complete.

Deuteronomy 16:13–15 (NIV)

PART THREE Feasts in honor of the saints and other special occasions

*C*hristian calendars have been, since the very beginning, variable, idiosyncratic. There is an open-endedness to the Christian calendar that gives it much of its charm and appeal, as the seasons roll around.

All the major Christian feasts focus, as well they should, on Christ, on God. But for centuries people have also wished to honor the Virgin Mary and many different saints, as well as particular aspects of the Divinity, such as the Trinity. Now the set of festivals that you will find in these pages has a particular idiosyncrasy of its own: it focuses essentially (don't say you're surprised!) on what people have eaten as part of their commemoration. There are great saints that you won't—alas—find here. Those who do appear do so at least in part because they inspired dishes; because they figure in some interesting or moving or amusing—or especially delicious!— way in the history of food in the Christian tradition.

Different readers may wish to use this part of the book in quite different ways. Some Protestant readers, wishing to focus exclusively on the major, Christ-centered feasts, may set aside the saints' days as outside of their tradition. A number of Protestants, however, are becoming convinced of the usefulness of honoring some of the saints—such as the Apostles, the Evangelists, some of the early martyrs—as models of heroism. And of course such traditional feasts as All Saints and All Souls have wide appeal, as do such commemorations as that of the great Archangel Michael. Protestant readers may also wish to insert into this calendar some of their own uncanonized but saintly figures, and honor them with feasts.

Catholic and Orthodox readers may also wish to modify somewhat the list of feasts and saints' days, and include yet other saints and occasions important to them. All to the good! This is, as I said, a very open-ended calendar.

But it is my hope that we can all learn something from each other's traditions: something about the richness, the diversity, the beauty—and the antiquity and universality—of the Christian heritage.

226

11

Winter

THE FEAST OF ST. ANTHONY
OF THE DESERT
January 17

St. Anthony of the Desert is very commonly represented in works of art with a pig next to him—and on his feast day it is traditional to eat pork. The pig has clear symbolic meaning.

Anthony was born in Egypt in A.D. 250 to a very wealthy family, but as a young man he took to heart the words "Go and sell what you have and give it to the poor." He went off alone to live in the Egyptian desert, and became one of the first great Christian hermits. He lived a life of great austerity, trying to pray constantly, and subsisting only on bread and water. Legend has it that the Devil tried to tempt him, taking many different forms—among them a hog, representing sensuality. But Anthony resisted all temptation, and that's what the pig (and the pork) are there to symbolize for the viewer (and the eater). Anthony died at the age of 105 in his cave on Mount Kolzim near the Red Sea.

Another charming feature of St. Anthony is that he is the patron saint of domestic animals. In various countries, among them Spain and Switzerland, animals—horses, mules, even dogs, cats and parrots!—have traditionally been groomed and decorated with ribbons, flowers and bells on his feast, and led in a procession to the church to be blessed with holy water and a special invocation.

I am struck by the humor of eating delectable pork in honor of a saint who ate only bread and water—and for whom the pig symbolized (among other things) gluttony. Well, if most of us can't *imitate* this saint very well, we can at least *honor* him.

There is poetry in a pork chop to a hungry man.

Philip Gibbs, quoted in the *New York Times*

228

Pork chops with sauerkraut

This recipe comes from Eastern Europe.

1 onion, finely chopped
2 tablespoons butter
1 teaspoon Hungarian (or
    other good) paprika
1 pound sauerkraut, drained
2–3 tablespoons dry
    vermouth
6 pork chops
Salt to taste
1 cup sour cream

In a large frying pan, sauté the onion in the butter. Stir in the paprika and the sauerkraut. Add the vermouth. Cover and simmer gently.

Sprinkle the pork chops with salt. In another pan, sauté the chops in their own fat, or in a little butter, until nicely browned on both sides.

Place the pork chops on top of the sauerkraut, cover, and cook gently until the pork chops are fully cooked (the length of time will vary according to the thickness of the chops).

Remove the pork chops from the pan. Stir the sour cream into the sauerkraut mixture, and taste for seasoning. Replace the pork chops on top of the sauerkraut.

Yield: 6 servings

ST. BRIDGID OF IRELAND
February 1

St. Bridgid is an extraordinary figure, inextricably entwined with Irish legend. She lived apparently in the sixth century, and is said to have been baptized by St. Patrick himself. She became a nun early, founded the nunnery of Kildare, and is considered to have been one of the great contributors to the spread of Christianity in Ireland.

Legends about her stress her charity and the miraculous (and occasionally amusing) multiplication of food. As a young girl, she once gave away all the family's butter to the poor—but God replaced it "with usury." A leprous woman once asked her for a glass of milk; Bridgid had none, but gave her cold water, which was turned into milk; when the woman had drunk it she was healed. Bridgid is said to have changed her bathwater into beer once to quench the thirst of some unexpected ecclesiastical visitors, and her cows gave milk three times one day so that some visiting bishops would have something to drink.

On the Eve of St. Bridgid's feast, every farmer's wife in Ireland traditionally bakes a bairn (or barm) brack—a spiced yeast bread. The neighbors are invited in and, as the folklore specialist Hazlitt puts it, "the madder of ale and the pipe go around, and the evening concludes with mirth and festivity."

May your laughter be from God.

Irish Proverb

Bairn brack

2 packages dry yeast
½ cup warm milk, about
    100–110° F.
1 cup brown sugar
1 stick unsalted butter
½ cup lukewarm water
4½ cups flour
2 teaspoons salt
4 eggs, well beaten
3–4 tablespoons caraway
    seeds
½ cup currants
1 healthy pinch each of
    nutmeg, allspice,
    cinnamon
Optional:
    1 small pinch cloves and
    ginger

OPTIONAL GLAZE:
1 tablespoon water
1 tablespoon sugar

Dissolve the yeast in the milk. Stir in 1 teaspoon of the brown sugar. Let the mixture sit for about 10 minutes, or until it is bubbly.

In a saucepan, melt the butter in the water; cool slightly. Pour into a large bowl. Stir in the flour and the salt. Add the eggs, stirring well, and the yeast, then stir in the remaining sugar, the caraway seeds, currants, and spices. Beat for 2 or 3 minutes.

Turn the dough out onto a floured surface, and knead for about 10 minutes, or until it is smooth and glossy. The dough should be fairly soft.

Place the dough in a buttered bowl; turn to grease the top. Cover and let rise in a draft-free spot until doubled in bulk, about 1 hour.

Punch the dough down, and form into a large round cake. Place on a buttered pan, cover lightly, and let rise until again doubled in bulk, about 1 hour.

Bake at 375° F. for 45 to 55 minutes, or until a skewer inserted into the center comes out clean, and the bread sounds hollow when tapped on the bottom. (If the bread begins to get too brown, cover it with a piece of aluminum foil or brown paper.)

Optional: Glaze the loaf, while hot, with a mixture of 1 tablespoon water and 1 tablespoon sugar.

Yield: 1 12-inch loaf

God is always opening His hand.

Spanish Proverb

ST. VALENTINE'S DAY
February 14

This day is celebrated with such enthusiasm in America—with hearts and flowers and chocolate candies, and tender or passionate or risqué greeting cards—we tend to forget that it commemorates a Christian martyr, a priest who died near Rome in the third century, during the persecutions of the Emperor Claudius the Goth.

How did this priest and martyr get mixed up with lovers? This point is unclear—and somewhat controversial. It has been suggested that the association between St. Valentine and love dates back to the old Roman Lupercalia, a pagan festival with strange fertility rites, that took place in mid-February. But our earliest evidence for the actual connection between the saint and lovers dates from the fourteenth century. Here is a charming quotation from the fifteenth century that clearly shows the tradition. A lady writes to her future son-in-law, encouraging him to come ask for her daughter's hand in marriage:

> And, Cousin, upon Friday is St. Valentine's Day, and every bird chooseth him a mate, and if it like you to come on Thursday at night, and so purvey that you may abide there till Monday, I trust to God that you shall speak to my husband, and I pray that we shall bring the matter to a conclusion.

This passage from *The Paston Letters* suggests what is in fact the likeliest connection between lovers and St. Valentine: it was thought, in England, that on or around this date, February 14, birds chose their mates for the season, and it came to be thought that human beings as well should choose their mates that day, under the patronage of St. Valentine.

The major symbols of this day—hearts, the color red, angels, and flowers—and the themes of tenderness, fidelity, the forming of bonds of love—all these belong strongly and beautifully to the Christian tradition. For example, the heart has often been used to represent the quality of love of several of the saints (such as Augustine)—not to mention (in the Catholic tradition) the love of Christ for humanity, and of Mary. Red has long been the color of martyrdom and the Passion; worldly lovers have borrowed this symbolism from Christianity precisely because of its power as a theme: to love someone is to be willing to suffer and die for him or her.

So, by all means, let's honor love and St. Valentine on his feast. Here are two recipes that pick up the major themes.

Love knots

It became a custom in the later Middle Ages to wear "love knots" on St. Valentine's Day. Gold pins, shaped like sideways figure 8s, they are symbols for infinity, and suggest love that is without end, eternal. The pins are traditionally made of gold, since that most precious of metals never tarnishes, never loses its perfection.

There is no need to give each other precious jewelry for St. Valentine's Day, but this theme of true love is a deep and beautiful one. Here then is a recipe for "love knots," edible ones, a sweet pretzel-like twist.

1 cup butter
1 cup sugar
1 egg yolk
2 eggs
¼ cup sour cream
1 teaspoon vanilla extract
Several drops yellow food coloring
2½ cups flour
1 teaspoon grated lemon rind
Yellow sprinkles

Beat the butter until soft. Gradually add the sugar, and blend the butter-sugar mixture until fluffy. Beat in the egg yolk, the eggs, sour cream, vanilla extract and yellow food coloring (to make the dough more "golden"). Sift and stir in the flour; add the lemon rind.

Chill the dough for several hours and only remove it from the refrigerator a little at a time: this will make it easier to handle.

Preheat the oven to 375° F.

Shape the dough into ropes about ½ inch in diameter and 12 inches long, and twist these into figure 8s. Place the twists on a greased baking sheet, and bake for about 15 minutes. About halfway through the cooking, gild with yellow sprinkles.

Yield: 12 to 14 love knots

St. Valentine's day cake

This is in one sense a perfectly conventional St. Valentine's Day cake: shaped like a heart, with red icing, etc. It is a nice cake to make with children. You might reflect with them on the meaning of the symbols. Red: the blood of martyrdom—and St. Valentine was a martyr. The heart: symbol of the very deepest and truest love. Angels? This time, why not skip the Cupids (symbols of intense, erotic desire) and instead turn to the Seraphim, the highest of the angels, who are all fire and love? Flowers? Roses are symbols of Mary, and are associated with several other saints as well, such as St. Elizabeth of Hungary. (Why? Because she was forever carrying bread to the poor, and—so says the story—her husband became cross at all her charitable activities. One day he met her in the road with a heavy basketful of something. He demanded to be shown what she was carrying, and when she opened the basket, it was full of . . . roses.)

You see the possibilities. . . .

*Any cake: made from
    scratch or from a mix*
*Any white icing: whether
    homemade or made from
    a mix*
Red food coloring
Optional:
*   Strawberry or raspberry
    jam*
*   Red decorative items,
    such as gum drops, jelly
    beans, red hots (these are
    ideal for small children)*
*   Red or white decorative
    icing, to be used in a
    decorating tube: you can
    make shapes such as
    hearts, roses, angels, etc.*

Bake the cake in a square pan, or in a sheet-cake pan. (Use heart-shaped pans if available.) When the cake is fully cooled, cut it into two heart-shaped layers. (Draw a heart carefully on waxed paper; cut it out. Then, placing the waxed paper on the cake, cut out the hearts. Remember that it is important that both layers be of identical shape!)

Prepare the icing according to directions, adding drops of red food coloring, to produce the desired shade of red. Ice the cake. Use the jam as icing between the two layers, if you wish.

Decorate the cake with whatever appeals to you and your children. With younger children I would recommend things that cannot go wrong: jelly beans in the shape of hearts, for example. If you are working with older children, or alone, you can try more complex and sophisticated motifs and techniques: angels or roses, made with the decorating tube.

CARNIVAL AND MARDI GRAS

"Carnival," "Mardi Gras": these words evoke in the imagination of many people visions of platters piled high with delicious pancakes or crêpes or blini, with fruit-filled beignets, meat-stuffed turnovers. These terms conjure up not merely a day but a whole season of indulgence in good foods, as well as in other pleasures.

Carnival is a rather peculiar season of the Christian year. No one knows just when it begins, whether at Epiphany, the day Christmas officially ends, or just three or four days before Lent. It *is* clear, though, when Carnival ends: in the West, the last day of Carnival is Fat Tuesday (also called "Butter" or "Shrove Tuesday"), the day before Ash Wednesday, which is the first day of Lent. For the Orthodox Lent starts on Clean Monday.

Whatever its exact dates, Carnival has always been understood to be the period before the rigors of Lent begin, before the elimination of meat and dairy products from the diet ("Carnival" comes from Latin and means "the removal of meat.") During this season people have traditionally prepared themselves for Lent. (Lent got them ready for Easter; Carnival got them ready for Lent!)

Christians had to clean out their larders—the places where they kept their lard, their bacon, their butter. Need I say that they generally "cleaned out" their larders by eating up everything in them? So the last few days before Lent were generally high in consumption of foods rich in butter, eggs, and cream, and often pies with meat fillings. Almost every country has its traditions for how best to dispose of these soon-to-be forbidden foodstuffs. They ate them at large social gatherings, which sealed the bonds of family and group solidarity; good cheer, hospitality, and generosity abounded. After that, they felt properly motivated to carry out an ancient rite: the burning (or burial) of King Carnival—often represented as a fat man with a necklace of fat sausages. Once Christians had cleaned out their larders, they also cleaned up their souls: on Clean Monday the Eastern Orthodox go to confession and also scrub all cooking utensils. The English term "Shrove Tuesday" refers to the old tradition of going to confession, being "shriven" or forgiven.

Carnival was a period not merely of gastronomic binging, but of blowing off steam in many other ways. Starting in around the fourteenth century, there were masquerades and mummery (pantomimes performed by masked actors), balls and festivities of all sorts. (In a number of cities of the world these traditions are still going strong.) This revelry drew on ancient pre-Christian traditions, in particular those of the Saturnalia, and, in northern Europe, those of spring rites. While much of this merrymaking was just good fun, there was also often an unleashing of violent (sexual and other) impulses.

Not officially a religious or liturgical season, Carnival has no spot on any church calendar. The Church, both in the East and in the West, has recognized its existence only to the extent of sanctioning pleasurable and unobjectionable activities such as processions, parades, horse races.

Carnival is perhaps best described as the tradition of saying an exuberant good-bye to foods and pleasures that Christians would not taste again for forty days. Mardi Gras is essentially a farewell party.

Russian Buckwheat Pancakes

BLINI

In Russia, it has been traditional to eat blini upon blini, with sour cream and caviar, during Carnival season. Blini are pancakes made with yeast and buckwheat flour. They have a very interesting and unusual flavor. Blini can be a whole meal in themselves (especially if served with several different toppings); they can make a hearty first course, to be followed by a meat dish and vegetables; or, preceded by zakuski (mixed hors d'oeuvres, such as cold sliced meats, and cold vegetables marinated in vinaigrette), blini can be served as the main dish.

1 cup milk
½ package dry yeast (1 teaspoon)
4 eggs, separated
1½ cups sifted buckwheat flour
¼ cup sour cream
½ teaspoon salt
1½ teaspoons sugar
3 tablespoons melted butter

Scald the milk, and allow it to cool to warm (100–110° F.—no hotter or it will kill the yeast). Stir in the yeast.

Beat the egg yolks lightly.

Place the sifted flour in a large bowl. Make a well, and mix in the softened yeast, egg yolks, sour cream, salt, sugar, and melted butter. Blend thoroughly. Cover the bowl, and allow the batter to rise for about 1¼ hours, or until frothy and about doubled in bulk.

Beat the egg whites until stiff but not dry. Fold them gently into the batter. Cover the mixture and allow it to rise for 20 to 30 minutes.

Preheat a griddle or frying pan. Brush lightly with butter. Pour the batter, a small ladleful (or large spoonful) at a time, onto the pan. (The batter, unlike that of ordinary pancakes, does not run in the pan.) Cook until lightly browned on each side, turning once.

Whip some sour cream lightly with a fork and spoon onto the blini. Sprinkle with red caviar. Alternatively you can serve with melted butter and crumbled bacon.

Variation:

You can substitute white flour for half (or all) the buckwheat flour, if you prefer. (Buckwheat flour is more authentic, and very tasty, but white flour produces lighter pancakes.)

Yield: about 30 three-inch *Blini*

Irish buttermilk pancakes

This is what Irish wives and mothers have served for hundreds of years to their families on Shrove Tuesday: Pancake Night—the eve of Ash Wednesday. Serve with bacon or sausage.

2 cups sifted flour
½ teaspoon baking soda
½ teaspoon salt
1 egg
Enough buttermilk to make a thick batter (about 2½– 3 cups)
Butter and sugar (or honey)

Sift together the flour, baking soda, and salt. Combine the egg and buttermilk. Mix the liquid into the dry ingredients. Do not beat: mix only enough so that the ingredients are well blended; the batter will be lumpy.

Drop the batter by large spoonfuls onto a hot greased griddle or frying pan. Butter the pancakes as they come from the pan, and sprinkle them generously with sugar (or dribble honey over them).

Yield: approximately 15 five-inch pancakes

Apple fritters from Normandy

BEIGNETS NORMANDS AUX POMMES

> *This recipe, only one of dozens of delectable French Mardi Gras recipes, produces fritters that are absolutely out of this world. What makes them "Norman" is the emphasis on apples and apple products: cider and Calvados (apple brandy, made in the Calvados region of Normandy). This recipe is adapted from a marvelous book entitled* Fêtes, Coutumes et Gâteaux, *by Nicole Vielfaure and Christine Beauviala.*

2¼ cups flour
1½ cups powdered sugar
Pinch of salt
1 cup milk
1 cup hard or sweet cider
1¼ pounds tart eating
  apples (Granny Smiths
  are my favorite)
1¼ cups granulated sugar
1 cup Calvados (or sweet
  cider)
Oil for deep-fat frying
Confectioners' sugar for
  sprinkling over the fritters

Mix the flour, powdered sugar, and salt in a large bowl. Make a well, and pour into it gradually the milk and the cider, alternating between the two, stirring constantly. Cover the mixture and let it sit at least 30 minutes.

In the meantime, peel and core the apples, and cut them into rounds ¼ inch thick. Stir the granulated sugar into the Calvados and let the apple slices sit in this mixture for 30 minutes or more.

Heat the oil to 370° F. Coat each apple slice with the batter and fry, a few at a time, in the hot oil until golden brown on both sides.

Drain well (brown-paper grocery bags are useful for this), then sprinkle with confectioners' sugar and serve hot.

Yield: 15 to 20 fritters

Carnival knots

SFRAPPOLE DI CARNEVALE

> *These delicious "knots" are served at Carnival time in northern Italy, the Emilia-Romagna region. Just slightly sweet and with a subtle flavor, they are wonderful served with a fruit salad or ice cream—or just with coffee.*

4 cups flour
2 tablespoons butter,
  softened
3 egg yolks, lightly beaten
1 egg white, lightly beaten
2½ tablespoons sugar
1 teaspoon salt
1½ teaspoons vanilla
  extract
Grated rind of 1 lemon
1–1½ cups white wine
Oil for deep-fat frying
Confectioners' sugar

Sift the flour into a large bowl. Work in the softened butter. Add the beaten yolks, the egg white, the sugar, salt, vanilla, and lemon rind. Mix in enough white wine to make a soft, smooth dough.

Place the dough in a plastic bag and refrigerate for 1 hour.

On a lightly floured surface, roll the dough out as thin as possible. Cut the dough into strips ½ inch wide and 8 to 12 inches long, as you prefer. The shorter length you can make into a simple knot; the longer strip can be formed into more of a bow.

Heat the oil to 375° F., for deep frying. Fry the knots (or bows) in the oil, a few at a time, until they are golden brown. Drain them on paper towels or heavy brown bags. Sprinkle with confectioners' sugar.

Yield: about 60 to 65 Sfrappole

ST. DAVID
March 1

On St. David's feast, it has long been a custom for Welshmen, whose patron he is, to wear or otherwise display leeks. I recommend that we honor him by *eating* them.

St. David is a delight to the lover of legends. He is said to have been related (collaterally!) to the Virgin Mary, to have been as well the uncle of King Arthur. They say that when he preached, the ground beneath his feet rose to form a natural pulpit for him.

A few hard and impressive facts are known about his life. A priest and monk living in the sixth century, he founded ten monasteries, among them the famous Glastonbury, where the monks lived like the early hermits of Egypt, devoting themselves to prayer, study, and hard physical labor, sustained by a simple diet of bread, vegetables, and water. At the synod of Brefi in Cardigan he spoke with such eloquence (apparently against Pelagianism, which denies the fallen nature of man), that he was made Archbishop of Wales.

Legends abound but no firm explanation has been offered as to why leeks are displayed on his day: Shakespeare called it "an ancient tradition begun upon an honourable respect" (*Henry V*, Act V, Scene 1).

Here are two leek classics to display upon your table on the feast of St. David and at other times as well.

Braised leeks

8 leeks, as identical in size as possible
5 tablespoons sweet butter
¾ cup broth or stock
2 tablespoons lemon juice or dry vermouth
½ teaspoon salt
2 teaspoons sugar

Wash the leeks carefully to remove all grit. The nozzle on your sink may be helpful. If you need to slit the leeks up one side to get the dirt between the layers, try to damage the leeks' appearance as little as possible. Trim off the roots and most of the green end, leaving only an inch or so of green. Pat dry.

Melt 4 tablespoons of the butter in a skillet and sauté the leeks until browned on all sides. Add the broth, lemon juice, salt, and sugar. Cover and simmer until the leeks are just tender. Remove and keep warm.

Boil the sauce down until it is reduced to a fairly thick glaze. Stir in the remaining 1 tablespoon butter and adjust seasoning. Pour the sauce over the leeks.

Yield: 2 to 4 servings

Cold leek and potato soup

VICHYSSOISE

6 medium potatoes
6 large leeks
6 cups water or chicken
  broth
Salt
About ½ cup heavy cream
Freshly ground white
  pepper
Juice of ½ lemon
Optional:
  1 cup sour cream
  4 tablespoons chopped
  chives

Peel the potatoes and slice thin. Wash the leeks carefully, slitting them up one or both sides to remove the dirt between the layers. Trim off the roots. Slice the leeks thin.

Place the potatoes and leeks along with the water (or broth) in a large saucepan. Add salt to taste. Simmer until the vegetables are tender, about 15 minutes.

Put the vegetables and cooking liquid in the blender and whirl at a fairly high speed until the soup is smooth. (You can also put the vegetables through a food mill.) Blend in enough heavy cream to make the consistency you like. If the soup gets too thick, it can be thinned with milk or more chicken stock or water.

Season with white pepper and lemon juice. Adjust seasoning, oversalting slightly. (If you are going to serve the soup hot, as you may, do not oversalt.)

Chill for several hours or overnight.

Serve, if you like, with dollops of sour cream and chopped chives.

Yield: 4 servings

ST. PATRICK
March 17

St. Patrick, apostle to the Irish. One of his early biographers, Tírechán, relates that late in life Patrick went up to the top of Mount Aigli, where he fasted for forty days. "God told all the saints of Erin, past, present and future, to come to the mountain summit . . . to bless the tribes of Erin, so that Patrick might see the fruit of his labors, for all the choir of the saints of Erin came to visit him there, who was the father of them all." What a scene to imagine!

Patrick was born in England, about A.D. 389. As a boy he was carried off by raiders to be a slave among the still-pagan Irish. He tended his master's herds in the mountains, and at that time (as he tells in his autobiography) "love of God and His fear increased more and more, and my faith grew." Eventually he escaped and returned home to England. But he began to have visions and heard "the voices of those who dwelt beside the wood of Foclut and thus they cried, as if with one mouth, 'We beseech you, holy youth, to come and walk among us once more.' " Patrick, apparently after being ordained to the priesthood, returned to Ireland and began his work of evangelization. Because of his holiness and, legend has it, his great miracles, he was astonishingly successful. He overcame the opposition of the druids, and many members of the great families of Ireland became Christians. There were, however, attempts on his life, and as an old man Patrick wrote, "Daily I expect either a violent death or to be robbed and reduced to slavery or the occurrence of some such calamity." But he goes on: "I have cast myself into the hands of Almighty God, for He rules everything; as the Prophet says, 'Cast your care upon the Lord, and He Himself will sustain you.' "

Patrick died in 461, as Archbishop of Armagh.

This saint has been honored by Christians and especially by the Irish for centuries. Numerous legends have grown up around him, among them this famous story. Patrick was trying to explain to some pagans (who were threatening to stone him) about the mystery of the Trinity, which is both Three and One. He picked up a shamrock and pointed out that it has three leaves but is still one plant. This trefoil, called "Patrick's Cross," became the symbol both of this saint and of Ireland itself. It figures prominently on the feast of St. Patrick, when people have traditionally honored the shamrock, often by wearing it pinned to their sleeves. In some parts of Ireland they have feasted St. Patrick with salmon. Let's combine the two customs in a molded salmon dish. In Ireland, this might be served with a "Patrick's pot" of ale or whiskey.

St. Patrick was a gentleman, and he came from decent people,
In Dublin town he built a church, and on it put a steeple;
His father was a Wollaghan, his mother an O'Grady,
His aunt she was a Kinaghan, and his wife a widow Brady.
  Tooralloo, tooralloo, what a glorious man our saint was!
  Tooralloo, tooralloo, O whack fal de lal, de lal . . .
Och! Antrim hills are mighty high, and so's the hill of Howth too;
But we all do know a mountain that is higher than them both too;
'Twas on the top of that high mount St. Patrick preach'd a sermon.
He drove the frogs into the bogs, and banished all the vermin.
  Tooralloo, tooralloo, etc.

Every Day Book by Hone, 1836
(reprinted in *British Popular Customs, Present and Past,*
by T. F. Thiselton Dyer)

Salmon mold

1 envelope unflavored
  gelatin
¼ cup cold water
1 teaspoon salt
1½ teaspoons dry mustard
Dash of cayenne pepper
1 tablespoon grated onion
2 tablespoons flour
2 teaspoons sugar
2 egg yolks
3 tablespoons cider vinegar
1 cup milk
1 tablespoon butter
2 cups canned red salmon,
  chopped
Lettuce
Sour cream
1 or 2 teaspoons chopped
  fresh or dried dill
1 chopped peeled cucumber

Soften the gelatin in the cold water.

Place the salt, mustard, cayenne, onion, flour, and sugar in a saucepan. Beat in the egg yolks. Gradually stir in the vinegar and the milk until the mixture is smooth. Add the butter, stirring over low heat until it is melted.

Cook over low heat, stirring constantly, until the mixture is well thickened. Stir in the gelatin. Drain the salmon. Remove dark skin and bones; flake or chop the fish. Fold into the hot mixture. Mix gently but thoroughly. Adjust seasoning.

Turn the mixture into a lightly oiled mold. You can use one large or several small shamrock molds in honor of St. Patrick; or you can use a cross, fish, or ring mold.

Chill for several hours, or until set.

Unmold on a bed of lettuce and serve with sour cream to which the dill and cucumber have been added.

Yield: 8 to 10 servings

FORTY MARTYRS OF SEBASTE
March 9, in the East

In a number of countries a special dish is prepared once a year to honor the memory of the Forty Martyrs of Sebaste. Forty Christian soldiers were condemned, during the persecutions of the Eastern Roman Emperor Licinius in 320, to be exposed, naked, on a freezing night, near Sebaste in Lesser Armenia.

In Armenia they eat forty stuffed wheat balls (whose central ingredients are, alas, hard to come by in this country); in Greece as well the Forty Martyrs are honored by the eating of dishes that stress the number forty. Thus there are pies made with forty layers of phyllo pastry, dishes consisting of forty pancakes or made with forty kinds of wild herbs.

Eat forty, drink forty, and give forty to save your soul.

A Greek proverb

Forty martyrs meat balls

This recipe is very much in the Middle-Eastern spirit.

1½ pounds ground lamb
2 cloves garlic, pressed
About 1 teaspoon salt
Freshly ground black pepper
3 teaspoons dried mint
½ cup pine nuts
½ cup finely chopped
   parsley
1 or 2 tablespoons vegetable
   oil
Lettuce

Combine the lamb with the garlic, salt to taste, pepper, mint, pine nuts, and parsley. Mix thoroughly. Form into 40 meat balls about 1¼ inches in diameter. (Make it easy: divide the meat into 4 parts; divide each part into 10 meatballs.)

Heat the oil in a large skillet. Sauté the meat balls until nicely browned on the outside but still a little pink in the inside. Turn them often with a spatula. Remove excess grease as it is rendered.

Serve the meat balls on a bed of lettuce in five rows of eight meat balls each, or in some other clearly numerical arrangement. With them serve Rice or Bulghur Pilaf.

Yield: 6 to 8 servings

Variations:
You can add in with the meat ½ teaspoon allspice or coriander.

Rice pilaf

1 stick (½ cup) butter
1 small onion, chopped
2 cups raw rice
½ cup sliced or slivered
   almonds, or pine nuts
4 cups water or chicken
   broth
½ cup dried currants
½ teaspoon allspice
1–2 teaspoons salt
Freshly ground black pepper

Melt the butter in a saucepan. Add the onion, rice, and nuts, and sauté for about 3 minutes, stirring frequently, or until they are golden.

Add the water or broth, currants, allspice, salt (less if using broth containing salt), and a few grindings of black pepper. Bring to a boil. Cover tightly, reduce heat, and cook for about 20 minutes, or until the rice is soft and the liquid has been absorbed.

Yield: 6 to 8 servings

Variations:
Here are some of the many ways you can modify this dish:
Sauté ½ to 1 cup finely broken-up vermicelli or thin spaghetti along with the rice.
Use brown rice instead of white.
In place of (or along with) the allspice, season the dish with a pinch of saffron or ¼ teaspoon curry powder.
Eliminate the currants and allspice, and substitute ½ teaspoon or more dry basil, or several teaspoons chopped fresh basil leaves.
Use part broth, part white wine as the cooking liquid.
Stir in a few tablespoons chopped parsley just before serving.
To make a risotto: Eliminate the spices. Use water or broth as

the cooking liquid. When the rice is done, remove from the heat. Stir in 1 or 2 additional tablespoons of butter if desired. Stir in 1 lightly beaten egg, 1½ cups freshly grated Parmesan cheese and 8 tablespoons lemon juice.

Bulghur wheat

Bulghur wheat is cooked cracked wheat. It has a nutty flavor. Buy it ground "large."

1 stick butter
1 small onion, chopped
2 cups bulghur wheat
½ cup pine nuts
4 cups water or chicken
  broth
1 teaspoon dry basil or mint
1–2 teaspoons salt
Freshly ground pepper
Optional:
  ¼ cup chopped parsley

Melt the butter in a saucepan and sauté the onion, bulghur, and pine nuts until golden brown. Add the water, basil, salt (less if using broth containing salt), and pepper. Bring to a boil. Cover tightly, reduce heat, and cook until the bulghur is soft and the liquid absorbed. If you like, stir in the parsley before serving.

Yield: 6 to 8 servings

Variations:
You can add a pinch of crushed red pepper or cayenne with the water or broth; or you can stir in a few tablespoons of sesame seeds at the end.

ST. JOSEPH, FOSTER FATHER OF CHRIST
March 19

St. Joseph is honored by Christians throughout the world. But devotion to him apparently originated in the East, and only spread to Western Europe at the time of the Crusades, in the twelfth and thirteenth centuries. He became the patron not merely of carpenters but of various other guilds of working men. Because of his kindness to Mary when he discovered that she was pregnant, he is considered the patron of unwed mothers. Because he was the father in the Holy Family, he is the patron of Christian families and homes. He is the patron of the interior or spiritual life. St. Teresa of Avila, one of those who encouraged the devotion to St. Joseph in Spain, declared that she always "went to him" when she needed light from heaven . . . In Roman Catholicism he is considered the patron of the Universal Church, the family of Christians.

Nowhere has St. Joseph been venerated with deeper feeling—or with greater gusto—than in Italy. Customs involving the sharing of food play an important part in his *festa*. In various towns and villages in Sicily the people prepare a *tavola di San Giuseppe*—"St. Joseph's Table." This is a great banquet, set at a table in the piazza, to which orphans and all the poor are invited.

Many regions of Italy have dishes that bear the name of St. Joseph, and these are served to family and friends on his feast day. Here are two of the most interesting and delicious—though it is hard to choose! From Sicily come absolutely heavenly ricotta-filled cream puffs called Sfinge. From Florence come the Frittelle, with raisins, orange rind, and pine nuts.

St. Joseph's cream puffs

SFINGE DI SAN GIUSEPPE

1 cup water
⅓ cup sweet butter
1 tablespoon sugar
Grated rind of 1 lemon
Pinch of salt
1 cup sifted flour
4 large eggs, at room
 temperature
1 tablespoon Cognac or
 vanilla

FILLING:
2 cups ricotta cheese
½ cup confectioners' sugar
½ teaspoon vanilla
¼ teaspoon ground
 cinnamon
⅓ cup grated milk
 chocolate, or mini-
 chocolate chips
2 tablespoons finely
 chopped pistachios
Optional:
 1 tablespoon candied
 orange peel, or other
 candied fruit peel
 Confectioners' sugar for
 sprinkling on top

For the cream puffs: Place the water, butter, granulated sugar, lemon rind, and salt in a large saucepan. Bring the mixture to a boil, and as soon as the butter has melted, remove the pan from the heat. Add the flour *all at once, stirring constantly and vigorously.*

Return the pan to the heat, and stir constantly until the mixture forms a ball and comes away from the sides of the pan. Continue to cook a little longer, until you hear a slight crackling or frying sound. Remove the pan from the heat, and cool slightly.

Add the eggs, one at a time. Be sure that each egg is thoroughly blended into the mixture before you add the next. Keep stirring until the dough is smooth and thoroughly blended. Add the Cognac or vanilla. Cover the dough and let it stand for 15 to 20 minutes.

Preheat the oven to 400° F.

Drop the dough by heaping tablespoonfuls on a buttered cookie sheet, leaving 2 inches between the Sfinge. Bake for 20 to 25 minutes, until they are golden brown. Remove them from the oven and cool. So that the cream puffs will be crisp, fill them just before serving if possible.

For the filling: Mix the ricotta, confectioners' sugar, vanilla, cinnamon, chocolate, pistachios, and peel, if using it. Cut each cream puff horizontally part way through the middle and fill with the mixture.

Optional: Just before serving sprinkle Sfinge with confectioners' sugar. Keep them refrigerated, if not serving immediately.

Yield: about 20 Sfinge

continued

Variation:

The cream puffs can be deep-fried instead of baked. For deep-frying, follow the directions in the recipe below. Other kinds of fillings can be used, such as vanilla custard or sweetened whipped cream (to which a little vanilla or a liqueur may be added).

St. Joseph's rice fritters

FRITTELLE DI SAN GIUSEPPE

2¼ cups milk
1 cup raw rice
Pinch of salt
¼ teaspoon vanilla
¼ cup sugar
2 eggs
1 tablespoon flour
1 teaspoon baking powder
2 tablespoons fruit brandy
  (optional)
Grated rind of 1 large
  orange
3 tablespoons golden raisins
3 tablespoons pine nuts
Oil for deep frying
Confectioners' sugar

Bring the milk to a boil in a saucepan. Add the rice, salt, vanilla, and granulated sugar. Cover the pan, and simmer gently until the rice is cooked and the milk absorbed. Let the rice cool overnight or for several hours. (Do not proceed with the next step until the rice is fully cool.)

Mix the rice thoroughly with the eggs, flour, baking powder, brandy, orange rind, raisins, and pine nuts.

Heat the oil to 375° F. for deep-fat frying. Drop the Frittelle mixture 1 tablespoon at a time into the oil. Cook a few at a time, keeping the Frittelle separate. Fry until golden brown.

Drain the Frittelle on paper towels. Serve them hot, sprinkled with confectioners' sugar.

Yield: about 25 Frittelle

12

Spring

ST. BENEDICT OF NURSIA
March 21

Benedict was born around 480 in Nursia, Italy. As an adolescent he was sent to Rome to complete his education, but, horrified by Roman decadence, he left to become a hermit. He hid away for three years in a cave at Subiaco, in prayer and penance. Many, however, came to join him, and he eventually established for his followers the famous Abbey of Monte Cassino. He wrote for them a Rule, to guide and regulate them in the monastic life. Benedict's Rule set out a balanced combination of prayer, study, and manual labor. It is a fascinating document—full of interesting details, full of wisdom and compassion; and it fixed to a substantial degree the practice of monastic life in the West for at least a millennium.

Benedict died around 547, and is buried at Monte Cassino near his sister, the great nun St. Scholastica.

For his day let's think in terms of a whole meal in the spirit of Benedict. First, we need bread. It is around good, wholesome monastery bread that we will build this meal. It is such bread that long formed the heart of the monastic diet—and still does, to some degree.

This recipe comes from a Benedictine arch-abbey called St. Vincent's, in Latrobe, Pennsylvania. It makes a hearty, nourishing loaf of bread, so substantial that, with gravy, it is jokingly referred to as "St. Vincent's Steak."

The bread is especially good when made with the stone-ground unbleached white flour produced and sold at the abbey farm itself. It is wonderfully gritty. But the bread is also good made with a mixture of unbleached flour and stone-ground whole-wheat flour.

I have used this mixture in the recipe, and, following the example of the nuns of St. Vincent's nearby sister convent, St. Emma's, I have increased the amount of yeast used, to make a somewhat lighter bread. If you prefer the full "steak" effect, you are free to reduce the yeast. I have also quartered the recipe: it called for 20 cups of flour, and produced three *very* large loaves of bread. In the amounts given here, it makes two average-sized loaves.

246

Monastery bread

2½ cups unbleached flour
  (for the sponge)
½ cup warm water (100–
  110° F.)
1 package active dry yeast
1 cup cool water
2½ cups whole-wheat flour
1½ teaspoons salt
½ to 1 cup more cool water
Melted butter

Measure 2½ cups flour into a large bowl.

Pour the warm water into a bowl. Sprinkle the yeast into the water; wait 5 minutes, then stir until the yeast is dissolved. Add 1 cup of cool water, and pour the yeast into the large bowl containing the flour. Mix thoroughly. This is the sponge and it will be very sticky and slimy.

Cover it with a cloth and let it rise to its highest peak. When you notice that the sponge is beginning to drop (this may take 3 hours or longer), add the 2½ cups whole-wheat flour.

Dissolve the salt in ½ cup of cool water and pour this into the flour. Mix thoroughly. The dough should be of a medium texture; if it is too sticky, add a little flour. Turn the dough out onto a lightly floured surface. Knead for 5 to 8 minutes.

Place the dough in a greased bowl, cover with a cloth, and let it rise until it has doubled in size. Then shape it into two loaves (oval or round, as you prefer). Place the loaves on greased baking pans, placing the seam side of the loaves down in the pans. Brush the loaves with melted butter. Cover them with a cloth and let them rise again until once more doubled in size.

Bake at 400° F. for about 40 minutes, or until the bottom of the loaf sounds hollow when tapped.

Yield: 2 loaves

Variations:

If you like your bread slightly sweet, you can add, along with the second batch of flour, a little sugar (the nuns at St. Emma's do). Add 1 or 2 teaspoons of sugar.

What shall we eat with this bread? No meat—it was forbidden to monks by Benedict in his Rule. (Not that he considered meat—flesh—evil, but as an act of renunciation and penance.) We might have some fish: many monasteries kept their own fishponds so that fresh fish would always be available.

But let's think primarily in terms of that great Benedictine tradition of monks as farmers, as vine growers and vintners, beekeepers, cheesemakers, and so on. Monks were celibate—but they were great husbandmen! They devoted a kind of inventiveness and care to the cultivation of the land and its fruits that often resulted in extraordinary breakthroughs. Some of the great cheeses, in particular, had monastic origins. Just think of the French Port-Salut and Munster, the English Wensleydale, the Swiss Bellelay cheeses. As for wines, one hardly knows where to begin, monks were so important in the development of the great wines and wine-growing areas of Europe.

So a glass of wine, some good, honest cheese, a fresh vegetable or piece of fruit, some honey—these can accompany our bread. A meal in the monastic spirit.

But there is more to it than that. Benedict's idea was that a monastic meal should not only be simple, it should be silent. There should be no talking among the brothers (or sisters) while they ate. This was not, however, to be an empty silence. One of the brothers would read aloud to the others (the brothers took turns at this task). There would be readings from Scripture, and from other worthwhile books. One interesting detail: the light meal that we still call a "collation" received its name from the title of the book that was generally read at the time: the *Collations* (or collected thoughts) of St. John Cassian.

What if you need to ask for something during this silent meal? The Benedictines and the Cistercians elaborated, from around the eleventh century on, a very complete and sophisticated sign language. These signs were necessary because the monks were to remain silent not just at mealtimes but virtually at *all* times.

THE ANNUNCIATION
March 25

On March 25, Christians have long celebrated the Annunciation, that is, the appearance of the Archangel Gabriel as a messenger of God to Mary, a young woman betrothed to a carpenter named Joseph. What is commemorated on this day is not only what the angel said to Mary ("Greetings, you who are highly favored. . . . You will be with child and give birth to a son, and you are to give him the name Jesus." Luke 1:28, 31, NIV), but what Mary *answered:* "I am the Lord's servant. . . . May it be to me as you have said" (Luke 1:38, NIV). These beautiful words have inspired many Christians, over the centuries, to try to follow her example of submission to the will of God.

This feast was held in the Eastern Orthodox world as early as the fifth century, and shortly afterward was introduced to the West. (Its date is placed nine months before the celebration of Christ's Nativity.) It was long celebrated throughout the Christian world as a major feast in honor of Mary. There were processions and mystery plays. Interestingly enough, though most of Sweden became Protestant at the time of the Reformation, this feast continues to be celebrated—in particular, with the eating of waffles.

Waffles (wafers, *gaufres*, it's all the same word) were eaten rather generally on feast days, in much of Europe, starting at least in the twelfth century. But they were eaten *especially* on the Feast of the Annunciation. In some places the crumbs were buried in the fields. The prayer was clearly that Mary, who was blessed on this day with fruit, would bless the harvest of the farmers.

Swedish waffles

Here are Swedish waffles for the Annunciation. Light and crisp, these make excellent dessert waffles. They are traditionally eaten with whipped cream and cloudberry preserves. Cloudberries are first cousins to our raspberries.

1¾ cups heavy cream, well chilled
1⅓ cups flour
1–2 tablespoons sugar
Pinch of salt
½ cup cold water
3 tablespoons melted sweet butter

Whip the cream until stiff.

Mix the flour, sugar, and salt in a bowl. Stir in the water to make a smooth batter. Fold the whipped cream into the batter. Stir in the melted butter.

Heat the waffle iron. (If it is well seasoned, it will not need to be greased.) Fill the grid surface about two-thirds full of batter. Bake until golden brown.

Place on a rack to keep crisp while you make the rest of the waffles.

Yield: about 8 waffles

ST. BENEDICT THE BLACK
April 4

See discussion of Euphrosynus the Cook, September 11 (page 264).

ST. HONORATUS OF AMIENS
May 16

St. Honoratus, bishop of Amiens in the sixth century and widely venerated in France from the eleventh century on, is the patron saint of bakers and pastry cooks. (Or rather, he is one of them: bakers also have as their patrons St. Elizabeth of Hungary, St. Nicholas, and St. Philip the Apostle.) This famous and exquisite cake is named for St. Honoratus, and it makes a fitting tribute, for those who love to bake, to prepare and serve on his feast day.

St. Honoratus cake

GÂTEAU ST. HONORÉ

A word of caution: this cake is an elaborate concoction, to be undertaken only when you have plenty of time. It involves the preparation of flaky pastry, chou paste (cream-puff pastry), caramel syrup, French pastry cream, and Chantilly cream.

FLAKY PASTRY

This basic pastry is also called "short pastry"; in French, pâte brisée.

5 tablespoons unsalted butter, well chilled
1 cup flour
¼ teaspoon salt
1 tablespoon sugar
¼ cup ice water

Cut the butter into ¼-inch cubes; refrigerate.

Sift the flour, salt, and sugar together into a large mixing bowl.

Add the butter to the flour mixture. Using your fingertips, or two knives, work the butter gently into the flour until the mixture resembles coarse meal.

Add 2 tablespoons of the ice water, distributing it evenly. If the mixture is still very crumbly, add a little more water—1 or, at most, 2 tablespoons.

Work the mixture gently into a ball, and flatten it slightly on a piece of waxed paper with your hand. Wrap it in waxed paper or plastic wrap and refrigerate for 15 to 20 minutes.

Roll out the pastry on a piece of lightly floured waxed paper or plastic wrap until it is about $^3/_{16}$ inch thick, and about 9 inches in diameter. Trim off the edges to form a perfect circle (you may use a pie pan as a guide). Transfer to a buttered baking sheet. Reserve until Cream-Puff Pastry has been prepared.

CREAM-PUFF PASTRY

1 cup water
6 tablespoons unsalted butter, cut into pieces
Pinch of salt
1 teaspoon sugar
1 cup sifted flour
4 large eggs
1½ cups small dried beans

Preheat oven to 400° F.

Combine the water, butter, salt, and sugar in a large saucepan. Bring to a boil. When the butter has melted, add the flour *all at once*. Reduce the heat to medium, and beat the mixture vigorously until it leaves the sides of the pan and forms a ball.

Remove the pan from the heat. Beat in the eggs one at a time. Stir until the eggs are completely incorporated, and the paste is shiny.

Spoon the mixture into a pastry bag (fill the bag only about one-third full). Pipe a rim about 2 inches high around the edge of the sheet of pastry. Cut a piece of aluminum foil to fit over the pie crust, inside the cream-puff rim. Roll up the edges of the aluminum foil (so that you will be able to remove it easily), and sprinkle 1½ cups dried beans on it.

Bake for 20 minutes. Remove the aluminum foil (and beans) and continue baking for about 10 more minutes, or until the cream-puff rim is puffy and golden, and the crust is nicely browned.

Increase the oven heat to 425° F.

With the remaining pastry, squeeze out 12 to 16 little cream puffs onto an ungreased baking sheet. Bake for 12 minutes. Then reduce heat to 350° F. and continue baking for 15 minutes longer, or until the puffs are golden brown. Turn off the oven and let the puffs sit in the oven for 10 to 15 more minutes. Cool on a cake rack.

CARAMEL SYRUP

1 cup sugar
½ cup hot water
½ teaspoon vanilla extract

In a saucepan, dissolve the sugar in the water, stirring with a spoon. Bring to a boil. Without stirring the mixture, continue to raise the heat until the liquid reaches 356° F. on the candy thermometer—or the "caramel" stage. Remove *immediately* from the heat. Stir in the vanilla extract.

Keep the Caramel Syrup fairly hot while you are dipping the cream puffs in it: as it chills, it hardens.

DIPPING THE CREAM PUFFS IN THE CARAMEL SYRUP

First, be very careful not to burn yourself with the hot syrup. Take one cream puff, dip the top into the syrup (kitchen tongs make this easier and less dangerous). Also spoon a little of the syrup onto the bottom of the puff, and using this as "glue," set the puff onto the rim of the cake. Follow the same procedure for the rest of the puffs, arranging them symmetrically around the cake. Exactly how many puffs you will have room for will depend on just how big your puffs are. (My children are always happy to dispose of any extras for me.) Leave ½ to 1 inch between puffs. Reserve one puff to set in the middle of the cake.

FRENCH PASTRY CREAM

½ cup sugar
6 egg yolks
6 tablespoons flour
Pinch salt
2 cups milk
1 teaspoon vanilla extract

With a whisk or a hand mixer, beat together the sugar and yolks until thick and cream-colored.

Gradually add the flour, blending thoroughly after each addition. Add the salt. Transfer the mixture to a nonreactive saucepan (such as stainless steel but not aluminum).

In another saucepan, bring the milk just to a boil. Add the vanilla. Remove from heat.

Pour the hot milk very gradually into the egg mixture, beating vigorously with a wire whisk. Bring the mixture just to the boiling point, stirring constantly. Reduce heat to medium and cook, stirring, for 3 to 5 minutes or until the mixture is fairly thick. (If it becomes lumpy, don't worry: just keep beating.)

continued

St. Honoratus cake, continued

Remove the pan from the heat, and continue to beat for a minute or two. As the cream cools, stir occasionally to prevent a skin from forming.

Yield: about 2½ cups

Variations:

Add about ½ cup whipped cream to the Pastry Cream, to lighten or extend it.

Add any liqueur you like.

Flavor the Pastry Cream with chocolate: when you remove the Pastry Cream from the heat add 4 ounces unsweetened or semisweet chocolate, melted; stir until well blended.

You might also try Frangipane Cream. This macaroon-flavored cream is named for a medieval Italian family. The Frangipani received their surname from their ancient reputation for "breaking bread" (frangi-pane) with the poor. Add to the Pastry Cream before cooling: ⅓ cup crushed macaroons or finely ground blanched almonds, 1 tablespoon butter, and ¼ teaspoon almond extract.

1 cup heavy cream
2 tablespoons sifted
  confectioners' sugar
½ teaspoon vanilla extract
Optional:
  1 tablespoon rum, brandy,
  kirsch, Cointreau, or
  other liqueur

CHANTILLY CREAM

Whip the cream until it stands in stiff peaks. Add the sugar, vanilla, and the liqueur if you wish.

Cake
Pastry cream
Chantilly cream
Optional:
  Green and/or red glacé
  cherries

INGREDIENTS AND INSTRUCTIONS FOR FINAL ASSEMBLY

Fill the center of the cake with the Pastry Cream. (You may make circular grooves, or another pattern, on its surface with the tines of a fork.)

Put the Chantilly Cream in a pastry bag. Use to fill the spaces between the Cream Puffs. Decorate the Pastry Cream surface of the cake with Chantilly Cream patterns. You can also stud the surface with cherries, or put a large Chantilly Cream "flourish" in the center of the cake and set a Cream Puff on top.

Yield: 1 ten-inch cake

13

Summer

ST. PETER THE APOSTLE
June 29

Simon Peter, a fisherman of Bethsaida, was called by Christ from his nets, along with his brother Andrew, to be a "fisher of men." In the Gospels and in Acts his name heads the lists of the Apostles, and he was clearly considered the foremost among the Twelve. Indeed, Jesus told him: "And I tell you that you are Peter [Rock], and on this rock I will build my church" (Matthew 16:18, NIV).

Simon Peter was very human. At the time of the Crucifixion, he three times denied ever having met Christ.

After Christ's Ascension Peter, and then soon Paul as well, became the acknowledged leaders of the new religion. (Indeed, this is in theory a joint feast for them, though in fact Paul has tended to be honored on the day that commemorates his conversion, January 25.) Peter served as the first bishop of Rome and is thought to have been martyred under Nero. He is honored by Christians of all denominations throughout the world, and is considered by Roman Catholics to have been the first Pope.

As a fisherman turned fisher of men, St. Peter is often shown with a fish, and in many countries it has been customary to eat fish on his feast day. (In various places, it was also long customary for fishermen and fishmongers to give fish to the poor, in his honor.)

A particular fish is associated with St. Peter, and in several languages it bears his name: the "St. Peter fish"—in English called the "John Dory." This very odd-looking (but delicious) fish—flat and spiny, with a thick skin—is connected, by legend, to one of Christ's miracles. When the temple tax collector came up to Peter and demanded to be paid, Jesus told Peter to "go and cast a line in the lake; take the first fish that comes to the hook, open its mouth, and you will find a silver coin, take that and pay it in" (Matthew 17:24–27). Peter did so, and the fish that he caught is said to have thenceforth borne on its side the mark of a coin.

Here is a recipe that originally called for St. Peter's Fish. This species is not available in American waters, but porgy makes a close and delicious substitute; other small fish, or fillets, can be used as well.

Sicilian St. Peter's fish in marsala

4 porgies, about 1 pound each (ask the fish dealer to fillet them, and to give you the heads and bones)
3 cups water
4 teaspoons minced shallots
2 bay leaves
A few peppercorns
Salt to taste
⅓ cup flour for dredging, seasoned with salt and pepper
4 to 5 tablespoons olive oil
1½ cups Marsala wine

Put the fish heads and bones in the water, along with the shallots, bay leaves, and peppercorns. Cook over moderately high heat until the liquid is reduced to about 1 cup. Strain the stock; add salt to taste. Reserve.

Dredge the fish fillets with the seasoned flour. Fry them in the olive oil until they are nicely browned and slightly flaky. Remove to a serving dish and keep warm.

Pour off all but a little oil. Pour the Marsala into the frying pan, and add the cup of fish stock. Boil for 2 or 3 minutes, until the sauce is reduced and is fairly thick. Pour over the fillets.

Yield: 4 to 6 servings

A Tuscan cake for St. Peter's day

TORTA GARFAGNANA

Wilma Pezzini in her Tuscan Cookbook *introduces this recipe as follows: "This tasty cake is made in the Garfagnana region as a fit ending for the big meal served on St. Peter's day. St. Peter is the beloved patron saint of this mountain region."*
The cake is indeed delicious.

¾ cup sweet butter
2⅔ cups flour
1 cup sugar
½ cup blanched almonds, finely chopped
1 tablespoon aniseed
Grated peel of ½ lemon
3 eggs
5 tablespoons cherry brandy
⅔ cup milk
1 tablespoon cream of tartar
1 teaspoon baking soda
Optional:
  Confectioners' sugar

Use about 1 teaspoon of the butter to grease a 9-inch square cake pan. Sprinkle it with a little of the flour.

Melt the remaining butter over a very low flame; allow to cool.

Preheat oven to 375° F.

Put the remaining flour, sugar, chopped almonds, aniseed, and grated lemon rind in a large bowl. Mix thoroughly. Make a well and break the eggs into it. Add the melted butter and cherry brandy. Work everything together until the mixture is smooth.

Warm the milk slightly, and add the cream of tartar and baking soda. When the milk foams up, add it to the flour mixture. Stir to blend well. Pour into the cake pan.

Bake for about 1 hour or until a toothpick stuck into the center comes out clean. Remove from oven. Sprinkle if you like with confectioners' sugar. Serve warm or cold.

Yield: 1 9-inch square cake

ST. JAMES THE GREATER
July 25

James was one of the most important of the Apostles: with his brother John and with Peter, he was a witness to the Transfiguration when Jesus appeared in glory with Moses and Elijah. James was there too in the Garden of Gethsemane. He and his brother must have been impetuous and hot-tempered: Jesus called them "the sons of Thunder."

James is known to have died around A.D. 42, by the sword, at the command of Herod Agrippa. According to legend, he first spent seven years in Spain, traveling throughout the land and preaching Christianity. After he was put to death, his followers are said to have brought his body back to Spain for burial. Then, somehow, the location of his body was lost. In the ninth century, a star miraculously revealed what was claimed to be his tomb. A great shrine was build at Compostela ("Star of the Sea"), and by the eleventh century great flocks of pilgrims were visiting it. From then on, only Jerusalem and Rome attracted more pilgrims than "Santiago" (Iago is Spanish for James.)

The festival in his honor in Compostela is a week-long affair, celebrated with dramatic liturgy and with beautiful local costumes, Galician bagpipe music, dancing, and of course wonderful, special food.

One of the traditional dishes is a scallop-filled *empanada*, or little pie. Nothing could be more appropriate, for the scallop shell has been, for hundreds of years, the symbol of Santiago. This shell

---

We beseech thee, Almighty God, to bless this crop of new apples, that we, who are doomed to a just sentence of death, by our first parents' eating of this deadly tree and fruit, may all be sanctified and blessed through the intercession of your only son, our Redeemer, the Lord Jesus Christ, and by the benediction of the Holy Spirit. And, the wicked deceits of the Temptor of that first crime being averted, may we from this day—the solemn anniversary of St. James—undertake in health the eating of these new fruits, through God in his unity.

"Christening" of the new apples on St. James's Day, from the Latin of the Old Sarum rite

was worn as an emblem by all pilgrims to the shrine at Compostella. (In French, scallops are called "St. James cockles": *coquilles St. Jacques.*)

Let's put these tasty little creatures back on their symbolic shells. This dish is lovely with rice and a green vegetable, and a good white wine.

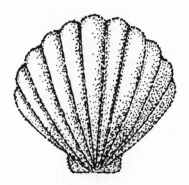

Scallops on the "pilgrim" shell

1 teaspoon each: finely
  chopped chervil, chives,
  parsley, tarragon
1 cup white wine
2 pounds scallops
Flour for dredging
Salt
White pepper
3 tablespoons butter
1 tablespoon olive or
  peanut oil
A little lemon juice
  (optional)
6 large (4–5-inch) scallop
  shells
¼ cup fresh breadcrumbs
2 tablespoons melted butter
For garnish:
  Chopped parsley
  Lemon wedges

A few minutes (better yet, an hour) before beginning to cook, put the herbs to steep in the wine.

Rinse the scallops, and dry them. If using large sea scallops, cut them into halves or quarters. Coat them with flour that has been seasoned with salt and white pepper. Shake off excess flour before cooking.

Heat 3 tablespoons of butter and the oil in a large frying pan. When the butter and oil are bubbling, add the scallops to the pan. It is important that the scallops not be crowded, and that the pan be hot. (You may need to cook the scallops in several batches.) Sauté the scallops, adding butter and oil as necessary, until they are nicely browned on all sides. Remove to a warm dish.

Pour the herb-steeped wine into the frying pan, boiling the liquid down slightly, and stirring in all the delicious little bits left in the pan.

Stir the wine into the scallops. Taste for seasoning. Optional: squeeze in a little lemon juice. Fill the scallop shells with the mixture. Sprinkle with breadcrumbs and moisten the tops with a little melted butter. Run briefly under a preheated broiler to brown the crumbs.

Garnish with chopped parsley, and lemon wedges.

Yield: 6 servings

Madeleines

While we are celebrating the feast of St. James, let's claim for him the Madeleine. This may seem a trifle pushy: the recipe for these delicious little cookies dates from the mid-nineteenth century, and has nothing whatsoever to do with the great Apostle (or with Mary Magdalene either). Madeleines get their name apparently from the name of the cook who first baked them. But the shell-shaped mold in which Madeleines are baked is, after all, the traditional cockle shell—the coquille St. Jacques—*just slightly slimmed out, à la française.*

Marcel Proust begins as follows one of the most famous scenes of his Swann's Way:

My mother, seeing that I was cold, offered me some tea. . . . She sent out for one of those short, plump little cakes called "petites madeleines," which look as though they had been molded in the fluted scallop of a pilgrim's shell. And soon . . . I raised to my lips a spoonful of the tea in which I had soaked a morsel of the cake.

Let's eat Madeleines in St. James' honor, and in honor of all pilgrims, all pilgrimages.

¾ *cup butter*
1⅛ *cups flour*
⅛ *teaspoon salt*
½ *teaspoon baking powder*
3 *large eggs*
1 *cup superfine sugar*
1 *teaspoon vanilla extract*
1 *teaspoon grated lemon rind*
Optional:
 Confectioners' sugar

Madeleine tins are available at most cooking-supply stores and at some department stores. Brush them with 2 tablespoons melted butter. Preheat the oven to 400° F.

Melt the butter and allow it to cool. Sift the flour with the salt and the baking powder.

Beat the eggs until light and lemon-colored. Add the superfine sugar gradually, beating constantly. Beat with an electric mixer until the mixture falls in a thick heavy ribbon. Stir in the flour gradually, folding it in gently but thoroughly. Stir in the melted butter, the vanilla, and the lemon rind. Pour the batter into the tins, filling them about two-thirds full.

Bake for about 10 minutes, or until the Madeleines are lightly browned around the edges and a toothpick stuck into the center of one comes out clean. Dust them with confectioners' sugar, if you wish.

Yield: about 30 Madeleines (tins vary in size)

ST. ANNE
July 26

"All Annes are beautiful," declares an old proverb, and Anne has ranked for centuries as one of the most popular of girls' names. She for whom they are named is the mother of Jesus' mother Mary.

Little is known about this figure. Her very name, like that of her husband Joachim, comes to us from ancient legend. One fact above all has explained the interest in and devotion to her that have existed for centuries, arising originally in the Middle East in around the fourth century and then spreading, at the time of the Crusades, to the West: She is the one and only grandmother of Jesus. Indeed—since Jesus is both man and God—she can legitimately be called "the grandmother of God." Quite a title! She has frequently been depicted in art as part of the Holy Family, in particular with Mary and the child Jesus. Sometimes she is shown with her husband, and often with Mary as a little girl, as in scenes in which she is teaching her daughter to read.

Many a grandmother has taken St. Anne as her special patron. Nannies as well (the word "nanny" apparently derives from Anne as the second mother of Jesus) invoke her; so do others who have little children in their charge. She has also been considered, since the Middle Ages, the patron of married women, and of special aid to childless couples in obtaining children. After all, she was—unlike many of the saints—married, and according to legend prayed for many years before God gave to her and her husband their extraordinary daughter.

There is a tradition of great devotion to St. Anne in Brittany. A Breton saying goes: "Anyone who does not love the mother of Mary is no Breton!" The French brought their love of St. Anne with them to Canada, where the shrine of St. Anne de Beaupré in Quebec draws tens of thousands of pilgrims each year. This saint is the official patroness of Canada.

July 26 has traditionally marked the feast not only of St. Anne, but, in many parts of Europe, of all "Annes": all pretty girls. Families often would honor their daughters. It has also been thought a fitting moment to honor grandmothers. (St. Joachim, who was long honored on August 16, is now commemorated along with Anne on July 26—so this makes a nice day to honor grandfathers as well! In the Eastern Orthodox churches the two are honored on September 9.)

In both France and French Canada what would commonly be served on this occasion is a fruit tart: such exquisite desserts are traditional at all patronal festivals (as well as other special occasions), especially those falling in the summer, when such a luscious assortment of fruits is available. Here are two fine French tart recipes.

Plum tart

This spectacular (but simple) tart with its creamy custard filling is a favorite in many parts of France. There it is commonly made with quetsches, *which are oblong purple plums, but any variety will do.*

1 *recipe for flaky pastry,*
  page 198
9 *or 10 good-sized plums*
  (about 2 pounds)
¾ *cup sugar*
½ *teaspoon cinnamon*
1 *egg*
¼ *cup flour*
½ *cup heavy cream*
½ *teaspoon vanilla extract*
Pinch salt

Butter a 10-inch tart tin.

Roll out the pastry very thin on a sheet of lightly floured wax paper or on plastic wrap. Lay the rolled pastry, paper side up, over the tart tin. Gently, using the edge of a dinner knife, pry the pastry loose and fit it into the tin. Don't stretch the pastry. If it should tear, you can repair it with scraps. Trim the edges, but not too close: the dough will shrink as it cooks.

To partly pre-bake the crust, preheat the oven to 400° F. Line the crust with a sheet of aluminum foil or wax paper large enough to extend over the edges of the pan. Press the foil carefully into place. In the foil place a layer of dried beans or raw rice. Bake for 10 minutes, then remove the foil and beans and return the crust to the oven for 5 more minutes or until the crust is turning golden. (Note: If you are using a tart tin with a removable bottom, it is essential that you *not* prick, or make any sort of hole in the crust: if you do, the custard filling will leak out. If any tears or holes occur during the pre-baking, you can often repair them with small scraps of uncooked dough.)

Let the crust cool before proceeding.

Halve and pit the plums. If they are large, you may wish to cut them into quarters or even smaller slices. Toss the plums in a bowl with ½ cup sugar and the cinnamon. Around the edge of the crust set a circle of plums standing up, as it were—points up, skins facing out. Against this row of plum slices lean another. Continue in the same fashion, packing the rows in fairly dense concentric circles, until the plum slices are used up—setting in the very center of the tart one plum slice, skin side up. (The design should resemble the petals of a flower.)

Bake the tart for 20 minutes in a pre-heated 400° F. oven. While the tart is baking, prepare the custard: Beat the egg and ¼ cup sugar for about 2 minutes with an electric mixer. The mixture will be light and pale yellow. Beat in the flour, then the heavy cream, vanilla and salt.

When the tart has cooked for 20 minutes, pour and spoon the custard in among the plum slices—trying to keep the part of the slices that extends above the custard as clean and crisp-looking as possible. Return the tart to the oven and bake for about 30 minutes, or until the custard is lightly puffed and golden brown, and the point of a knife when inserted comes out clean.

Yield: 1 ten-inch tart, serving about 6

Apple tart

This apple tart is made with a pâte sablée *crust—a French cookie-type crust—and crisp apples. Aside from its appeal to diners of all ages, one of its charms is that it requires no complicated tart pan: you can make it on any large baking sheet.*

CRUST:
2 cups flour
4 tablespoons sugar
1 teaspoon salt
8 tablespoons (1 stick)
    unsalted butter, softened
1 egg
1 teaspoon vanilla extract

FRUIT FILLING:
4 large tart apples
3–4 tablespoons sugar
1 tablespoon butter
About ½ cup apricot jam
Optional:
    1 tablespoon or so
    Calvados (apple brandy)

Sift the flour, sugar and salt together into a bowl. Make a well and put in the butter, egg and vanilla. Using your fingers, a rubber spatula or a fork, work the ingredients together. Knead briefly in the bowl to blend ingredients thoroughly. Wrap the dough in plastic wrap and refrigerate for 1 to 2 hours, or overnight. (You can hasten the chilling process by placing the dough initially in the freezer for 20 minutes or so.)

Just before you are ready to roll out the dough, peel and core the apples and cut them into thin slices. (If you should need to prepare the apples earlier, place them in a bowl of cold water to which a tablespoon or two lemon juice has been added: this will prevent discoloration. Dry them thoroughly before proceeding.)

On lightly-floured waxed paper or on plastic wrap, roll the dough out thin to a large circle 13 to 14 inches in diameter. Trim the edges to form as perfect a circle as possible. (You can use a pizza pan as a guide, or a piece of brown paper bag cut into the proper shape.) Transfer the dough to a buttered baking sheet. Pinch the edges up to make a border about ½ inch high. With your fingers or the tines of a fork, make the edging attractive.

Set the apples in place on top of the crust, by placing them in two concentric circles. The apple slices should be so densely packed that they stand virtually upright. Sprinkle with the sugar and dot with butter.

Bake in a preheated 375 oven for about 45 minutes, or until the crust and the apples are nicely browned. Melt the apricot jam and strain it; add the Calvados, if you like. Brush over the surface of the hot tart.

Allow the tart to cool for a few minutes on a rack, then transfer to a serving platter by sliding it off the baking sheet.

Yield: 1 twelve-inch tart

Variations:

You can make this tart in any shape you like, such as a square or rectangle: set the apples in straight rows. (Try a triangle in honor of the Trinity?) You can also make several small tarts instead of a large one.

ST. LAURENCE
August 10

St. Laurence, honored by Christians since at least the fourth century, is one of the most famous of the martyrs. In the third century he was one of the deacons in Rome in a time of persecution. Ordered by the Roman prefect to surrender the treasures of the church, he assembled the poor and took them to the prefect, saying, "Here is the church's treasure." According to legend he was put to death by being roasted on a grill, or gridiron. In one of those marvelous quips attributed to the saints, he is said to have remarked to his torturers: "One side is done now; you can turn me over."

Which brings us to the foods traditionally eaten on St. Laurence's Day. In some places, nothing hot is served at all, in compassion for his martyrdom; it is a day for cold soups and salads. But in Spain they make in his honor a chestnut-flavored Bizcocho de San Lorenzo. Now the word *bizcocho*, like our word *biscuit*, really means "twice-cooked"! Is the pun intended? In any case, you can either serve cold dishes, to help cool off St. Laurence; or you can serve twice-cooked or barbecued dishes, to signify his triumph over the fire. After all, St. Laurence is one of the patron saints of cooks!

St. Laurence sweets

BIZCOCHO DE SAN LORENZO

This unusual and delicious recipe is adapted from the Spanish classic Manuel de Cocina, Recetario.

½ pound chestnuts (or 1 six-ounce can puréed chestnuts)
Milk
¾ cup sugar
1 tablespoon orange-flower water, or 1 teaspoon orange extract and grated rind of ½ orange
6 eggs
1 cup cornstarch (see Note)
Orange marmalade (optional)
Confectioners' sugar

If you are using fresh chestnuts (which may be hard to get at this time of year), proceed as follows: cut an X into the surface of each chestnut. Cover the chestnuts with cold water in a saucepan. Bring them to a boil and boil for 1 or 2 minutes. Remove from the heat. Take out the chestnuts one at a time and remove the shell and the skin.

Return the peeled chestnuts to a saucepan. Cover them with milk, and cook gently until they are just soft enough to be put through a sieve or puréed in a food mill. Purée, and reserve.

Combine the sugar, orange-flower water, and eggs in a large saucepan. Beat vigorously with a whisk over low heat until the mixture is light and spongy. Add the chestnut purée, and then the cornstarch, a little at a time. Blend thoroughly, and pour the mixture into a generously buttered ring mold.

Place the mold in a pan of hot water in the oven, and bake

at 350° F. until the chestnut mixture is set, about 1 hour. Remove from the oven and let cool.

When the Bizcocho has cooled, turn it out of the mold, and cut it into slices about ¾ inch thick. If you like spread the slices with marmalade. Sprinkle them with confectioners' sugar.

Yield: about 20 slices

Note: This seems like an astonishing amount of cornstarch to the American cook, but the cornstarch takes the place of flour, and makes a delicate, fine-textured cake.

THE ASSUMPTION (OR DORMITION) OF THE VIRGIN MARY
August 15

August 15 is the day on which Eastern Orthodox and Catholic Christians have long celebrated what is called the Dormition ("Falling Asleep") or Assumption of the Virgin Mary. This feast commemorates the ancient tradition that the Virgin's body, when her life on earth ended, was preserved from corruption, and was united with her soul in Heaven.

This feast, which is said to have been established before the sixth century, is both solemnly and joyfully celebrated in much of the Orthodox world, and, for example, in Italy. Here are the moving words of an elderly man—an eighty-nine-year-old Sicilian—describing his recollection of the Inclinata, or "Bowing Procession," in which he took part as a youngster. This beautiful account was given to me by a student of mine, Carol Rovello, who transcribed it from her grandfather's Italian.

I was dressed in my Sunday best, I had my father's tie on, and was all prepared to take my part in such a holy day. I was eleven or twelve, I'm not sure. The priest told me to be very careful not to let go, at any point, of the Statue. [He was one of a number of men and boys honored by being allowed to carry through the town the great statue of the Virgin.] A lot of the others were older men of the town. I was one of the youngest. Everyone was so proud to be there, but not as proud as I was. We carried the statue through the village and at the end, the finish, there was an arch, almost like that of a gazebo, adorned with flowers of every sort, I remember the gladiolas the most. I don't know exactly why. [The gladiolas and other flowers represent the gate of heaven.] There was another statue that was held by very strong men. That was the statue of Jesus Christ. These men were, oh so tall and strong, they scared me with their strength. Both sets of us, those that were holding the statue of Jesus

Christ and those that were holding the statue of the Virgin Mary, bowed three times . . . one bow after another. I'll never forget how that felt to me, all I know is that I believed I was as strong as all of the other men, no matter how big they were. After that, the two statues were taken back to the village church, and a most beautiful mass was celebrated. I was so proud of myself, and my mother was so proud of me that we both cried in each other's arms with tears of joy and love.

Before the celebration of the Assumption there is a traditional fast throughout much of the Christian world—especially among the various Orthodox groups. (The Copts in particular keep this fast with the greatest devotion.) In Sicily and throughout much of Italy this fast and the subsequent feast take an interesting form: for the first fourteen days of August no fruit at all is eaten. Then, on the day of the feast itself, every possible kind of fruit is eaten, along with an assortment of cheeses and breads. But no meat. This is, then, a little like Christmas Eve: a "joyous fast." This tradition may also be related to the fact that on this day it has long been customary to implore the blessings of the Virgin over herbs, fruits, and flowers.

ST. EUPHROSYNUS THE COOK
September 11

There are a number of saints, and other holy figures as well, who are famous for being (among other things) *cooks*. Let's take this opportunity to remember and honor them.

Let's begin, and end, with an Eastern Orthodox saint, Euphrosynus. He was born of peasant stock and was an uneducated man. When he became a monk, he was made to serve in the kitchen, and was mocked by some of the other monks because of his "coarse country up-bringing," as the story puts it. But there was in the monastery a very pious priest who was ever asking God to show him the good things that they who love God shall enjoy. One night in his sleep he saw a garden, which was clearly the kingdom of heaven, and in it he beheld Euphrosynus the cook, who was enjoying the many beautiful things, in particular some incredibly tasty and fragrant apples, which he shared with the priest. When the priest awoke, lo and behold, he was still holding the apples— and it became clear to him that this was not just a dream, but a *vision;* that the humble Euphrosynus had deeper enjoyment of God than anyone else in the monastery. For his feast day, I suggest Baked Apples.

But Euphrosynus is not the only saintly cook, far from it!

Another is Benedict the Black. Born an African slave in Sicily (in the sixteenth century), he was freed by his owner. He became a hermit, then a Franciscan. He was first—and for a long time—a cook for the order. Eventually, for his obvious holiness, he was made the superior of the house although he was illiterate. (He was famous as a healer throughout Italy.) On retirement, he returned to his beloved kitchen. He is quoted as saying these (oh, how true!) words, that "the greatest mortification is not to fast altogether, but to eat a little and then stop."

Another extraordinary figure, Brother Lawrence, served in the Carmelite monastery kitchen in Paris in the late seventeenth century. The beautiful book *The Practice of the Presence of God* was compiled from recollected conversations with him. What was Brother Lawrence's message? "That we should establish ourselves in a sense of God's presence by continually conversing with Him." As regards the kitchen: he had a natural aversion to it, but "having accustomed himself to do everything there for the love of God, and with prayer," having always asked for "His grace to do his work well, he had found everything easy, during fifteen years that he had been employed there."

People said of him that "in the greatest hurry of business in the kitchen he still preserved his recollection and heavenly-mindedness. . . . He was never hasty or loitering, but did each thing in its season, with an even, uninterrupted composure and tranquillity of spirit."

I hope this sounds more like you in the kitchen than it does like me. At any rate, we could all take lessons from Brother Lawrence. Since, like many other holy people of all denominations, he has never been canonized, we can honor and try to imitate him any day—every day.

Baked apples

6 large tart apples
⅓ cup brown sugar
½ teaspoon mace
½ teaspoon ground ginger
Grated rind of 1 orange
Chopped walnuts or pecans
  (optional)
Butter

Preheat oven to 350° F.

Core the apples to within ½ inch of the bottom (but not *through* the bottom).

Combine the brown sugar, mace, ginger, and orange rind. Add the nuts, if you wish. Fill the apple cavities with this mixture. Dot the tops with butter.

Place them in a baking pan with ¾ cup boiling water. Cover and bake for 45 minutes to an hour, or until the apples are tender but not mushy.

Yield: 6 servings

THE EXALTATION OF THE HOLY CROSS
September 14

This ancient feast honors the cross itself, as the instrument of Christ's redemption of the world. The cross, which disappeared after the Crucifixion, was believed to have been discovered by St. Helena, around 335, in the course of excavations in Jerusalem. Helena's son, the Emperor Constantine, newly converted to Christianity, was in the process of building the basilica of the Holy Sepulchre on Mount Calvary. By the end of the fourth century, relics of the cross were being venerated in Jerusalem, and this honor paid to the cross spread both east and west.

This holy day is one of strict fasting among the Eastern Orthodox. In Greece, the priest distributes sprigs of sweet basil to his congregation, because tradition says that basil grew all over the hillside where Helena discovered the cross. In honor of this ancient tradition, here is a recipe for Pesto, a wonderful sauce for pasta, whose primary ingredient is fresh basil. With this dish you can keep the spirit of the day as one of abstinence from meat—and still serve something delicious and symbolic.

Here are some other possible uses for finely chopped basil: try stirring it into scrambled eggs or omelets, adding it to vegetable soups, tossing it with fresh vegetables such as peas, mixing it in with salad dressing.

Pesto

2 cups chopped fresh basil leaves
1 teaspoon salt
¾ teaspoon freshly ground pepper
2 teaspoons finely chopped garlic
3 tablespoons pine nuts (pignoli)
1–1½ cups olive oil
½ cup freshly grated Parmesan or Romano

This dish is very easy to make in a blender: Combine the basil, salt, pepper, garlic, pignoli, and 1 cup oil in the blender. Blend until the mixture is smooth; stop the blender every few seconds to stir the mixture slightly, and to press the leaves down.

The mixture when puréed should be slightly runny; if it is still too thick, add more olive oil. Pour the sauce into a bowl, and stir in the grated cheese.

Pesto can also be made by hand, with a mortar and pestle, or a bowl and a heavy wooden spoon. In that case, start by crushing the basil leaves, then add the other ingredients one at a time.

Serve on hot pasta.

Yield: 1½ to 2 cups

Cross cake or cross tart

There could hardly be a more fitting day to bake something in the shape of or in honor of the cross. One can of course purchase cake pans in the shape of a cross. But why not try something a little different? The cross, as a devotional object and as a shape, has been a source of great inspiration to artists across the centuries, and there are many beautiful designs derived from the basic cross shape.

Any cake—homemade or store-bought, large or small—can be decorated with one of these crosses. With a large sheet cake, you can make an "ecumenical" cake, using several different crosses.

For the decorating, you can use:

Whipped cream or Chantilly Cream (see page 252) squeezed from a pastry bag.

Cake icing in a color contrasting with that of the cake, squeezed from a pastry tube.

Blueberries or raspberries or halved (seeded) grapes, or other small pieces of fruit.

You can also make a lovely fruit tart, on which the fruits are arranged in the shape of a cross.

Fill any prebaked pie or tart crust or crumb crust (below) with French Pastry Cream (see page 251). On top of the Pastry Cream, lay out the fruits (blueberries, raspberries, halved green or red (seeded) grapes, etc.) in the desired pattern. If you like, glaze the entire surface with red currant jelly that you have melted in a saucepan and strained.

CRUMB CRUST

This simple crust is a great addition to family life. Not only is it easy for even a youngster to make; it can be made with various kinds of crumbs. Here is a basic recipe with some variations suggested:

6 tablespoons sweet butter, at room temperature
3 tablespoons white or brown sugar
Pinch salt
Optional:
 About ⅛ teaspoon cinnamon or nutmeg
1½ cups cookie crumbs (graham-cracker, vanilla/ chocolate wafer or gingersnaps, or part cookie crumbs, part ground nuts)

Preheat the oven to 350° F.

Cream the butter with the sugar. Add the salt and, if you wish, the spice. Stir in the crumbs, mixing well with a fork.

Using a spatula or the back of a spoon, spread the crumbs evenly into a 9-inch pan, covering the bottom and sides. Press the crumbs firmly into place.

Bake the crust for about 12 minutes, or until the edges are getting crisp and dry. If the crust has bubbled up in the center, flatten it gently with a fork. Let the crust cool before proceeding. (If you prefer, instead of baking the crust you can chill it in the refrigerator for about 30 minutes.)

Yield: 1 nine-inch pie crust

ST. NINIAN
September 16

Chances are you have never heard of St. Ninian. But he *is* known in Scotland, where a number of places still bear his name. And visitors and pilgrims still go to see the cave that was his hermitage, long ago, on the southwestern coast.

Living in the fourth century, son of a Galloway chieftain, Ninian was the very first of the great Scottish missionaries. He traveled a great deal, in particular taking the Gospel message to the Picts, and he sailed as far north as the Orkneys and the Shetlands—a dangerous trip in those days. He also built at Whithorn the first stone church ever seen in Great Britain: his *candida casa*, or "white house."

St. Ninian gingery muffins

In Scotland they eat spicy, gingery St. Ninian Muffins. Just why ginger and why muffins I haven't been able to ascertain. But they are so tasty that I am willing to eat first and ask later. Let's eat these muffins in honor of St. Ninian, and that old Scots courage. The recipe is from The Highland Fling Cookbook *by Sara M. Walker.*

1½ *cups flour*
1 *teaspoon baking soda*
¼ *teaspoon salt*
¼ *teaspoon cinnamon*
¼ *teaspoon nutmeg*
¼ *teaspoon cardamom*
1 *teaspoon ground ginger*
½ *cup molasses*
¼ *cup brown sugar*
¼ *cup (½ stick) butter*
½ *cup boiling water*
1 *egg*

Preheat the oven to 400° F.

Sift together the flour, baking soda, salt, and spices into a large bowl. In another bowl, combine the molasses, sugar, butter, and boiling water.

Add the liquid mixture to the dry mixture a little at a time. Beat in the egg. Do not overbeat. The batter may be lumpy. Leave it that way for best results.

Pour it into buttered muffin pans and bake for 20 to 25 minutes.

Yield: 12 muffins

14

Fall

ST. MICHAEL
West: September 29; East: November 8

Michael is not in fact a saint but an angel, indeed an archangel. He is (along with Raphael, Gabriel, and Uriel) one of the messengers of God to men. He has long been considered by the Jews the protector of Israel, and in Christian tradition he is seen as the protector of the Church. Michael is referred to as "the captain of the Heavenly Host"—our great defender against the Devil. Michael is also (as our protector) charged with the care of all departed souls.

Like St. Martin's Day, his feast, Michaelmas, was to some degree a thanksgiving festival. In Ireland, it has been customary to eat goose on this day; in much of northern Europe, Michelsminne "St. Michael's Love" wine was drunk—and still is in Denmark.

In the northern and western islands of Scotland there was long-abiding devotion to the archangel, and an ancient tradition of eating on his feast a St. Michael's Bannock. This large, flat cake, cooked on a "girdle," or griddle, is a big first cousin to a scone. Everyone present, whether member of the family or stranger or servant, must eat of this bread dedicated to St. Michael. This interesting recipe from the Hebrides is adapted from Marian McNeil's fine *The Scot's Kitchen, Its Traditions and Lore with Old-Time Recipes.*

St. Michael's bannock

STRUAN MICHEIL

I undertook the preparation of this cake the first time with considerable trepidation—and I was far from persuaded that my family would find it appealing. I was very much surprised: it is not very hard to make. My husband, children, and various friends all loved it. It is good plain, or (as I like it) with butter and honey.

270

1⅓ cups each barley, oat,
  and rye meal
1 cup flour
½ teaspoon salt
2 scant teaspoons baking
  soda
2½–3 cups buttermilk
3 tablespoons honey, or
  molasses, or brown sugar
Optional:
  Any or a combination of
  the following: ½ cup
  blueberries, ¼ cup raisins
  or currants, 1–2
  tablespoons caraway
  seeds
2 eggs
1 cup cream
4 tablespoons melted butter

Put the barley, oat, and rye meal into a large bowl. Add the flour and the salt. Mix well. Stir the baking soda into 2½ cups buttermilk, and add to the flour mixture. Stir in the honey, and the berries or other additions if you wish.

Turn the mixture out onto a well-floured board. Mix the ingredients only long enough to make a soft dough. Add more flour, or more buttermilk, as necessary (more flour if the dough is too sticky, more buttermilk if it is too dry and doesn't hold together).

Divide the dough in half. On a sheet of floured waxed paper or foil, roll out one half of the dough into a circle about 8 to 9 inches in diameter and ½ to ¾ inch thick. Do the same with the other half of the dough. (You may choose to make more, smaller bannocks; see below.)

Mix together the eggs, cream, and melted butter.

Heat the griddle and grease it lightly. (If you have a large griddle you can cook both bannocks at once. Otherwise you will have to do them one at a time.) To cook: paint one surface of the bannock with the egg mixture, and, loosening the bannock from the waxed paper, place that surface down on the griddle. (This flipping of a large bannock is the only tricky part of the recipe. But if your bannock breaks, never mind! It tastes just as good. Just push it back together as well as you can. Another solution is to make *smaller* bannocks.) Cook over moderate heat until the under-surface is brown. While it is cooking, paint the upper surface of the bannock with the egg mixture. Turn and cook the other side, and paint the new top side. The idea is to repeat this procedure until each side of the bannock has been painted and cooked three times.

Yield: 2 large Struans (bannocks) or 4 or 5 smaller ones

And there was war in heaven. Michael and his angels fought against the dragon, and the dragon and his angels fought back. But he was not strong enough, and they lost their place in heaven. The great dragon was hurled down—that ancient serpent called the devil or Satan, who leads the whole earth astray. He was hurled to the earth, and his angels with him.

Revelation 12:7–9 (NIV)

Archangels on horseback

16–20 sea scallops
8–10 pieces thin-sliced
  bacon; cut each piece in 2
Buttered toast

This Victorian specialty is theoretically a "savory," served toward the end of a dinner, but it is popular as a first course as well.

Wrap each scallop in half a piece of bacon; fasten with a toothpick. Grill under the broiler until the bacon is browned and crisp. Serve on rounds or squares of hot buttered toast.

Yield: 4 servings

Variation:

To make *Angels* on Horseback, replace the scallops with shucked oysters, and proceed as above.

DEVIL'S—AND DEVILED—FOOD

The Devil, they say, must always have his due. And there are a good many foods associated with him (at least in name). What better—what safer—place to take them up than apropos of St. Michael, Satan's ancient opposite number and the protector of the faithful?

The foods of the Devil—"deviled" or "devil's" foods—are of two kinds. The first category includes dishes that the Devil (or his minions) might cook in "hell's kitchen"; or that he might, one assumes, like himself. These are the hot and spicy foods, generally meats rubbed or painted with a sauce, then grilled. There are thus two kinds of heat involved: that of the spices in the sauce and that of the fire itself.

I give only one of the many, many recipes for "devil" sauces; there are also recipes for rather friendlier, as it were, deviled dishes, such as the various Italian *fra diavolo* (brother devil) dishes. None of these sauces or dishes appears to go back further than the late seventeenth or eighteenth century; the term "devil" in this sense is of late coinage.

Whereas *deviled* foods evoke the hotness of hell, *devil's-food* cakes and bakery items evoke the theme of darkness. One of the names of the Devil is "The Prince of Darkness"; the allusion here is, however, hardly fearsome! These devil's-food items are American inventions of the nineteenth century—as are their opposite numbers, the angel-food cakes, angelic, clearly, in their whiteness and lightness.

There are other creatures and plants that bear (and have borne for centuries) the name of the Devil, but the name almost always indicates that these should not be eaten or that care must be taken in their eating. The Devil's apple is the thorn apple; the Devil's fig, the prickly pear; there is also the devil fish. In all these cases the imagery is clear: either the object is clearly painful to pick or eat (the tortures of hell are alluded to); or else it is deceptive (like the Father of Lies): it looks good, but isn't.

A fairly hot barbecue sauce for deviling meats

2 medium onions, chopped
2 cloves garlic, minced
⅓ cup olive oil or butter
1½ cups tomato purée
¼ cup vinegar
¼ cup Worcestershire sauce
2 tablespoons brown sugar
1 teaspoon salt
¼ teaspoon paprika
1 teaspoon dry mustard
Grated rind and juice of 1
   lemon
Dashes of Tabasco to taste
Optional:
   ¼ cup dry red wine

In a large skillet sauté the onion and garlic in the olive oil until soft and golden brown. Add the tomato purée, vinegar, Worcestershire sauce, brown sugar, salt, paprika, mustard, lemon rind and juice, and Tabasco. Simmer for 10 to 15 minutes. Add the wine, if you like.

Brush on meat or fowl as you are barbecuing it. For meats that take long to cook, such as spareribs, brush this sauce on only during the final 30 to 45 minutes of cooking.

Yield: about 2 cups sauce

Variations:

To make this sauce hotter, you can add: more onion and garlic (don't sauté them first), cayenne pepper, chili powder, or grated horseradish.

ST. FRANCIS OF ASSISI
October 4

Hardly a saint has won more hearts than Francis of Assisi. Some are drawn by his love of nature, others by his romantic yet cheerful disposition, yet others by his deep and evident holiness.

He was born in Umbria, in 1181 or 1182, the son of a wealthy cloth merchant. Though his family was middle class, as a young man Francis was imbued with chivalric ideals and wanted to be a troubadour and a knight. The experience of captivity and illness in war, however, began a conversion process that was intensified by a vision he had before a crucifix. Christ spoke to him and said, "Francis, go and repair my house, which you see is falling down." He began by literally repairing dilapidated churches, selling his family's merchandise to pay the cost of supplies. His father was outraged, and Francis eventually in the public square renounced his inheritance and even his clothes; the bishop provided him with simple apparel.

Francis embarked on a new quest—to live the Gospels faithfully—and he wedded (as he said) Lady Poverty. He and the followers who soon came to join him lived by begging from door to door and by menial labor. They preached repentance and cared for the poor and lepers.

Eventually Francis was given permission to found a new religious order, the Friars Minor (or Franciscans), committed to poverty and humility. The order drew thousands of members, and soon there were as well an order for women, the Minoresses or Poor Clares headed by St. Clare, and a group of Tertiaries, or lay people following a religious rule. There are today around 13,000 members of the Order of St. Francis in its various branches.

Francis yearned to convert the Saracens, and in 1219 he went to the Holy Land. The Sultan of Damietta was deeply impressed by Francis, though he did not become a Christian. "Remember me in your prayers," he begged Francis, "and may God, by your intercession, reveal to me which belief is more pleasing to Him."

In 1224 Francis, who had asked Christ to allow him to share in his sufferings, is said to have received on his body the Stigmata, the marks of Christ's wounds, which remained with him until his death in 1226.

There is one and only one earthly food that Francis is known to have loved, and this particular delicacy he enjoyed so much that he asked for some on his deathbed. Here is a recipe for this Italian almond pastry called Mostaccioli.

Mostaccioli

1 pound blanched almonds
½ cup honey
1 teaspoon cinnamon, or 1 teaspoon vanilla
2 egg whites, lightly beaten
Approximately 1 cup flour

Chop the almonds very fine or coarsely grind in a blender.

In a bowl combine the nuts, honey, cinnamon, and egg whites. Mix thoroughly. Gradually stir in enough flour to form a thick paste.

On a lightly floured surface, knead the paste until smooth and stiff. Roll out to about ¼ inch. Cut into diamond shapes, about 2½ inches long. Place the diamonds on a lightly buttered and floured baking sheet. Let dry for 1 to 2 hours.

Bake in a preheated 250° F. oven for 20 to 30 minutes or until set. Do not let brown.

Yield: about 3 dozen

ST. TERESA OF AVILA
October 15

Spanish mystic, with trances and visions and moments of levitation. Reformer, woman of action, founder of a new branch of the Carmelite Order. Essentially uneducated, and writing only under obedience to her superiors, but one of the greatest writers of Spain's Golden Age. Under suspicion of heresy for her visions, yet the first woman to be named a doctor of the Roman Catholic Church. Charming, loving, witty. So strong and fearless that one awe-struck prelate declared that she was "worthy to wear a beard." The poet Crashaw spoke of "all the eagle in thee, all the dove." A complex and fascinating woman, and saint.

Fortunately for us, several dishes are traditionally associated with her memory. St. Teresa's Bread and St. Teresa's Egg Yolks might well have been cooked by the saint herself. Even when she was the head of her order, she always took her turn in the kitchen— and to aristocratic Spanish nuns who resisted having to learn how to cook, she declared: "The Lord walks among the pots and pans!" Since one of the vows of her order was perpetual abstinence from meat, Teresa and her nuns must have worked hard to find appealing ways to serve bread and eggs, their most basic foodstuffs.

St. Teresa's bread

PAN DE SANTA TERESA

This dish, which makes a tasty breakfast or brunch, is a first cousin to French toast, but with a flavor and texture all its own.

2 cups milk
3 tablespoons sugar
1 cinnamon stick
1 good piece of lemon peel
12 slices Italian/French bread (a little stale) ½–¾ inch thick
3 eggs
Pinch of salt
Cinnamon-sugar for sprinkling on the toast
Olive oil for frying

Combine the milk with the sugar, cinnamon, and lemon peel. Simmer gently for 5 to 10 minutes, until the milk has become well flavored. Place the bread in a large flat dish or pan, and strain the milk over it.

Beat the eggs in a shallow bowl with a pinch of salt. With a spatula, lay the slices of bread in the egg, turning them to coat both sides. Beat additional eggs and salt together if necessary to finish coating bread slices. Fry the bread in the olive oil until it is browned and crusty on both sides.

Sprinkle with cinnamon-sugar.

Yield: 4 to 6 servings

St. Teresa's egg yolks

YEMAS DE SANTA TERESA

Yemas make an unusual dessert, or a lovely snack for a special occasion. They are particularly popular in the Avila region of Spain—but they are beloved of people of the Spanish tradition everywhere.

6 tablespoons sugar
¼ cup water
1 stick cinnamon
1 twist lemon peel
6 egg yolks, lightly beaten
A little superfine or
  confectioners' sugar
Optional:
  Small white paper cups

In a saucepan, mix the 6 tablespoons sugar, water, cinnamon stick, and lemon peel. Simmer, stirring frequently, until the mixture begins to become viscous, and until a drop of it forms a hard ball if placed in a glass of water.

Place the egg yolks in a saucepan. Beating constantly, gradually add the hot syrup to the yolks. Place the saucepan over medium heat, and stir constantly until the mixture has thickened to a paste and no longer adheres to the sides of the pan.

Turn the paste out onto a plate, and allow it to cool.

When the paste is fully cool, form it into a long roll. Cut it into 12 pieces, and form each piece into a little ball. Roll the balls in the sugar. In Spain these little balls would be put into little paper cups, such as the ones that chocolate candies are put in. Such little cups are not necessary—the Yemas taste just as good without them!—but they can be purchased anywhere that sells candy-making equipment. Or, same idea, you could serve them on pretty white paper doilies.

Yield: 12 Yemas

ALL SAINTS DAY
October 31

Since the fifth century Christians have honored the memory of the many unknown "saints"—people who have died, or lived, for Christ, but whose names are not known, and who thus cannot be honored individually. This feast honors all "the apostles, martyrs, confessors, and all the just and perfect servants whose bodies rest throughout the world." Many have believed, since at least the third century, that people can ask the saints who stand before the throne of God for their prayers.

The day before this feast is what we call Halloween: the Eve of All Hallows—another term for All Saints. Despite its name,

Halloween is not observed in America as a Christian holiday. Many of its practices are of ancient druidic origin—such as dressing up as evil spirits; the purpose originally was to appease the forces of evil abroad in the world by joining with them, at this changing of the seasons. In Europe, Halloween has also functioned partly as a harvest home festival.

Here is a recipe for a wonderful Italian All Saints Day bread inspired by a recipe in Giuliano Bugialli's *The Fine Art of Italian Cooking*.

Italian All Saints Day bread

PANE CO' SANTI

2 packages dry yeast
2 cups warm water (100–110° F.)
2 tablespoons sugar
1 cup olive oil
¾ cup chopped walnuts
½ cup chopped blanched almonds
2 teaspoons salt
About 7 cups flour
Grated rind of 1 orange
Grated rind of 1 lemon
2 teaspoons aniseed
½–1 teaspoon freshly ground black pepper
¾ cup raisins

Sprinkle the yeast into the warm water in a large bowl. Stir in the sugar and let the mixture sit until frothy.

Heat ½ cup of the olive oil and sauté the walnuts and almonds until golden brown. Reserve.

Add the salt to the yeast mixture. Gradually stir in about 5 cups of the flour. Mix in the remaining ½ cup olive oil. Gradually add enough of the remaining flour to make a fairly firm, nonsticky dough.

Turn the dough out onto a lightly floured surface. Knead it for about 5 minutes. Work in the orange and lemon rinds, aniseed, black pepper, and raisins. Knead for another 5 minutes, or until the dough is shiny and elastic.

Place the dough in a greased bowl, turning the dough to grease the top. Cover and let rise in a draft-free spot until doubled in bulk, about 1 to 1½ hours.

Preheat the oven to 400° F.

Place the dough on a lightly floured surface. Work in the olive-oil-and-nut mixture, kneading for about 5 minutes to work them thoroughly into the dough; the olive oil must be fully incorporated.

Form the dough into a large round loaf on a lightly greased large baking sheet. Cover lightly and let rise until the dough is almost doubled in bulk, about 45 minutes.

Bake for about 45 to 55 minutes, or until the bread is golden brown. If you pick up the loaf with a kitchen towel and tap the bottom, it should sound hollow.

Yield: 1 loaf about 14 inches in diameter

> The glorious company of the apostles praise Thee. The goodly fellowship of the prophets praise Thee. The white-robed army of martyrs praise Thee. All Thy saints and elect with one voice do acknowledge Thee, O Blessed Trinity, one God!
>
> Feast of All Saints (November 1), Antiphon at Lauds.
> From *Te Deum*

ALL SOULS DAY
November 1

The day after All Saints is All Souls Day. The desire to remember the dead is of course by no means exclusively Christian. In many pagan cultures—cultures in which there has been a deep belief in the immortality of the soul—there has been not only a concern for the happiness and well-being of the dead but also a fear of them: a feeling that their spirits needed to be appeased. Food was often brought to their graves, to keep them happy, so they wouldn't want to come back and haunt the living.

The early Christians living in the Roman Empire maintained the pagan practice of honoring the dead, but with some major modifications. The appeasing of the spirits was replaced with an emphasis on honoring their memory and praying for them. This came to be seen as a central implication of the concept of the "communion of saints": those in heaven can pray for the living, and the living can pray for the dead. (This similarity in theme explains why All Souls falls right after All Saints.) In some Roman Catholic countries, there used to be a pious superstition that I find very appealing: people kept windows open on that day as they prayed, so that the souls in Purgatory could hear the prayers being said for them, and be consoled and encouraged.

The term "soul food"—which today has taken on a new meaning—is very old, originally referring to dishes, especially cookies and cakes, prepared for All Souls Day. These were either eaten at communal meals in the home, or given to the poor, in memory of the dead. In pagan times these foods would commonly have been left on the graves for the dead themselves to enjoy, but this practice was frowned on by the Church as smacking of paganism.

Here is an old "soul" rhyme, such as begging children used to sing in England at All Souls:

Soul! Soul! for a soul cake!
I pray, good missis, a soul cake!
An apple, a pear, a plum, or a cherry,
Any good thing to make us merry.
One for Peter, one for Paul,
Three for Him who made us all.
Up with the kettle and down with the pan.
Give us good alms and we'll be gone.

And here is a recipe for Italian "soul" cookies called Fave dei Morti, "Beans of the Dead." The theme of beans suggests, among other things, the idea of burial in the ground and rebirth. Sometimes "soul" cookies are called *Ossi* dei Morti—"*Bones* of the Dead"— and are made in the shape of bones. In fact, the central ingredient in all the forms of this cookie is ground or crushed nuts, which are understood to suggest bones. (This theme is also common in bakery items for this day in other countries, such as Mexico.) These perhaps morbid considerations notwithstanding, Fave (and Ossi) dei Morti are delicious.

Beans of the dead

FAVE DEI MORTI

⅔ cup blanched almonds
¾ cup sugar
¾ cup flour
1 teaspoon ground cinnamon
4 tablespoons butter, cut into small pieces and softened
1 egg
1 teaspoon vanilla extract
Grated rind of 1 lemon

Place the almonds on a baking sheet and dry them out for 10 minutes or so in a slow oven: 200° F. Reset the oven for 350° F.

Grind the almonds very fine. Place them in a large bowl. Add the sugar, and blend the mixture well with a fork. Add the flour and the cinnamon, then the butter, then finally the egg, the vanilla, and the grated lemon rind, mixing well with each addition. With a fork or floured hands, work the mixture to a smooth paste.

Break off large-bean-sized pieces of paste (about 1 inch long), and place them about 2 inches apart on a greased, floured baking sheet. Squash each piece slightly to produce an oval shape like a lima or fava bean.

Bake for about 15 minutes, or until they are a golden color.

Yield: about 100 one-inch beans

Variation:
Form pieces of dough into the shape of bones, 1 or 2 inches long.

ST. MARTIN OF TOURS
November 11

Martin was born in Pannonia (Hungary today), the son of a pagan soldier in the Roman army. Martin joined the army, and also became a Christian catechumen (that is, he decided to learn about the Christian faith). While in the army in France, in Amiens, one bitter cold night Martin shared his military cloak with a naked beggar, and that night Martin had a dream: he saw Christ wearing the halved cloak he had given to the beggar. (As Christ had said: "What you do to the least of my brothers, you do to *me*.") Soon after, Martin was baptized and left the army, determined to be a "soldier of Christ."

He became a hermit, and founded a hermitage at Ligugé in France. He was elected bishop of Tours because of his reputation for holiness—and because he was already famous for his miracles: he is said to have raised a dead man to life, to have cured a leper with a kiss, to have conversed frequently with angels and with saints. At his episcopal ordination, some complained that he was not a nobleman, and he had "dirty clothes and unkempt hair." (He was forever giving his nice things away to the poor.) Be that as it may, Martin's holiness was universally recognized, and when he died in 397, he became one of the very first non-martyrs to be venerated as a saint. His shrine in Tours drew pilgrims from all over Western Europe.

His feast, called Martinmas, became a major one in Europe, largely no doubt because it took on the character of an in-gathering festival: a thanksgiving celebration. On this day it has been traditional to eat young goose and to taste the new wine of the season. In Germany, they make a cake in a special mold, showing St. Martin on horseback. In Holland, they roast chestnuts and apples and give them to the children; in Italy, they make a Pizza di San Martino (actually a coffeecake), with trinkets hidden inside.

This feast, like that of St. Nicholas, continued to be celebrated in a number of Protestant countries even after the Reformation abolished most saints' day festivities. When the American Pilgrim Fathers decided to establish three days of rejoicing after their first harvest in the New World, they apparently modeled their celebration in part on the old Martinmas tradition, which some of them had come to know in Holland where they had been exiled before coming to America. Before the first Thanksgiving, they went out hunting for goose in the European tradition. As we all know, they came back with wild turkey as well—and the rest is history.

Swedish roast goose, stuffed with prunes and apples

Why goose on St. Martin's Day? There may be some connection with his legend. Martin is said to have wanted to avoid being elected bishop, and to have hidden; a goose gave away his hiding place.

Goose is delicious served with Spiced Red Cabbage (recipe below), Brussels sprouts, and stewed apples or applesauce. For dessert have a beautiful cake made in a St. Martin mold.

Follow the basic roast goose recipe (page 148), but use this stuffing:

20 large prunes, pitted and plumped until soft in hot water
6–8 tart apples, peeled and quartered
½ teaspoon allspice

Mix the ingredients well. Stuff the goose loosely. As it cooks baste the goose with the pan drippings.

If you wish to make a gravy: Pour off the drippings, strain them, and degrease them as much as possible. Thicken with cornstarch that has been dissolved in a few tablespoons of cold water or stock. Add—to taste—salt, pepper, brandy, if you wish, and a few teaspoons of red currant jelly.

Spiced red cabbage

There is a charming legend attached to red cabbage, and it concerns another bishop, better dressed apparently than St. Martin, but just as charitable. As Waverley Root (the late, great expert on our culinary heritage) tells it:

Though unromantic botanists explain the color of red cabbage (blue cabbage, Blaukraut, in German) by its chemical composition, the French have a prettier story to account for it. In the days when unmarried mothers were considered to have disgraced themselves, an obviously pregnant young woman of Périgueux returned from the fields balancing an enormous cabbage on her swollen stomach, a spectacle which obliged her to run the gauntlet of the sort of pleasantries you can easily imagine. The charitable bishop of Périgueux happened to pass by. Taking the cabbage from her, he wrapped it in a fold of his mantle and, taking her hand, escorted her to her door. There he handed back the cabbage; it had taken on the color of his episcopal robes.

1 two- to three-pound head of red cabbage
3 tablespoons bacon fat
½ cup red wine
Salt and freshly ground pepper to taste
2 tart apples, cored and diced but not peeled
2 tablespoons brown sugar
2 tablespoons vinegar

Remove any outer wilted leaves of the cabbage. Core, quarter, and shred or grate the cabbage. Soak for about 30 minutes in lightly salted cold water. Drain well.

In a large skillet heat the bacon fat, and sauté the cabbage. Add the wine, salt, and pepper, and simmer for 5 minutes. Add the apples, brown sugar, and vinegar. Cover and simmer until the cabbage and apples are just tender, but still crisp.

Yield: 4 to 6 servings

St. Martin's Day cake

This cake is made in a special mold. St. Martin molds can be ordered from the Broadway Panhandler, 520 Broadway, New York, N.Y. 10012

2 cups sifted flour
¾ teaspoon baking powder
¼ teaspoon salt
½ teaspoon nutmeg
1 cup butter
1 cup plus 2 tablespoons sugar
2 teaspoons grated lemon or orange peel
½ teaspoon almond extract
2 teaspoons vanilla extract
4 eggs

ICING:
½ pound (1¾ cups) confectioners' sugar
1 teaspoon vanilla
¼ cup milk (more if needed)
Vegetable food coloring; small paint brushes

Remove the racks from the oven, and place a sheet of aluminum foil, or a baking pan, on the bottom of the oven. Preheat the oven to 375° F. Grease the inside of the mold thoroughly with shortening, and dust with flour.

Resift the flour with the baking powder, salt, and nutmeg.

Cream the butter. Gradually add the sugar, creaming until fluffy. Add the lemon peel and extracts. Alternately beat the eggs and the flour mixture into the butter mixture.

Pour one-half of the batter into the mold. (Refrigerate the rest of the batter, for the second cake.) Make sure that the batter fills the heads of Martin and his horse. Set the mold on its legs on the bottom of the oven and bake for 40 to 45 minutes, or until a straw comes out clean.

Let the cake cool in the mold for 5 minutes on a wire rack. Remove one half of the mold and allow the cake to cool 5 more minutes. Then remove the other half of the mold, turn the cake out onto the rack and allow it to cool thoroughly. If necessary, trim the bottom of the cake so that it stands up well.

Repeat the above procedure, to make the second cake.

Mix the confectioners' sugar, vanilla, and enough milk to make a smooth, not too runny icing. Spread this icing over the surface of the cake. Allow it to dry thoroughly—2 hours or so.

Mix (in a muffin tin or small cups) the vegetable colors to make the colors you want, such as red for Martin's robe, yellow for his miter and bishop's crook, brown (red plus blue) for his beard and his horse, green for the grass, etc. Paint the colors on the dried icing.

Yield: 2 smallish cakes (each serves about 4);
you can easily halve this recipe

ST. CATHERINE OF ALEXANDRIA
November 25

The legend associated with St. Catherine of Alexandria is truly fascinating. She is said to have grown up in Alexandria in the third century and to have been extremely well educated. She was converted to Christianity, and when the Emperor Maxentius tried to force her to sacrifice to the pagan gods, she refused. He brought in (so the legend says) fifty pagan scholars to argue with her; she confounded them all, and convinced them of the truth of Christianity—whereupon Maxentius had them burned. Catherine was then scourged and imprisoned, but she managed to convert the Empress herself, and a general with his soldiers. Maxentius then had her placed on a spiked wheel; it broke as soon as she was fastened to it. She was finally beheaded, and angels (or possibly monks) carried her body to Mount Sinai, where it can still be venerated at the Monastery of St. Catherine (founded in her honor in the eighth or ninth century).

St. Catherine is the patroness of the most varied assortment of groups: of philosophers in general, and female students in particular, because of her deep wisdom and learning; of wheelwrights, mechanics and spinners, because of her association with the wheel; of spinsters, because she was, and remained until her death, a virgin; but also of young women desirous of finding husbands (Catherine is one of a number of saints to whom the young have confided their desire of finding a suitable mate). Catherine's voice is one of those that Joan of Arc heard.

In northern France, there is a lovely old custom: on Catherine's Day, heart-shaped cakes are given to young women who have reached, unmarried, the age of twenty-five—who have, as the saying goes, *coiffé Sainte Catherine* (who wear her headdress, who have taken her as their patroness). The idea is to encourage them in their search for love.

St. Catherine's hearts

LES COEURS DE SAINTE CATHERINE

Butter or shortening for
  greasing the pan
7 tablespoons butter,
  softened
½ cup plus 2 tablespoons
  sugar
3 eggs
2 cups sifted flour
2 teaspoons baking powder
¼ teaspoon salt
½ teaspoon cinnamon
¼ cup mixed candied fruit
½ teaspoon orange extract
1 tablespoon grated orange
  rind
3 tablespoons water
Optional:
  Confectioners' sugar

You need a 1-quart heart-shaped pan for this.

Preheat the oven to 300° F. Butter and flour the baking pan.

Cream the butter. Gradually add the sugar, mixing well; beat in the eggs, one at a time. Resift the flour with the baking powder, salt, and cinnamon.

Stir the flour into the butter mixture. Stir in the fruits, orange extract, and orange rind, and the water. Mix thoroughly. Pour the batter into the baking pan.

Bake for 20 minutes, then raise the heat to 425° F. and bake for another 15 to 20 minutes, or until a straw inserted in the center of the cake comes out clean. Remove from the pan when cool.

Optional: Sprinkle with confectioners' sugar.

Yield: 1 cake

AFTERWORD

Those of us who prepare the food want it always to be as delicious as we can make it. Feeding others is part of our mission in life, and we strive to do it as perfectly as possible. But this book can also serve as a reminder to us all that the true feast is in the hearts of those who prepare and share the meal; it is not in the quality or quantity of the viands but in the breaking of the bread in love.

The Lord bless you and keep you;
the Lord make his face to shine upon you and be gracious to you;
the Lord lift up his countenance upon you and give you peace.

Numbers 6:24 (RSV)

Index